Minnesota Lacrosse: A History

J. Alan Childs

Copyright © 2015 J. Alan Childs
All rights reserved.

No part of this book may be used or reproduced in any manner whatsoever without written permission of the author.

For information regarding permission, write to Flamethrower Productions via email at
`flamethrowerprod@gmail.com`

Lacrosse History Blog
laxhistorygeek.com

ISBN-13: 978-1468022179
ISBN: 1468022172

Special pricing available for lacrosse clubs for fundraising opportunities in bulk orders. Please contact us at the above email for more information.

DEDICATION

This book is the result of many hours of research, journeys, and time spent with people who share a passion for this sport. I would to thank my family for their support in letting me pursue this passion for lacrosse.

CONTENTS

	Introduction	1
Chapter 1	First Nations	7
Chapter 2	First Observers	19
Chapter 3	Fort Michilimackinac	29
Chapter 4	Fort Snelling	37
Chapter 5	Treaty, Trading, and the Traditions of Lacrosse	49
Chapter 6	First Rules	63
Chapter 7	Exported to the United States	73
Chapter 8	National Champions	81
Chapter 9	First Minnesota Lacrosse Team	93
Chapter 10	First Championship	103
Chapter 11	First East Coast Trip	117
Chapter 12	First State Fair Lacrosse Game	131
Chapter 13	First St. Paul Winter Carnival	137
Chapter 14	Lost Championship 1886	139
Chapter 15	Ugly Era of the Game	149
Chapter 16	20th Century Lacrosse Begins	161
Chapter 17	Northwest Lacrosse League	171
Chapter 18	1904, The First American Olympics	195
Chapter 19	1905, International Champions	211

Chapter 20	1906, The End of Midwest Lacrosse	221
Chapter 21	Gopher Lacrosse	233
Chapter 22	The Boarding School Experiment	241
Chapter 23	Olympic Lacrosse Memories	247
Chapter 24	Women's Lacrosse	261
Chapter 25	Lacrosse Restored to Minnesota	269
	Epilogue	299
	References	303
	Bibliography	309
	Appendix A – Minnesota Hall of Fame	313
	Appendix B – Minnesota and Lacrosse timelines	321
	Appendix C – Evolution of Men's Lacrosse Rules	329
	Appendix D – Lacrosse vs Base ball	335
	Appendix E – Language of Lacrosse	339

ACKNOWLEDGMENTS

There are many people who have helped me on this journey of discovery, research, and writing. The lacrosse community is still relatively small. When you attend a game, clinic, or other event, people love to share stories of adventures in lacrosse. I did not have nearly enough room or time to write everything I heard.

Thank you to all who helped with this project.

Erin George, Assistant Archivist at the University of Minnesota Archives, who tracked down the Minnesota Gopher rosters and articles.

Joe Finn, Archivist, US Lacrosse Museum, who gave me a special tour of the museum, contacts, confirmed ideas, found articles, and always responded to my many requests for more information.

Roger Godin, Historian for the Minnesota Wild, and author of *Before they were Stars – Early Major League Hockey and the St. Paul Athletic Club*. Roger took the time to meet with me and help fill in the gaps from lacrosse to hockey in the state of Minnesota. His insights and research helped me obtain names of lacrosse players who led the charge into hockey.

City of Savage Library Staff, who helped with endless hours of finding data on the Pond Brothers, Fort Snelling, Dan Patch, many other local resources, and always pointed me in a new direction when I hit a wall.

Dr. Anton Treuer, at Bemidji State University, whose passion for language gave me insight about the Ojibwe culture and history.

Dave White, founder of Twin Cities Lacrosse Club, who generously shared his private papers, photos, and stories from the early days in the Twin Cities Lacrosse Club.

Maxwell Kelsey for sharing his knowledge about Ojibwe stick-making, many resources about Beltrami, and his photo collection.

Dan Ninham for his time, books, and stories about the culture of lacrosse and retelling of his efforts to restore the game throughout Minnesota, with a large focus on the native communities he serves.

Franky Jackson at Lower Sioux, Lukas Fineday at Pine Point Lacrosse on the White Earth Reservation, and Pete Neadeau at Red Lake who along with Dan Ninham are bringing back the game.

Jay Ludwig, Cultural Arts Coordinator, Bloomington Parks and Recreation, who pointed me in the right direction at the Pond House, and helped me find the next round of people when I struggled to connect the Pond house to the Treaties and Oak Grove lacrosse games.

Mark Hellenack, who shared his papers and documents from the early days in the Minnesota Chapter formation. Mark's commentary was instrumental in putting some pieces together in Chapter 25.

Mark Erickson, for his review of the stories, feedback, and for always being willing to show me my gaps.

Janet Holdsworth, who has since moved out of state, took the time to write down her memories of the early days and provide insight on how the girls' lacrosse programs got started and achieved high school sanction status.

John Crampton, Minnesota Historian, who helped me find the modern-day setting of Seth Eastman's painting of the Dakota on the Minnesota River.

John Hunter of the Twin Cities Native Lacrosse Club and Randy Blackdeer of the Ho-Chunk Mission Lacrosse Club for their inspiration and leadership of First Nation Lacrosse teams returning to play the game. They have been very generous in allowing me and my family to attend and even participate in wooden stick lacrosse games.

Thanks to the many First Nation players and coaches like Corey Holiday, Dawi Huhá Máza, Matt Childs (no relation), Chase Childs (no relation), Dave Turner, Sasha Brown, and so many others I have met along the way.

Of course a thank you to my editor, Cindy Wilson, whose patience and diligence in teaching me to write with proper spelling and grammar has no end.

INTRODUCTION

My interest in writing about Minnesota lacrosse started during the research my son Brody and I did while writing the Flamethrower books. We created a fictional lacrosse tradition in Minnesota based on ideas from Brody's 2008 summer project, a comic book. As we finished the first Flamethrower book (*Flamethrowers Guardians of the Game*), and started the second one based in Canada, we stumbled across newspapers announcing the appearance of the United States Lacrosse Champions, the St. Paul Lacrosse Club.

I was surprised to learn about a Minnesota team winning a lacrosse national championship. Local books such as *The 75 Memorable Moments in Minnesota Sports*, by Joel Rippel, and Sid Hartman's *Great Minnesota Sports Moments* mention nothing of the St. Paul Lacrosse Club and their magnificent back-to-back national lacrosse championships.

So off on a "squirrel moment" we went. Brody and I put the Flamethrower books on hold (sorry fans)! This history book represents over five years of research, with countless hours spent at the Minnesota Historical Society, museums, and other locations tracking down information.

History shows that there are many versions of cultural stories. For this book, I relied upon Thomas Peacock's book *"Ojibwe Waasa Inaabidaa,"* as it is well documented. There are other perspectives of the Ojibwe stories that are not included.

Throughout this book, some standards are incorporated to help the reader keep track of my words versus newspapers or other quotes.

> **SIDE WALL:**
> *Side walls are items that I want to call attention to. These include items like a Fun Fact, Did You Know, or Research Notes.*

Newspapers and journals

There are many newspaper and journal articles in this book. Most are from the St. Paul Globe, which is no longer published. A different font is used to call out these articles. The misspellings and bad grammar has been kept as is. It was fun to learn how people wrote and talked during these earlier times and I wanted to pass that on to the reader.

Stories

Scattered throughout the book are stories told by native speakers. These stories are shared in this font, with wording kept as told.

Naming conventions

Realizing that it is not possible to find the names of the original lacrosse game developers, you will see them referred to as Nations or First Nations. Why? Using the name First Nations seems to carry the most credibility to who they are. *Indians* is of course based on Columbus mistakenly thinking he had arrived in India. So to give proper honor to those who created the game of lacrosse and lived here before the Europeans arrived, I use the name First Nation.

Spelling

American English has evolved over the years and some words were spelled differently in previous eras. Language continues to evolve. To maintain the historical culture of Minnesota, I have kept those original spellings.

For example, you will see baseball represented as "base ball" before it became one word. Other examples show the Canadian influence on the game in St. Paul, including words like centre and defence.

Some words have disappeared from the world of lacrosse, like "frisking." Frisking was when a player used his feet to grab a lacrosse ball, flip it up in the air, turn around and catch the ball in his crosse. This was used to avoid picking up a ground ball with the stick. This skill, used by the First Nation players, is no longer used in today's sport of lacrosse.

In the chapters about modern lacrosse, the current US Lacrosse naming conventions are used: boys', girls', men's and women's.

For the Nations of Minnesota I use the names most commonly referred to now as the Dakota and Ojibwe. There are many variations of these names like the Dakota (eastern), Lakota (western), Anishinaabe, Chippewa, and others. Most First Nations refer to themselves by band and not the overall names on the treaties or reservations. In the end, no matter which names I choose, there will be those who say it is incorrect wording. For consistency, Ojibwe and Dakota will be used.

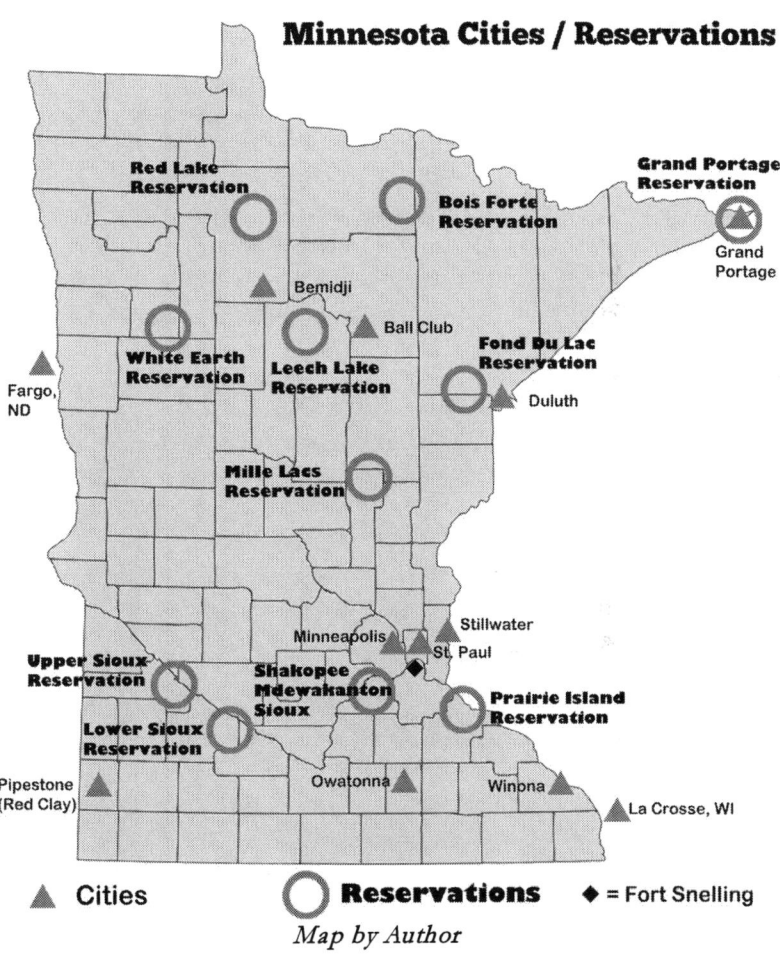
Map by Author

The Haudenosaunee, located in Canada and upper New York, are also known as the Six Nations, Iroquois Confederacy, or the People of the Longhouse. Some people are familiar with their lacrosse team, the Iroquois Nationals, so to honor their lacrosse team I will refer to them as the Iroquois.

Minnesota's history, like other states, was not a kind one for the First Nations. Unfortunately Minnesota holds the distinction of performing the largest public mass execution of First Nation people in the United States. After the US-Dakota War of 1862, Abraham Lincoln approved the execution of 38 Dakota in the town of Mankato (303 men were convicted).

This book starts with the movement of the Ojibwe Ancestors and their journey to Minnesota. Their travels through the "Cradle of Lacrosse" in the St. Lawrence River area is where they most likely helped to create the game and eventually brought it to Minnesota. The book then discusses the First Observers of the game, the French Jesuit Missionaries who saw and recorded the game. Next we will visit specific lacrosse games before any white settlers began playing. This will include figures like George Catlin who painted the game in Minnesota, places like Fort Snelling that hosted the games on Catlin's visits, and natural resources like the great red clay of Pipestone that played a large role in the Dakota and Ojibwe culture.

From there we will explore a brief history about how Canadians created rules for the modern game of lacrosse, followed by the expansion of the organized game in the United States, and specifically Minnesota. We will then show cultural context around the state when white settlers began to play the game of lacrosse in 1883.

After the creation of the St. Paul Lacrosse Club, other communities formed teams including Minneapolis, Owatonna, Stillwater, Duluth, and Winona. Next the midwest exploded with successful lacrosse teams in Chicago, Detroit, Louisville, and of course La Crosse, Wisconsin.

St. Paul became a powerhouse in the midwest and won the national championship. They traveled what were then great distances to play teams not only in the midwest but also New York, Boston, Winnipeg, Toronto, and the birthplace of modern day lacrosse, Montreal.

After the early struggles of lacrosse nationally, lacrosse was successfully brought to the University of Minnesota, only to face a terrible tragedy that ended the program before it could truly compete. Soon afterwards, the sport of lacrosse gave way to hockey in Minnesota. Yes, lacrosse developed before hockey in Minnesota and many of the hockey positions and rules mimic those in the original lacrosse culture. Many people in Minnesota struggle with the influx today of hockey players playing lacrosse "hockey" style. The reality is that lacrosse influenced the hockey culture first.

Introduction

Even though lacrosse in Minneapolis and St. Paul ended in 1912, the Ojibwe and Dakota continued to play until the end of WWII. After that time, the game of lacrosse appears to have declined and left the general culture of the state. The Ojibwe and Dakota tried to bring it back several times, but with limited success.

We will cover the return of the game to Minnesota and how those events unfolded. The game has reached a larger audience in Minnesota, and those who brought the game back have played a role in growing the sport.

Included at the end of the book is a timeline for Minnesota, connecting events in lacrosse to events in the history of the state. This includes a brief review of how the rules have changed over the years in men's lacrosse. I am often asked why women's lacrosse is so different from the men's game. We will review how the two sports developed and why the women's game more closely resembles the original game developed by George Beers.

Should Minnesota ever have a Hall of Fame for lacrosse, I have included my nominations for those who went before and brought honor to lacrosse; Minnesota has many heroes who taught the game and brought multiple championships to the state.

Enjoy.

CHAPTER 1

FIRST NATIONS

Before there was hockey, baseball, basketball, or football, there was lacrosse. The First Nations had many games using sticks and balls, but lacrosse was special, a medicine game that could heal a person, place, or nation.

The inventors of the game of lacrosse are those First Nation people who have lived here since the creation of Turtle Island (North America). The "cradle of lacrosse" is considered the area surrounding the St. Lawrence River Valley in what is now modern day Quebec, Ontario, and upstate New York. It is in this valley that lacrosse was born and played by the First Nation people for centuries.

This book begins with stories of the ancestors of the Ojibwe, called the Algonquians, starting with the formation of Turtle Island and the First Nations having lived here for 50,000 years or longer. [1]

The Algonquians moved through the centuries from one coast to another. Their history starts with a shared ancestor called the Lenni Lenape, also known as the "grandfathers." The grandfathers recorded their story on bark and song sticks. This story is the oldest North American written record dating back to 1600 B.C. [2] The story is known as the "Walam Olum" or the migration story. [3]

The Walam Olum story begins in the west—perhaps as far west as California—where their shared ancestors, the Yuroks and Wiyots, lived. From there the Lenni Lenape migrated east to the Rockies and Great Plains. They encountered the great mound builders of the Mississippi, and met with those who became their traditional enemy, the Iroquois.

Other Nations with Lenape roots include the Cheyenne, Arapaho, Cree, Blackfeet, Shawnee, and Miami. (4) These groups may have stopped along the journey eastward and developed their own settlements. At some point the Lenni Lenape reached the Atlantic Ocean and settled along the Delaware River. From there some moved northward into the New England area becoming the Montauk, Wampanoag, Pequot, Narraganset, Nipmuc, Penobscot, Passamaquoddy, and others. These Nations are the groups that eventually meet and welcome the pilgrims upon their landing.

Still more groups continued north into the St. Lawrence River Valley. This included the ancestors of the modern day Ojibwe Nation.

Birch bark scroll image from "The Midewiwin, or 'Grand Medicine Society', of the Ojibwe" in Smithsonian Institution, U.S. Bureau of Ethnology Report, v. 7, pp. 149-299 by Walter James Hoffman. (Washington, DC: Government Printing Office, 1891).

It is in this time and in the area along the St. Lawrence River that the Ojibwe most likely helped develop or learned the game of lacrosse. Lacrosse was considered the favored of their many games, used primarily as a "healing" game for a Nation. A game could be called to heal a person or the whole Nation if the situation called for it. A current Ojibwe member said to me, "How could you not feel better if a whole Nation was playing to heal you?"

The first documented game observed by an outsider was to heal an old man (this will be discussed further in the next chapter.)

Chapter One – First Nations

In the St. Lawrence River Valley, the Algonquian had contact with the "People of the Longhouse" or the Iroquois Nation. These contacts might have shared in the evolution of the game. Algonquian descendants, like the Ojibwe, use a very different lacrosse stick than those of the Iroquois, as seen in the next image.

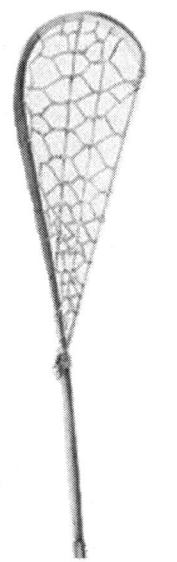

Ojibwe/Dakota Stick *Iroquois Stick*

The Algonquians lived along the Atlantic Ocean somewhere in the area of New Brunswick and Newfoundland. This area is where the St. Lawrence River empties into the Atlantic. (5)

SIDE WALL:
The furthest tributary of the St. Lawrence River originates in Minnesota from the North River in the Mesabi Range near Hibbing. (6)

It is said that during a time when the Ojibwe lived a full and peaceful life, seven prophets came to the elders and delivered teachings and prophecies. These teachings came to be known as the seven fires of the Ojibwe. (7) The seven principals taught were Love, Respect, Wisdom, Honesty, Humility, Bravery, and Truth.

- The first fire foretold that the Ojibwe were to follow the Sacred Seashell westward.
- The second fire told that they would find a new great body of water.

- The third fire said they'd know when they reached their destination when they found "food that grows on water."
- The fourth fire told of the coming of a light-skinned race.
- The fifth fire told of a time of great struggle when many would abandon the old teachings.
- The sixth fire told that children would be taken away and turn on the elders, bringing a new sickness to the nation.
- The seventh fire told of children returning, but that the elders would be asleep. Two roads will face the children: stay on the path or seek the peace.

Soon the elders saw a great Sacred Seashell rise up and they began their journey westward. Long before the Pilgrims arrived in 1620, the Ojibwe began a slow exodus westward. Starting around 900 A.D., the journey took over 500 years to complete. (8)

Researchers of the game agree that lacrosse first appeared around 1000-1100 A.D. This timeline seems to confirm that the Ojibwe ancestors saw or helped develop the game.

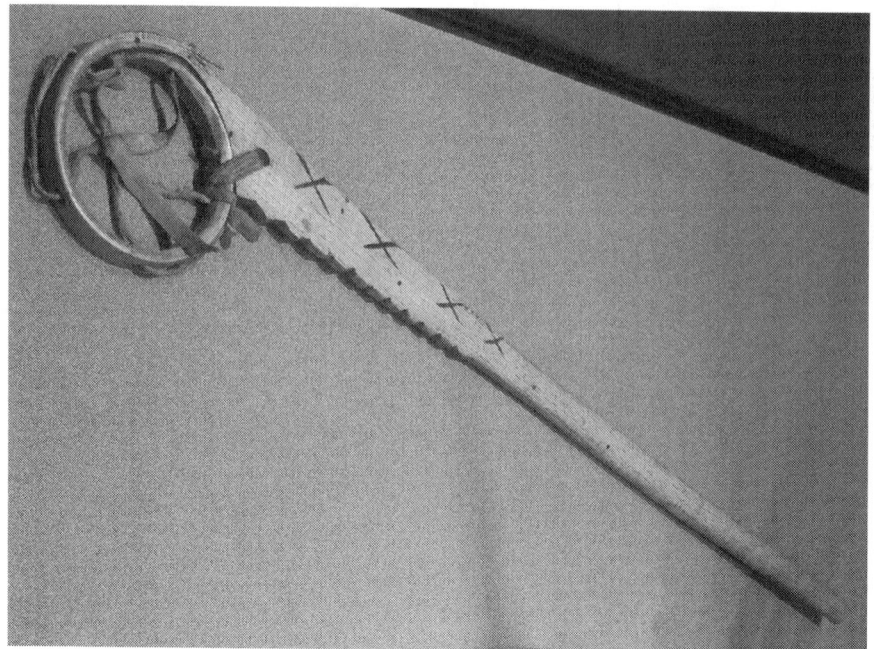

The Beltrami 1823 Ojibwe Lacrosse Stick – Bergamo Museum, Italy
Photo provided by Maxwell Kelsey

Chapter One – First Nations

The oldest known surviving lacrosse stick is Ojibwe. It's from 1823 and is located in Bergamo, Italy, the hometown of explorer Giacomo Costantino Beltrami. Beltrami acquired the lacrosse stick during his journeys to what he erroneously thought were the headwaters of the Mississippi River, Lake Julia. He named the lake after his friend Giulia Spada de Medici. [9]

The Ojibwe started their journey by heading south along the St. Lawrence River. It was here they met resistance with the Iroquois. At first they lived peacefully together, but hostilities eventually broke out and the Ojibwe were forced further west along the Great Lakes.

The Ojibwe traveled with the Odawa (Ottawa) and the Potawatomi Nations, and formed a union known as the Council of Three Fires. At Sault Ste. Marie the three Nations were being pursued by the Iroquois. One evening the Ojibwe snuck into the Iroquois camp and unleashed a brutal attack, leaving only a few alive to tell the story. After this battle the Iroquois no longer pursued the Ojibwe westward. [10]

Around 1612, as the group migrated westward along the Great Lakes, they met the "Black Gowns." [11] Black Gowns were French Missionaries and the first Europeans to meet the Ojibwe, followed by French explorers. The Ojibwe began to trade with the French and enjoyed a comfortable relationship. These early Europeans respected Ojibwe beliefs, didn't laugh at their ceremonies, and admired their great hunting skills. At first there were no formal trading posts, but each spring the French came to trade with the Ojibwe.

Stories handed down indicate that by the time they reached the Great Lakes, the Ojibwe were playing the game of lacrosse. Ball-play was called baggataway, pronounced "baaga`adowe."

Native author William Warren (1825-1853) describes the love of the game of lacrosse by the Ojibwe and how the young men played their "favorite and most beautiful game." [12] The Ojibwe described their spring activities in the following way: "before the warmth of the spring sun it was time for recreation, ball-play, racing, courtship, and war." [13]

The game of lacrosse, as developed by the First Nations, was called a medicine game. The shape of the lacrosse pocket on the oldest sticks were made with four sections, possibly designed after the medicine wheel.

Minnesota Lacrosse: A History

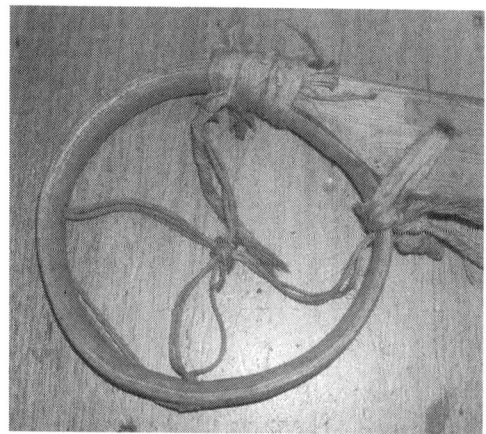

*Ojibwe Lacrosse Stick with four sections similar to Medicine Wheel
Photo provided by Maxwell Kelsey*

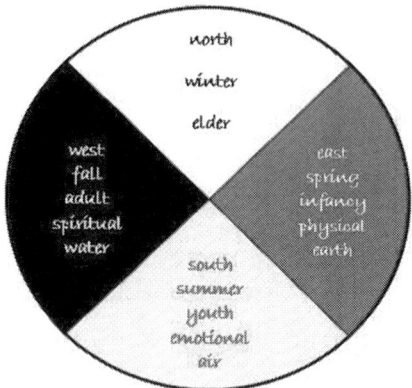

Ojibwe Medicine Wheel

A great split of the Ojibwe occurred near Sault Ste. Marie. One group headed north along the shores of Lake Superior and the other group headed south into the areas now called Michigan and Wisconsin. The Minnesota Ojibwe followed the south shore of Lake Superior with stops in the Apostle Islands, including Madeline Island, and ended up in northern Minnesota via Duluth. The French established the first trading post in 1679 at or near Grand Portage, Minnesota. (14)

The Ojibwe enjoyed a great relationship with the early French Traders, and they gained the advantage of being able to trade for weapons such as metal axes and guns. These weapons helped as they arrived in the area that is now Minnesota and began to push the existing Dakota Nation south and

Chapter One – First Nations

west. The Ojibwe experienced peace and war with the Dakota over the next two centuries.

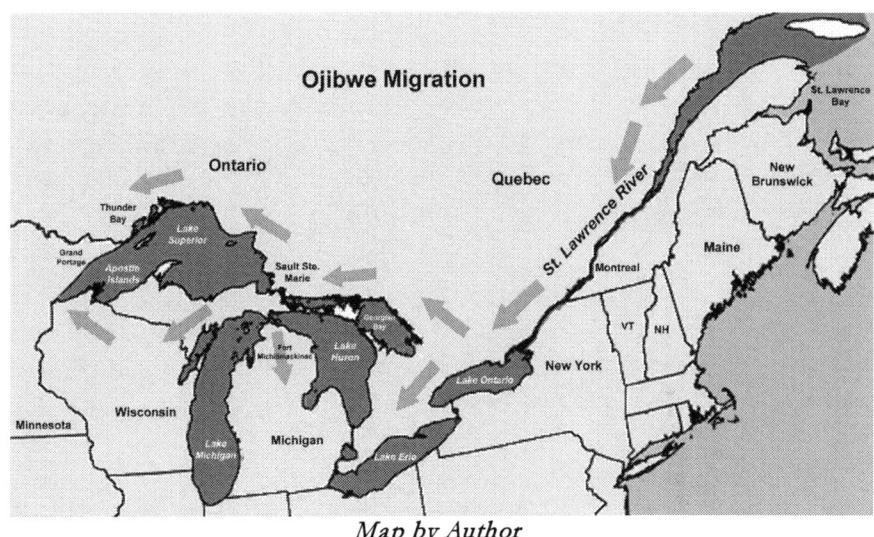
Map by Author

The Ojibwe moved into many places in northern and eastern Minnesota. They met with the same challenges with disease that other Nations faced. Small pox and measles wiped out large numbers of their population in the coming years.

This decrease in population reduced their cultural traditions and the prophecies of the sixth fire would come true. Starting in 1879, the children of the First Nations were taken from their parents and sent to boarding schools where their language was not to be spoken. Minnesota and other US states moved children off the reservations in an attempt to educate and indoctrinate them in the American culture. This was another dark episode in American history where cultural traditions were lost and lives changed. Lacrosse was not allowed to be played at these boarding schools, except for Carlisle in Pennsylvania (more about the boarding schools will be discussed in chapter 22.)

First Nation cultures are full of wonderful stories about nearly everything in their surroundings, such as how a mountain was made, a lake was formed, or why a tree has a special shape. These stories also teach lessons to pass on traditions, and some involve lacrosse games. Here are two stories that teach a lesson about acceptance and how the game is for everyone to share, not just a chosen few.

Game between animals with teeth and those with no teeth.

This story is from a book named *The Great Ball Game*. The story teaches the concept of including everyone on your team; don't reject players, because you never know when their unique skill will be needed to win a game. (15)

Long ago there was a great argument between the birds and animals. We who have wings are better than you they cried. That is not so, we who have teeth are better the animals replied. The crane the leader of the birds, and the bear, leader of the animals agreed to play a game of ball to settle the dispute.

They agreed the loser of the game had to accept the terms of the winner. So they began to divide into two teams. Those with wings on one team and those with teeth on another. One player went back and forth between the teams because he had wings and teeth! The bat.

The bat first went to the bear and declared I have teeth; I must be on your side. But the bear answered, you have wings it would not be fair, you must be a bird.

Then the bat went to the birds and said take me on your side for you see I have wings. But the birds just laughed at him, you are too small to help us, we do not want you on our team.

The bat again approached the bear who this time took pity on the bat and said he join the team but he must wait to play and let the big animals play first.

Two poles were setup and the game began. Each team played hard, the deer and fox were swift and the bear cleared the way for his team. The crane and hawk were even swifter and stole the ball each time they got close to scoring.

Soon it became clear the birds had the advantage because each time they got the ball the birds would climb in the air and the animals could not reach them. The animals guarded their goal well but they grew tired as the sun began to set.

Just as the sun fell below the sky the Crane took the ball and flew toward the goal. Bear tried to stop him but in the darkness he tripped and fell. It appeared the birds were going to win.

Suddenly a small dark shape flew onto the field and took the ball from the Crane. It was the bat. He darted from side to side dodging around the field and no one could catch him.

The bear looked up as the bat carried the ball toward the goal and watched the bat score for the animals. That is how the bat came to be accepted as an animal and not a bird.

The Bat was allowed to set the terms for the birds. He declared for half the year the birds must leave this land. So that is why birds must fly south each winter.

Now every day at dusk the bat still comes out flying to see if the animals need him to play a game of ball.

This first story talks to one of the great lessons—that everyone is meant to play lacrosse. The game is for everyone to play and not just those who are strong and fast.

The next story tells why only some birds fly south for the winter. This story comes from the book *Tales the Elders Told, Ojibway Legends*. (16)

Long ago there was only summer. Days were always warm and sunny. For children it was a time of happiness and they played lacrosse. Mong the Loon was like others but the game he loved the most was lacrosse. As soon as one game would end he wanted to play another. But the other birds were not as fond of lacrosse as he was.

One time when no one would play with him he approached Kaikaik the hawk and challenged him to a game. But Kaikaik said it was too hot to play. Mong said let's play tomorrow, but pick teams now. Kaikaik answered lacrosse was too easy. So Mong offered a bet. If his team won Kaikaik had to play lacrosse whenever he asked and if Kaikaik won he had to do whatever he asked.

They picked teams and Kaikaik picked the Raven, Cardinal, Owl, Woodpecker, grouse, pheasant, and snow bird. Mong selected the Canadian Goose, kingbird, robin, sparrow, thrasher, and swallow. They agreed the first team to score would win the game.

The game began the next day and soon Mong could see his team was quite slow. The Raven was knocked down and laid on the field rolling in pain But the game was not to stop until a goal was scored. The Swallow got the ball and flew past the Raven who leapt up and stole the ball and scored on Mong.

Mong supporters now groaned and wondered what Kaikaik would require of Mong for losing. Kaikaik approached Mong and said this is your punishment, from now on when the east wind blows it will bring rain, and thunderstorms and you will not be able to play lacrosse. No one had ever heard of such a thing.

Mong did not want to not play lacrosse so he declared the Raven had cheated pretending to be hurt. He asked to play again and the terms would be the same the loser had to do whatever the winner says. But Mong asked for the Raven to be on his team.

Kaikaik agreed to the terms and believed he could win without the Raven. The next day a great game of lacrosse was played again. This time the Raven played hard for Mong. As the day wore on Mong's team began to tire. As Raven was flying towards the goal the Grouse tripped the Raven and stole the ball. The Grouse then scored the winning goal. Mong cried foul but the vulture who was the referee did not see the trip and he declared Kaikaik the winner.

Everyone now rushed the field to hear what Kaikaik would now give a punishment. He told Mong from now on when North Wind blows it will bring snow and cold.

That very night the North Wind began to blow and the snow and cold came. Mong and his friends did not like the snow and the cold so they left the land they loved. From then on every time the North Wind blows and winter comes Mong and his friends fly south for the winter. If Mong had not made that foolish bet, winter would have never come.

This story focuses on greed and foolishness. A greedy Mong brought winter on everyone because he wanted to play the game of lacrosse all the time even when others did not.

The Dakota

The Ojibwe story of how they arrived in Minnesota is well documented. However, the Dakota story begins with the Nation already existing in Minnesota. The Dakota Nation is made up of three primary groups: Dakota (eastern), Nakota (central), and Lakota (western). Each of these speak a different dialect such as Santee, Yankton and Teton.

The Dakota history is rich and complex, but less information is publically available. Some Dakota bands, like Prairie Island, say that their tribe had very limited or no history of playing the game. However, documentation shows that the Dakota played in some very significant lacrosse games in the area of modern day Bloomington. This will be discussed further in the Fort Snelling chapter.

SUGGESTED FURTHER READING

- *American Indian Lacrosse – Little Brother of War*, Thomas Vennum
- *Games of the North American Indians*, Stewart Culin
- *Tales the Elders Told – Ojibway Legends*, Basil Johnston
- *Ojibwe in Minnesota*, Anton Treuer
- *Ojibwe Waasa Inaadidaa – We look in all directions*, Thomas Peacock
- *History of the Ojibway People*, William Warren
- *The Great Ball Game - A Muskogee Story*, Joseph Bruchac

CHAPTER 2

FIRST OBSERVERS

Word of a New World spread throughout Europe and stories of new Nations emerged. Like many early travelers, it was the religious who went to new places looking to spread the word of God. Our story starts with these first men who traveled to the New World as missionaries. These missionaries listened as the Spanish and French explorers returned home to Europe and told grand stories of the New World and Nations of "untamed" people.

Jean de Brébeuf was one of those men who heard the tales of people who had never heard the story of Jesus, and he longed to travel to the New World to find a way to convert what he considered lost souls.

Brébeuf was born in the small town of Condé-sur-Vire, just outside of Normandy, France. He grew up with a passion for Christianity and became a Jesuit priest.

Minnesota Lacrosse: A History

> **SIDE WALL:**
> *Thunder Bay, Ontario, is a city located just north of Grand Portage, Minnesota. The city gets its name from local Ojibwe stories about Thunderbirds.*
>
> *The Thunderbirds are mythical creatures who in many stories control the wind, rain, and keep evil creatures away from the Nations. Thunderbirds in Ojibwe traditions are believed to have provided the Ojibwe with the first lacrosse sticks.*
> (17)

Brébeuf was a dedicated priest who had an unwavering belief in Christ, wanted to prove his worthiness, and desired to sacrifice his life to Jesus.

Jesuits, like Brébeuf, believed that going to this new world was like Jesus going among the Jews, and they would be successful by becoming martyrs for their beliefs.

Jesuit Background

The information provided here comes from *The Jesuit Relation*, missionary reports published from 1632 – 1673 and sent back to Europe. These annual reports were the activities and observations of the Jesuit missionaries and their attempts to convert the "savages." (18)

The Jesuits were members of the "Society of Jesus," and took special oaths of poverty and obedience that separated them from other priests.

In Central and South America the Jesuits were very successful in converting the First Nations because they followed the conquering Spanish soldiers. In those areas, the Jesuit's were in a better position to force their ideals upon the local populations. However, the French did not conquer the First Nations in North America as the Spanish did. Instead, the French embraced the First Nations, intermarried, and traded with them. Because of this, Jesuits were less successful in converting and indoctrinating the northern First Nations.

When the Jesuits arrived in the St. Lawrence River Valley they found two distinct groups of people, the Algonquians and the Iroquoians. The Nations inside the two groups spoke different dialects. Their way of living was also different. The Algonquians relied on hunting and fishing for food, while the Iroquoians planted and cultivated crops.

The Jesuits worked with both Nations and spent considerable time learning and documenting their languages and activities. The Jesuit approach was to live with Nations, adopt their lifestyle, observe and only take food and shelter if offered.

Map by Author

New France

The French established a presence in the New World, calling it New France. Here is a quick overview of the events that occurred before Brébeuf arrived.

- 1534, Jacques Cartier arrived near Newfoundland and claimed the country by erecting a cross with the words "Long Live the King of France"
- 1604, First year-round settlement established in Arcadia
- 1608, Samuel de Champlain founded Quebec
- 1611-1613, two Jesuits tried to establish a mission in Quebec but failed
- 1625, Jesuits returned and established a mission in Quebec
- 1629, Jesuits returned to France as the mission in Quebec was lost
- 1630s, Lake Huron became the central focus of the fur trade
- 1632, Jesuits returned again to Quebec and stayed

Jean de Brébeuf personal timeline:
- 1593, Born in Condé-sur-Vire, France
- 1617, Joined the Jesuit order at age 24
- 1622, Ordained a priest
- 1625, Arrived in New France
- 1629, Returned to France when mission was lost
- 1630, Took final vows as a Jesuit
- 1633, Returned to New France to work with the Hurons
- 1636, Wrote in his journal about a game he calls lacrosse
- 1638, Left the Huron mission and turned it over to Jerome Lalemant
- 1640, Broke his collar bone, lived in Quebec
- 1643, Returned to the Hurons
- 1649, Tortured and murdered by the Iroquois

The Jesuits chose to work with the Hurons because they were the largest, most settled, and influential group in the area. [19] Brébeuf documented the language of the Hurons and lived among them for many years. The Hurons became the middlemen between fur-rich Algonquians and the corn and tobacco growers to the south. The Hurons developed contacts with Samuel de Champlain and King Henry IV in France. This alliance provided aid to the Hurons against their enemy the Iroquois Nation. [20]

Jean de Brébeuf was an outstanding Jesuit. He lived the longest among the Hurons, was fluent in their language, and developed a keen insight into their society. His fellow Jesuits described him as the kindest and most charitable man they knew. Brébeuf was a large man with broad shoulders and considerable strength. He typically sported a full black beard that matched his Jesuit black robes. The Hurons referred to Brébeuf as the "Echon," the most powerful sorcerer of the Christian French. [21]

The first record of a lacrosse game was in Brébeuf's journal and published in *The Jesuit Relations*. However, the placement of the recorded event was not with recreation activities, but in the *"Medical Practices of the Hurons."* Brébeuf wrote about two cures for illness they practiced: first was curing by a game of crosse, and the second was curing through gambling. [22]

Brébeuf was not happy that they thought healings or cures could be achieved by playing a game or by gambling. He believed the only true healer was Jesus. Brébeuf went on to document that any person in the Nation could call for a game of crosse. If a person was ill or had a dream that he may die, they could call for a game of crosse. If a medicine man saw that the Nation

Chapter Two - First Observers

was sick, or that the Nation was suffering from famine, bad crops, or disease, they could also call for a game to be played.

After a game was called for the captains formed teams and all young men did their duty and played the game. If a player refused to play, it was believed he would bring misfortune to his family for not participating.

The medicine man in the First Nation culture served as the coach for lacrosse players and was considered responsible for the success or failure of the team. Thomas Vennum compared the medicine man to the Greek God Apollo and his role in Greek athletic contests. (23) Nearly all young men learned to play the game lacrosse as a child. (24)

St. Paul Globe 1885 Sketch

Bishop's Crozier

Much discussion has occurred over the years as to why Brébeuf called the game la crosse. There are no surviving Huron lacrosse sticks. Since the Hurons had significant contact with them during the Ojibwe migration, it may be surmised that the stick Brébeuf saw is similar to the Ojibwe stick.

An 1885 sketch from the St. Paul Globe, when compared to a bishop's crozier or cross, show the similarity.

SIDE WALL:
The book "Lacrosse technique and tradition" by Bob Scott refers to the area where Jean de Brébeuf first sees lacrosse being played as "near Thunder Bay, Ontario." (25)

Upon further research, the area Bob called Thunder Bay was most likely Thunder Falls near Niagara Falls.

After additional research, the actual area appears to be the Georgian Bay area in Ontario.

This is an explanation that experts such as Thomas Vennum and Donald Fisher dismiss. Instead they have suggested that back in France, other games involving sticks, such as bandy and field hockey at the time, used the term crosse to describe those sports.

Whatever the reason for Brébeuf to use this name, it stuck with his brethren, who in future journals confirmed that the same game was played by many Nations. They used the phrase a "game of crosse" to describe this activity.

In lacrosse circles, Brébeuf's story normally ends when he wrote the name of the game in his journal, linking his name to the game forever. And what did he do with his life? The continued story is quite interesting.

Though the French did not conquer in the same way that the Spanish did, they had a major impact on the First Nations. Their trading and favoring of the Hurons led the Iroquois to war on several of their neighbors.

Prior to these wars, disease had major impacts on the Nations. Diseases brought from Europe included measles and small pox, which wiped out over 50% of the Hurons. (26)

In addition to these losses the Huron faced a new rising enemy to the south.

The Iroquois, seeing the losses suffered by their neighbors, seized the moment by conquering many Nations between 1645 and 1655. (27) In ten years, the Iroquois destroyed the Huron, Petun, Neutral, and the Erie Nations. Each Nation was at least ten thousand strong before the conflict started.

The Iroquois reached Huron country in 1648. The Hurons were already suffering losses from disease and now had internal leadership conflicts. Some believed that only the Jesuits and French could save them from the Iroquois. It was this belief that allowed the Jesuits to have success in baptizing and converting the Hurons to Catholicism.

In 1649 the Iroquois reached the fortified settlement of St. Ignace (near the eastern end of Lake Huron). The town was surrounded by a 50-foot ditch and 15-foot wall, based on advice from the French. However, due to cold temperatures, the river and ground were frozen and provided excellent footing for the Iroquois to climb and scale the walls. St. Ignace fell on March 16, 1649. The Hurons knew this would be their last stand. The next day the

Chapter Two - First Observers

Iroquois reached the nearby town of St. Louis Ontario, where Brébeuf and Lalemant resided with the Hurons. Although 500 Hurons fled and begged the missionaries to join them, the Jesuits stayed, knowing their fate.

The Iroquois were informed that the great Echon (Brébeuf) was in St. Louis Ontario. Part of Echon's power was that he dictated who could trade for goods. Additionally, diseases were starting to kill off the Iroquois, who feared that he was causing their deaths for not converting to Christianity. While he had been respected among the Hurons, he was the most hated and feared Blackrobe by the Iroquois. They agreed that at all costs, Echon must be captured and saved for torture.

Brébeuf and his companion Lalemant were captured. Brébeuf stood tall and encouraged the new Huron Christian converts by crying out that God was witnessing the deaths of Brébeuf and Lalemant's. The Iroquois, incensed by his courage, dragged Brébeuf and Lalemant and tied them to posts. The torture that was about to begin would last all afternoon.

The Iroquois gathered iron hatchets and put them in the fire until red hot. Placed on Brébeuf and Lalemant's shoulders, the hatchets burned both chests and backs. But Brébeuf would not call out nor scream in pain. Instead he prayed silently as the torture continued. Next they wrapped him in bark and set him on fire.

Brébeuf was then tortured by a mock baptism of boiling water poured over his head and body. Instead of asking for mercy, Brébeuf continued to pray and bless his assailants. The Iroquois, now infuriated by his calmness and continued prayers, gagged him and cut off his nose and lips, then watched the blood pour from his face. Brébeuf continued to call on God to forgive his captors, just as Jesus had done on the cross.

Finally at 4pm on March 16, 1649 an Iroquois warrior buried his hatchet into Brébeuf's jaw, ending his life. The Iroquois had admiration for the strong warrior they had just killed. Brébeuf had never cried out, never begged for mercy, and must indeed be the strongest man they had ever met.

In 1649, Father Paul Ragueneau wrote in *The Jesuit Relation* that Brébeuf died a martyr as he had dreamed and crowned his life in holiness. (28)

Jean de Brébeuf was sainted, along with five other early French missionaries, by Pope Pius XI on June 29, 1930.

- *Saint René Goupil, Jesuit novice, (Born in 1608, martyred in 1642)*
- *Saint Jean de La Lande, layperson, (Born in 160?, martyred in 1646)*
- *Saint Isaac Jogues, Jesuit priest, (Born in 1608, martyred in 1646)*
- *Saint Antoine Daniel, Jesuit priest, (Born in 1600, martyred in 1648)*
- *Saint Jean de Brébeuf, Jesuit priest, (Born in 1593, martyred in 1649)*
- *Saint Charles Garnier, Jesuit priest, (Born in 1606, martyred in 1649)*
- *Saint Gabriel Lalemant, Jesuit priest, (Born in 1610, martyred in 1649)*
- *Saint Noel Chabanel, Jesuit priest, (Born in 1613, martyred in 1649)*

Holy card for the North American Martyrs

Chapter Two - First Observers

The lore of lacrosse has referred to writings of Brébeuf and his naming of the game, but few understood his sacrifice for his beliefs and commitment to his God.

SUGGESTED FURTHER READING

- *Jean de Brébeuf 1593-1649,* Joseph Peter Donnelly
- *The Jesuit Relations,* Allan Greer

CHAPTER 3

FORT MICHILIMACKINAC

Fort Michilimackinac was the site of an infamous lacrosse game involving the Ojibwe Nation. Not many resources discuss why the game of lacrosse was used as a ruse to take over the fort or the purpose for attacking the fort.

The location of Fort Michilimackinac was a key area to the Ojibwe, Ottawa, and Potawatomi during their migration from the east coast.

A century after Brébeuf became a martyr, France and Great Britain entered a war, often referred to as the Seven Year War or French and Indian War. In May of 1754, a 22-year-old British Major George Washington ambushed a French patrol. This later led France and Great Britain to declare war in 1756. The British were victorious and the war ended with the Treaty of Paris on February 10, 1763.

Map by Author

France was given a choice at the end of the war. One option was to keep the lands in New France (Canada and United States east of the Mississippi River). The other option was to keep their islands in the Caribbean. France, believing sugar cane was a better economic value, left behind New France.

The reason to explain this background is to point out that France had left their trading posts and forts to the British. The British were not as generous as the French and did not understand the First Nation culture as the French had. The British began to limit trade on many items like weapons. These limits showed that the British did not trust the First Nations.

The British treated the First Nations as subjects won in war. The First Nations watched as the British colonists pushed them off their land, cleared the trees, and grew crops. They feared that under British rule this would continue without interruption. It is on this canvas we will now explore how a game of lacrosse allowed the capture of a fort.

In the east, a man known as the Delaware Prophet Neolin warned his fellow First Nation people that living among the British was bringing the wrath of disease and death upon them, and that they must reject the British ways and cast them out. (29)

Chapter Three - Fort Michilimackinac

Pontiac, a leader in the Ottawa Nation, saw his people suffer under the British and began to plot an attack. Pontiac used his "light-footed messengers," sending them to neighboring villages with offerings of tobacco. He asked them to attend a general meeting to discuss his plan. On April 27, 1763 the tribes assembled near Detroit and Pontiac spoke to the council.

Pontiac spoke of the arrogance and injustice of the British, and how they drove the French and the First Nations from their lands. He spoke of the Delaware Prophet and his vision from the Great Spirit that declared they must drive the British out of their lands to regain respect from the Great Spirit. After he spoke, the Ottawa, Ojibwe, and other Nations began their attack on the British. [30]

As was custom for the Ojibwe and Ottawa, they came down to Detroit in the spring to assemble for trading. They assembled in the open fields in front of the fort. Many soldiers thought they were going to play lacrosse, but instead they approached the fort gates. On May 1, their first ruse was to enter Fort Detroit by offering to perform the calumet dance. During the performance at the Fort, they took note of each area within the fort and any weakness they could attack.

As the story goes, an Ojibwe girl lived nearby and was friendly with Fort Detroit's commander, Major Gladwyn. On May 6 she visited the Major and shared that Pontiac planned to visit the Fort the next day with sixty of his leaders armed with guns cut short and hidden under blankets. [31]

When Pontiac arrived at Fort Detroit on May 7, he was met by fully armed British soldiers dressed in full gear to show their readiness. Major Gladwyn invited Pontiac to speak as he had asked. Pontiac saw the fear in the eyes of his men and wondered how the British could have known of their intentions. Among his deceptions, Pontiac spoke of sharing the peace pipe with his new British friends. The Major did not believe him, but did not really understand the threat posed by Pontiac, either. The Major allowed Pontiac and his men to leave unharmed.

The next day, to cover his guise of peace, Pontiac called for a game of ball play (lacrosse), while he and the leaders plotted again to find a way to defeat the British. The next day Pontiac again tried to enter the Fort, but the Major would not allow it. At this point, Pontiac began to plan attacks upon British settlements in the area. Pontiac stayed and continued to fight in the area and against Fort Detroit throughout the summer. [32]

Meanwhile Pontiac's allies had more success at other forts in the Great Lakes region. From May 16 to June 2 the First Nations captured five forts. The first fort to fall was Fort Sandusky on May 16. The ruse to capture Fort Sandusky was the same as Fort Detroit: an offering of a peace council. However, word had not reached Fort Sandusky about the betrayal at Fort Detroit and that the Wyandot Nation was successful at taking the Fort, killing the British soldiers and burning the fort to the ground. (33)

On May 25 Fort St. Joseph was taken in the same manner, using the guise of a peace council, by the Potawatomi Nation.

The next to fall was Fort Miami on May 27. The deception this time was changed. The fort commander was lured out of the fort. The Miami Nation shot the commander and surrounded the fort. The remaining soldiers surrendered the fort.

On June 1 Fort Ouiatenon was taken using the ruse of a peace council outside the fort. The Weas, Kickapoos, and Mascouten Nations took the fort without bloodshed and spared the British soldiers.

Three forts in the Ohio country were taken in a second wave of attacks in mid-June. Senecas of the Iroqious confederacy took Fort Venango (near the site of present Franklin, Pennsylvania) around June 16, 1763. They killed the entire 12-man garrison, keeping the commander alive to write down the grievances of the Seneca. Possibly the same Seneca warriors attacked Fort Le Boeuf (on the site of Waterford, Pennsylvania) on June 18, but most of the 12-man garrison escaped to Fort Pitt.

Fort Michilimackinac was located in the Straits of Mackinac between Lake Michigan and Lake Huron. This fort was a key area for trading in the northern region. Word of the attacks had not yet reached British Major George Etherington, commander of Fort Michilimackinac. The Major observed that the local Ojibwe Nation was assembled outside the fort to trade as they normally do in the spring. They played lacrosse for several days and now had invited the Sauk (a rival Nation), to join them for a big game to celebrate the King's birthday.

Unknown to the Major, the Ojibwe chiefs Minweweh and Madjeckewiss had been planning an attack for days. Pontiac's attacks used the deception of peace offerings, dances, celebrations, and even luring Commanders out to see their mistresses. Minweweh, however, wanted to try a different plan of attack.

Chapter Three - Fort Michilimackinac

The Major heard rumors of unrest and possible attack. He had served in the French and Indian War, and felt the rumors were not worth any concern. On June 2 he joined his men in wagering on the Ojibwe Nation to win the game and watched with great interest. The game was said to have had over 500 players, a large number compared to the population of the fort which had around 35 soldiers.

The next day the priest delivered this letter at the gates of Fort Detroit. The letter is from the commander of Fort Michilimackinac, Major Etherington:

June 12, 1763
"*Sir:*
Notwithstanding what I wrote you in my last, that all savages were arrived, and that everything seemed in perfect tranquility, yet on the second instant the Ojibwe, who live in the plain near the fort, assembled to play ball, as they had done almost every day since their arrival. They played from morning until noon; then, throwing their ball close to the gate, and observing Lieutenant Lesley and me a few paces out of it, they came behind us and seized and carried us into the woods.

"In the meantime, the rest rushed into the fort, where they found their squaws, whom they had previously planted there, with their hatchets hid under their blankets, which they took, and in an instant killed Lieutenant Tracey. They wounded two, and took the rest of the garrison prisoners, five of whom they have since killed.

"They made prisoners all the English traders, and robbed them of everything they had; but they offered no violence to the persons or property of any of the Frenchmen..." (34)

The Major went on to detail more about the attack and requested that reinforcements be sent to reclaim the fort. But Fort Detroit was still under assault from Pontiac and Major Gladwyn could not spare any forces.

Ojibwe historian William Warren recorded this version of the story: (35)

On the morning of the 4th of June, after the firing of the cannon for the King's birthday, an exciting game of lacrosse would begin. Two hundred players painted and dressed in feathers, ribbons, and with fox and wolf tails played up and down the fields in front of the fort. Players leap to avoid hits as opponents tried to knock the ball loose from their sticks. They would make sudden dodges and run swiftly towards the goals.

The commander of the fort came out and watched outside the open gates. His soldiers were carelessly unarmed and intermingled with the Indian women who had taken positions near the open gates. The ball would then be thrown near the open gates of the fort and with a loud yell the player dropped their sticks and grabbed tomahawks, shortened guns, and knives hidden under the blankets of their women. The massacre would begin and soon the bodies of the unsuspecting British soldiers would be scattered about the grounds of the fort. The careless commander would be taken captive.

Another version of the story is told by a survivor of the attack, a British Trader at the fort named Alexander Henry. Mr. Henry had befriended an Ojibwe named Wa-wat-am or Whirling Eddy, and it would be this Ojibwe who spared Henry's life during and after the attack. Here is the diary account from Alexander Henry: (36)

The morning was sultry. A Chippeway came to tell me that his nation was going to play a game at Baggataway with the Sacs or Saukies , another Indian nation, for a high stakes wager. He invited me to witness the sport adding that the commandant was to be there, and would bet on the side of the Chippeways. In consequence of this information, I went to the commandant and expostulated with him a little, representing that the Indians might possibly have some sinister end in view, but the commandant only smiled at my suspicions.

I did not go myself to see the match, which was now to be played without the fort, because, there being a canoe prepared to depart on the following day to Montreal, I employed myself in writing letters to my friends; and even when my fellow trader Mr. Tracy, happened to call on me, saying that another canoe had just arrived from Detroit, and proposing that I should go with him to the beach to inquire the news, it so happened that I still remained to finish my letters, promising to follow Mr. Tracey in the course of a few minutes.

Mr. Tracey had not gone more than twenty paces from the door, when I heard an Indian war-cry and a noise of general confusion. Going instantly to my window, I saw a crowd of Indians within the fort, furiously cutting down and scalping every Englishmen they found. In particular, I witnessed the fate of Lieut. Jenette.

Chapter Three – Fort Michilimackinac

I had, in the room in which I was, a fowling piece, loaded with swan shot. This I immediately seized, and held it for a few minutes, waiting to hear the drum beat to arms. In this dreadful interval, I saw several of my countrymen fall, and more than one struggling between the knees of an Indian, who holding him in this manner, scalped him while yet living!

At length, disappointed in the hope of seeing resistance made to the enemy, and sensible of course that no effort of my own unassisted arm could avail against four hundred Indians, I thought only of seeking shelter. Amid the slaughter which was raging, I observed many of the Canadian inhabitants of the fort calmly looking on, neither opposing the Indians nor suffering injury. From this circumstance I conceived a hope of finding security in their houses.

Next on June 7, Mr. Henry's friend and adopted brother, Wa-wat-am, approached and defend him to Chief Wen-ni-way. Mr. Henry was released.

Pontiac learned of the successful attack after Father Jonois (a Jesuit priest of the Ottawa mission near Fort Michilimackinac) and the son of Ojibwe chief Minavavana arrived. Pontiac then reached out to the Ojibwe villages on Lake Superior with a request to join the rebellion.

Jean Baptiste Cadotte, a French trader who possessed great influence over the Ojibwe in the Lake Superior area, advised them not to join the rebellion. He told them that the French soldiers had returned to France and were not available to help Pontiac, as was being promised by Pontiac's messengers. The Lake Superior Ojibwe took his advice, and this saved the Lake Superior Ojibwe villages from attack by the British. The Nations that had joined Pontiac were not as fortunate. (37)

Even though the Ojibwe had successfully taken Fort Michilimackinac, they had no interest in maintaining the fort and quickly abandoned it. The fort remained empty until after a peace treaty was signed later that year. Colonel Bradstreet sent Captain Howard to head north from Detroit and take possession of Fort Michilimackinac again.

SUGGESTED FURTHER READING

- *The Conspiracy of Pontiac Volume 1*, Francis Parkman
- *The Conspiracy of Pontiac Volume 2*, Francis Parkman

CHAPTER 4

FORT SNELLING

After the 1803 Louisiana Purchase, an anxious President Jefferson sent Louis and Clark to map the new territory. In Clark's report to the President he cited that a fortified trading post should be established near St. Anthony Falls. [38] Lieutenant Zebulon Pike was sent in 1805 and acquired 100,000 acres in the area from St. Anthony Falls to present Mendota.

Nothing more was done with the land Pike acquired near Mendota until 1819 when the Army founded Fort St. Anthony on a bluff overlooking the conjunction of the Mississippi and Minnesota Rivers. This *bdote* (the confluence of two great rivers), was sacred ground to the Dakota.

In 1820 Colonel Josiah Snelling took command and oversaw the construction of the fort. When the fort was completed in 1825 it was renamed to Fort Snelling to honor its commander and architect.

Earlier on his journey, Lieutenant Pike had observed a lacrosse game being played on the eastern shore of the Mississippi River in what is now southwestern Wisconsin.

In an 1805 journal entry, Pike expressly stated that the area's name originated from the "French name of the game of ball played by the Indians at this place." The place Pike referred to was "Prairie de La Crosse," which when settled in 1844 kept the name La Crosse. [39]

Fort Snelling was the first fort established after the War of 1812 and its purpose was to promote the interest of the United States in activities such as

Minnesota Lacrosse: A History

the growing fur trade. The fort's location was considered strategic for trading routes and to protect the new Louisiana Purchase.

At first the Fort's role was to keep white settlers out of the region and to only allow the rivers to be used for business trade. The Fort kept the peace and did not allow settlements until treaties were reached.

> **SIDE WALL:**
> *One of the more interesting guests at Fort Snelling was Count Zeppelin in 1863.*
>
> *Zeppelin is reported to have made his first trip in a captive air balloon at Fort Snelling, which led him to return to Germany and develop the Graf Zeppelin, the model of future flying blimps.*

In the spring of each year the local Nations of the Dakota and Ojibwe visited, traded, debated government policies with the Indian Agency, and played ball.

After a long Minnesota winter, the spring was a great time to perform dances and play lacrosse games around the fort.

Over the years Fort Snelling hosted many visitors. George Catlin was one of the first artists who traveled west of the Mississippi River and recorded on canvas the First Nation people. Catlin was very fond of the people he painted and sketched. He was also an admirer of the ball play game now called lacrosse. Catlin made some of the most famous paintings seen in lacrosse books today.

Catlin was born in Pennsylvania in 1796. The majority of his art was created during his travels of the Great Plains from 1830 to 1836. [40]

Catlin's work was not without controversy and people criticized him for his sympathy towards the Nations he visited. Some have also criticized that his paintings, such as the lacrosse games, showed an over-estimation of the number of players involved in games. But without him, we would not have the record of how the Nations dressed and played games.

In 1834 Catlin recorded his first lacrosse game near Fort Gibson, in present-day Oklahoma. He was visiting the Choctaws who had been relocated from Alabama and Mississippi. It was here that Catlin became a huge fan of ball play. He wrote that he would make every effort to attend each lacrosse game he heard of. He traveled 20-30 miles in a day to watch games. He watched these men play with high energy, tricks, and scuffles in a superhuman effort to control the ball. [41]

Chapter Four - Fort Snelling

George Catlin by William Fisk, National Portrait Gallery

Catlin goes on to define the game as goals being erected with two 25-foot poles placed about six feet apart at both ends of the field. The goals were about ½ mile apart. The ball was tossed at mid-field with the firing of a gun. After a team scored, the game paused for a moment, then began again. Catlin said the Choctaw played to 100 goals. (42)

The Choctaws played the game with two sticks and dressed in a breach cloth with beading and wore a tail.

Catlin continued his journeys on the Great Plains. In the spring of 1835, he reached Fort Snelling. A tribe of Ojibwe had recently arrived from the north to trade furs. There was also a presence of Dakota in the area. The commander at the fort was Major Lawrence Taliaferro. Catlin shared that he had witnessed many lacrosse games and asked if the Dakota or Ojibwe played the game. Catlin said he had come to the area to see if the Dakota and Ojibwe played with the same intensity as the other Nations. (43)

The Major invited the Dakota and Ojibwe to play a game of lacrosse at the fort. In exchange, the fort's cannon would be fired twenty-one times. The Major asked them to play on the Fourth of July because the cannons were already set to be fired off for the celebration.

On July 4, 1835 they played a game of lacrosse at Fort Snelling dressed in their best. Catlin noted that the Dakota and Ojibwe played a different style of lacrosse from the Choctaws, using only a single stick compared to the Choctaws who played with two.

George Catlin's No. 21 Ball Players - Smithsonian American Art Museum

Catlin painted the player he felt was most distinguished, *Ah-no-je-naje (He Who Stands on Both Sides)*, who is featured on the far right of the painting. The other Dakota player, pictured in the center, was named *We-Chush-Ta-Doo-Ta (The Red Man)*. The Choctaw player on the left was known as *Tul-lock-chish-ko (Drinks the Juice of the Stone)*.

Chapter Four - Fort Snelling

Catlin also marveled at the influence of the Fort, noting that the two Nations, which seemed to be continually at war, now posted camps outside the Fort and worked with trade agents without the threat of war.

Ojibwe and Dakota had played games of lacrosse to help keep the peace. William Warren describes games of lacrosse in the Red River area along the banks of the Platte River with Sisseton, Wahpeton, and Mdewakanton tribes. Some games turned violent, and all had wagers on the outcome. Lacrosse always seemed to involve a wager between the opponents. (44)

George Catlin left Fort Snelling in 1835 and returned in 1836. This time he returned to seek the famed red clay west of the fort. Catlin makes very little mention of this trip in his diary, but the Fort Commander, Major Lawrence Taliaferro, had noted that Catlin left for the Pipestone Quarry on Sunday, August 21, 1836. (45)

Catlin had written in his previous travel journals that tobacco was a major tradition of all Nations he visited. He also noted that most Nations had their pipes or bowls made of the same red clay material.

Catlin departed with his English companion, Robert Wood, and traveled by canoe up the St. Peter River (now known as the Minnesota River) as far as they could go. From there they acquired horses and made it to a trading post named Le Blanc.

> **SIDE WALL:**
> *The territorial legislature asked the US Congress to officially change the name of St. Peter River back to the Dakota name, Minnesota. On June 19, 1852, the name was changed and all official maps would now say Minnesota River, meaning sky-tinted or cloudy sky water.*

The Dakota had heard of his intention to see the sacred pipestone quarry and met him at the trading post, "filling each avenue of the cabin." This contingent of Dakota was there to stop him, telling him to turn back and that no white man had ever seen Pipestone. (46)

The Dakota went on to declare that the red clay was a gift to all native peoples from the Great Spirit. After giving the warning the Dakota left, but Catlin continued his journey. He received more warnings along the way.

Catlin and Wood reached the quarry, which is located in what is now southwestern Minnesota. Traditions relate that this is the mysterious birthplace of the red pipe, given by the Great Spirit and that has blown its fumes of peace and war across Turtle Island. It was here the Great Spirit brought all Nations together, brought out a great bowl, and smoked it over them. To the North, South, East, and West the Great Spirit told them the stone was red, the color of their flesh, and belonged to them and must be used only for making pipes of peace. The scared ground could never be used for war.

*George Catlin, Pipestone Quarry on the Coteau Des Prairies. 1836-37
Smithsonian American Art Museum*

Catlin painted an image of the quarry with a 30 foot wall and an area where the Nations dug out the red clay. Catlin took back a sample of the clay and sent it to mineralogist Dr. Charles Jackson in Boston. Dr. Jackson declared it a new mineral and named it "catlinite" to honor George Catlin.

First Nations have various reasons to hold this area sacred. One story involves the Great Spirit himself visiting the area and feasting on bison. The Great Spirit feasted so much that the blood of the bison stained the earth the red color that it is today.

Another story is that the area was a meeting place of all nations, and that this resulted in war. The blood of those who died in the battle is said to have seeped into the ground causing the red clay to form. To the First Nations, this area remains very sacred and pipes and other items made from this clay hold a special meaning. (47)

The reason for telling the Pipestone story is to remind people that this place exists today in Minnesota, and that the St Paul Lacrosse Club had their greatest rivalry against a team named the "Calumets," a word that means *peace pipe*.

Seth Eastman

Artist and West Point graduate Seth Eastman served at Fort Snelling for two tours, and was later the Fort Commander.

In 1830, Eastman received a 3-year assignment to Fort Snelling. Eastman was a map-maker and illustrator. He learned the Dakota language and sketched and painted the Dakota Nations in the area. In 1833 he was assigned to West Point to teach map drawing and illustration.

In 1841 Seth Eastman was promoted to Brigadier General and appointed commander of Fort Snelling. During this time Seth and his wife Mary studied and documented the Dakota in the area.

From their time at Fort Snelling, Mary Henderson Eastman wrote a book called *Dacotah, or Life and Legends of the Sioux Around Fort Snelling* (1849), illustrated by Seth Eastman.

Mary and Seth Eastman were admirers of lacrosse and watched many games played near the fort. Mary wrote about the game in her books and Seth recorded the games in his artwork. Mary wrote a chapter in her book, *The American Aboriginal Portfolio*, where she described the lacrosse game depicted in Seth's Ball Play painting: (48)

The game of ball is universally popular among the North American Indians. Almost all of the tribes play it, though each tribe has its peculiar mode. They play it in small parties or in large; on the ice in winter, or on the prairie in the summer.

In some tribes it is customary to use one bat-stick in throwing the ball; in others, one is held in each hand. In winter, the Indians adorn themselves with their choicest finery, dressing in their very best; in summer, they hardly dress at all; so that the same game makes a variety of pictures, seen at different times, and under different circumstances.

It is not necessary that the parties should be equal number; braves of villages send a messenger to those of another, challenging them to a game of ball; or those of a large village invite those of two or more villages to the contest.

The challenge is always accepted; old men, young men, and boys, are eager for the fun. It must here be remembered, that each Indian feels it a sort of duty to enjoy himself in the same customs as did his ancestors; and in the game of ball, duty and inclination meet most harmoniously.

The time appointed has come, and the men are assembled on both sides. Two marks are set up on the ice about half a mile apart. The game is to commence at a point halfway between these points. Each side has its limits, and the object in this game is for the combatants on one side to get the ball beyond the limits of the other. Whichever side shall accomplish this will be entitled to all the prizes that are displayed to induce emulation.

The ball is caught up in a bat-stick three feet in length, curved at the end so as to form a hoop, three or four inches in diameter. Through this hoop a few thongs of raw hide are drawn, so as to form a kind of net, which holds the ball when it is caught.

One of the Indians, catching it in his net, throws it towards the boundary of the other party; it is caught by one of that party, and thrown back again; and so on. The utmost strength and agility are exercised, and often with little effect; for the ball is often kept going from one side to the other all day without exceeding either boundary. Sometimes the game continues several days, the parties stopping to eat and sleep a little, and then arousing, with a double energy, to renew the contest.

Before the game commences, heavy bets are made on the result; a gun is bet against a blanket, a pair of leggings against a tomahawk, an embroidered coat against a buffalo robe. These bets are given charge of some old men of the tribe, who distribute them to the winners when the game is over.

While the game is going on, these men cheer the different parties, laugh aloud, call to them to exert themselves, and being too old to use their legs, make up for it by an extra use of the lungs. Sometimes one of the players become much injured; he is struck by the ball or bat-stick, of falls, and is trodden upon by some one running over him; but he must not expect any sympathy.

Sometimes an Indian is so expert as to catch the ball, and run to the limits of the opposing party in time to throw it back to his own. This is allowed by the rules of the game. The picture represents this movement. The one that has the ball is running against time, pursued by the crowd. If, however, one of the opposite party overtake him, he can knock it out of his net by a mere touch of the bat-stick. This

Chapter Four - Fort Snelling

his own party are trying to prevent, by warding off blows, so as to enable him to get as near the limits as possible before throwing the ball.

I saw the game played on the St. Peter's River, in the depth of winter. The surrounding hills were white with snow, and the ice, dark and heavy-looking in some parts, glistened like the sun in others.

The scene was inexpressibly wild. The long, gaunt boughs of the trees, leafless, and nodding with the wind towards the dark, heavy evergreens among them; the desolate appearance of nature contrasted with the exciting motions and cries of the Indians. It was impossible even for the mere spectator to be unmoved; he must feel an interest in the game, until the ball has been at length thrown beyond one of the limits, and the tired and hard-breathing men receive the prizes awarded them.

Seth Eastman's Dakota Ball Play on the Minnesota River

Seth Eastman's painting *"Ball Play"* depicts a winter version of lacrosse being played by the Dakota Nation on the Minnesota River. The painting was made in 1848 while he served as commander of Fort Snelling.

> **SIDE WALL:**
> *The area depicted in the painting is located just east of the current I-35W bridge over the Minnesota River in Bloomington.*
>
> *This area was perfect for a controlled lacrosse game with the shores as boundaries.*

Eastman was intrigued by this winter version of the game and its surroundings: bare trees, a rosy-gray sky, and the Dakota sliding on the frozen river. The players are shown testing their strength and endurance while competing for prizes. Scholars suggest that the buffalo robes, trade cloths, pots, spears, arrows, quiver, and medicine bundle in the lower left corner of the painting are items wagered on the outcome of the game. For some contests, entire villages were at stake.

Modern day Bloomington, Minnesota located near I-35W and the Minnesota River - Photo by Author

Fort Snelling served a pivotal role in Minnesota lacrosse history by attracting artists such as George Catlin and Seth Eastman to document and preserve the game. Game accounts and the Ojibwe and Dakota way of life are well documented by the Fort Snelling staff and visitors. These accounts serve to remind us that lacrosse was alive and well long before Minnesota became a state.

Chapter Four - Fort Snelling

SUGGESTED FURTHER READING
- *Letters and notes on the manners, customs, and conditions of North American Indians*, George Catlin
- *Old Fort Snelling*, Marcus Lee Hansen
- *Fort Snelling – Colossus of the Wilderness*, Steve Hall
- *Dahcotah Life and Legends of the Sioux Around Fort Snelling*, Mary Eastman
- *The American Aboriginal Portfolio*, Mary Eastman

CHAPTER 5

TREATY, TRADING, & TRADITIONS OF LACROSSE

The Ojibwe and Dakota in Minnesota, and the surrounding areas in Wisconsin and Canada, had a very different lacrosse style than the east coast version played by the Six Nations. This chapter discusses many of the historical aspects of the game of lacrosse as it was developed in the western Great Lakes area.

Thomas Vennum and Stewart Culin did a great service to the history of lacrosse by recording many traditions of the Nations in the western Great Lakes area. Stewart Culin documented the cultural traditions and practices of the First Nations for the Smithsonian. Thomas Vennum, who was by training a music major, fell in love with the game of lacrosse when he researched Ojibwe drumming traditions. He became fascinated that the drum stick, war club, and lacrosse stick shared very similar designs. (49)

Let's begin with the Ojibwe stories of the Thunderbirds, who are believed by tradition to have given the game of lacrosse to the Ojibwe Nation. Many cultures (Fox, Iroquois, Ho-Chunk, Winnebago, Dakota and others) have similar stories of the Creator or Great Spirit teaching them the game. Originally, the purpose of lacrosse was for the entertainment of the Creator.

The Ojibwe version of this story is that Thunderbirds presented lacrosse sticks to the people and showed them how to play the game. The Thunderbirds delivered the first lacrosse items in a bundle that included a war club, lacrosse stick, dance wand, drum stick, and a canoe. (50)

Each spring, after the snow had melted, the men started their ball-play or lacrosse games. From the beginning lacrosse was a spring sport. Lacrosse could be played in any season as a healing or medicine game, but spring was when most games were played. Lacrosse was even played on ice if a game was called.

Sticks and Balls

The Western Great Lakes Nations learned to make lacrosse sticks from the local trees, mostly ash in northern Minnesota and other trees as available in southern Minnesota. The ash tree allowed sticks to be made quickly from young saplings and to be the style of the Great Lake stick pictured below.

George Beers sketch of an Algonquian Lacrosse Stick, 1869

Many traditions talk about which trees should be used to make a lacrosse stick. Often, the players sought out a tree that had been struck by lightning, which served as a sign from the Creator that this tree should be used to make lacrosse sticks. A hoop end would be created to symbolize the medicine wheel—as this is a medicine game—and this end was used to scoop, carry, catch, and throw the ball. (51)

Each lacrosse stick was made with personal markings or ornaments. This practice was also used to allow the player to customize his lacrosse stick to represent a certain animal trait or spirit to help him in the game. This is still done today.

The first balls used in Great Lakes lacrosse were from a tree knot. The knot was carved out and then burned. The burnt outside was then carved off to create a round ball. Sometimes at special games the wooden ball was carved with holes that made whistling sounds as the ball was thrown. The ball was passed and the whistling sound alerted players that the ball was near.

Chapter Five - Treaty, Trading, & Traditions of Lacrosse

The knot-wood balls were replaced over time with deer skin or other leather-based outsides. This new style allowed the medicine men to conjure special powers into the lacrosse balls.

It was tradition for grandparents to present a miniature lacrosse stick, about 8 inches long, to a newborn child in their family. All boys in the Nation were expected to play lacrosse.

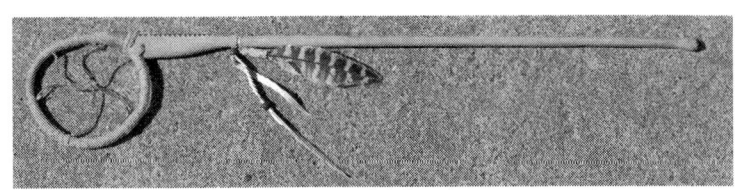

Grandparent Lacrosse Stick given to a newborn
Source: Mark Hellenack

The tradition of having a lacrosse stick in your hands continued even in death. Many players were buried with their lacrosse stick so they could continue to play the game in the next life.

In the northern culture of lacrosse, the Aurora Borealis (northern lights) are signs of the departed lacrosse players still playing in the afterlife.

Invitation Sticks
There were many ways a person or Nation could call for a game. It could be for a healing, to settle a dispute, or to play at a major event such as a treaty. One form of requesting a game was to send an invitation lacrosse stick with tobacco tied to it. A messenger delivered the stick and offering for a game of crosse. Having tobacco tied to the stick represented the commitment of the offering tribe to hold a game. (52)

Preparation Rituals
After a game of lacrosse was agreed to, the teams assembled and sticks were made for the event. Medicine men prepared players for the game.

Medicine men prepared drinks for players in order to induce vomiting and purge the body. After this, players prepared sweat lodges to further purify their bodies through sweating out the impurities.

Western Great Lakes players offered items like tobacco to the thunderbirds and thunder spirits who ruled the game of lacrosse so that they would be successful in the game.

Players were required to stay away from their women for a period of time before the game and were separated from the tribe. As game time grew closer, the players colored their bodies or marked themselves. They had no jerseys to tell who was on their team, so headbands or body paint made from trees was used to help players identify each other. Body paint including facial designs died out as white settlers made fun of the players, calling it "war paint." Elders and players today note that lacrosse was never played as a preparation for war; this was a white settler reference only.

Players did not wear protective equipment. Instead they applied oils, eel skin, slippery elm, and turtle blood to make clutching or grabbing difficult for an opponent. (53)

Medicine men were viewed as coaches preparing their team for a game. They had many tricks to help their team win—for instance, they would bless or curse balls, sticks, or even players.

Medicine men carved symbolic images into the wooden balls. Many painted or dyed the ball various colors. Red and blue were favorites, where red represented the warm summers, and blue represented winter and cooler temperatures. A medicine man may dye a ball a certain color to track it throughout the game, and he knew the blessing or curse he had placed upon it.

As animal hide began to replace wood, the medicine men found a new way to modify the ball, enhancing it with the attributes of certain animals. They may add worms, wings from a bat, or even place a small snake into a ball to make it hard to carry. Imagine trying to cradle a lacrosse ball today that moved and bounced around in your stick because it had a snake in it.

Medicine men were known to wage war over the control of lacrosse sticks.(54) Strong medicine men were thought to have the power to control lacrosse sticks or remove the power of an opponent's lacrosse stick.

Field Layout

Lacrosse fields were often located near water because it was treeless, flat ground.

Chapter Five – Treaty, Trading, & Traditions of Lacrosse

Mississippi River in Ball Club, Minnesota – Photo by Author

The Ojibwe made their lacrosse fields facing east to west. East to west was also the orientation for a medicine lodge in most First Nation traditions, and since lacrosse was a medicine game the field followed the same orientation.(55)

In the Great Lakes lacrosse game, unlike other Nations, the field was set up with one post or tree that would be scored upon. Other Nations used a two goal-post approach, but the western Great Lake area Nations developed a single goal post tradition. To score a goal one needed to hit the post with the ball or touch the post with his stick while the ball was in the stick pocket.

Pregame Rituals
Like today, the Great Lakes Nations had traditions before a game. Pregame music was a tradition, with flutes and drums being the most popular to create a game-like setting for the players and the fans.

Players assembled on the field and circled their goal post in a counterclockwise direction. To the Ojibwe, the home goal post was not the one you defend, as is the tradition in today's game, but instead was the one on which they scored. (56) The circling of the goal post was to prepare the players to recognize how and where they would be scoring their goals.

A tradition of many Nations before a big lacrosse game was for the medicine man or spiritual leader to give a speech. The speech included stories of great plays, big wins, and other challenges the players had overcome to win a game for their community. The stories included the game leader's personal experiences and that it was now the player's turn to create a story that would be told to future teams.

A game started with the ball being tossed or thrown into the air. By tradition the strongest players were in the center of the field and the weakest players would play near the goals.

Community Event

Lacrosse games were a big part of the community, and fans participated in the games through gambling. Gambling gave fans a stake in the game and made them feel a part of it. Cash or greed was not a part of the gambling; often items were made specifically to wager on the game. If the item was lost, it simply became a part of the community and it might be won back in the next game. Elders held items wagered and watched them during the game. The elders played many roles, including being officials.

Spiritual leaders in the Nation embraced the gambling and even encouraged members of the community to make bets. The leaders thought it built a sense of community if everyone participated in the game in some way. Greed became a problem after the white settlers introduced cash and betting to make a profit.

Fans were not allowed on the field and if someone dared to interfere in a game, other fans stopped them and they were removed. It is said that fans truly enjoyed watching a game of lacrosse and often observed in silence, marveling at the skills of the players.

Player Skills

Frank Mayer, who sketched the Dakota at the 1851 Treaty Signing near St. Peter, showed players using two hands to pass and catch the ball. Vennum writes that players could throw and catch the ball with amazing accuracy. Game accounts report that the ball rarely touched the ground during play. (57)

As the Dakota assembled along the river, they held days of lacrosse games against one another. Frank Mayer recorded these games in his artwork with sketches of the players, which he drew like ancient Greek warriors. His sketches show us that players used both hands on the stick to throw great distances.

When horses were introduced, some Nations adopted the game to be played on horseback. Mainly it was the Plains tribes that played the game on horses. Other Nations began using horses for the officials to ride around and cover ground quickly to enforce rules.

The Ojibwe and Dakota in particular did not tolerate *"ball hogs"* in a game. Violent behavior was allowed if a player did not pass the ball. The defending player would yell "bagadoon" (throw it, get rid of it) up to three times. If the player still held the ball the defender was allowed to hit the ball carrier over the head with his stick to separate the ball from the player. (58)

Concluding a game

Games were played according to agreed-upon conditions. Play could continue until the sun went down, or to a certain number of goals, or until they ran out of players. Some games went on for hours or days, when players reached exhaustion and were unable to go on. If that happened, the other team gave up a player on their side to match the numbers.

This reduction of team players could result in each team having only one player. In some lacrosse tournaments today, when regular time and overtime has not settled a game, they will reduce the size of the team to one player per team, with goalies and no substitutions. First one to score wins the game for their team. This is called a "Braveheart," beckoning back to the tradition of fewer players to end a game.

Post-game rituals

Fire played an important role in war for the First Nations. Fire was carried into war and warriors protected it so it would not be lost. Fire was used to predict success or failure by the medicine man. If a fire went out, the war journey would end and warriors returned home. If the fire remained intact the warriors continued their quest. (59)

As war became less common, this practice continued with lacrosse and fire was brought to games to inspire the players. A leader might light a pipe and walk behind a goal and blow smoke to conjure the ball to come and score a goal.

Following the game, players had to again be purified before returning to the community. After purification, winning teams invited the losing team to a celebration meal. Once a game was over there were rarely bad feelings towards the other team. Instead, both teams celebrated the great day of lacrosse together.

Pickup Lacrosse

Pickup lacrosse games in local communities were common. A spiritual leader had all players put their sticks in a pile, then mixed up the sticks and moved them into two piles. The concept was that through the spiritual leader, the spirits of former players picked the teams. Players then found their sticks and knew which team they would be playing for that day.

Women in Lacrosse

Although the eastern tribes such as the Iroquois did not allow women to play in lacrosse games, the western Great Lake Nations like the Ojibwe and Dakota allowed it. After the men played, a women's lacrosse game followed and then a mixed game was played with men and women on the same team.(60)

Legends

As discussed in the earlier chapters, many stories in First Nation culture revolve around lacrosse. Thomas Vennum wrote an entire book about these stories called *"Lacrosse Legends of the First Americans."*

These legends contain deep meaning to both the storyteller and the listener, and were passed on during the storytelling time of long cold winters.

One story told of how the rabbit's leg was injured in a lacrosse game and why his descendants still carry the injury today — and that is why the rabbit leaves only 3 foot prints in the snow.

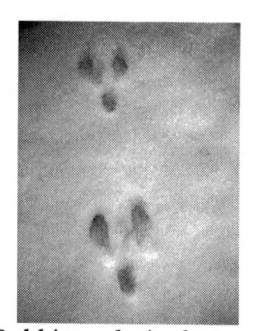

Rabbit tracks in the snow

Another story focuses on the origin of the moon. During a game of lacrosse, a player dared to pick up the ball with his hand. The ball was taken away from the player by the Creator and placed in the sky. At night the ball in the sky (the moon) was visible to everyone to remind them not to touch the ball with their hands and not to cheat the game.

Another tells of a frog who talked too much during a lacrosse game, and his friend the hare became frustrated and kicked his teeth out, and that is why frogs have no teeth.

Spring for Lacrosse

There are many stories of spring being the season of lacrosse. In Lieutenant Zebulon Pike's journal he confirms the game being played at

Chapter Five – Treaty, Trading, & Traditions of Lacrosse

various times in the spring when he met with the area Nations. In his journal entry of April 20, 1806, Pike recalls his encounter with the Sioux, Puants, and Reynards. The next day Pike wrote about a game:

"this afternoon they had a great game of crosse on the prairie, between the Sioux on the one side and the Puants and Reynards on the other. The ball is made of some hard substance and covered with leather, the crosse sticks are round and net-work, with handles of three feet long.

The parties being ready and bets agreed upon (amount of some thousand dollars), the goals are set up on the prairie at the distance of half a mile. The ball is thrown up in the middle, and each party strives to drive it to the opposite goal; and when either party gains the first rubber, which is driving it quick round the post, the ball is again taken to the centre, the ground changed, and the contest renewed; and this is continued until one side gains four times, which decides the bet.

It is interesting sight to see two or three hundred naked savages contending on the plain who shall bear off the palm of victory; he who drives the ball round the goal is much shouted by his companions.

It sometimes happens that one catches the ball in his racket, and depending on his speed endeavours to carry it to the goal, and he finds himself too closely pursued, he hurls it with great force and dexterity to an amazing distance where there are always flankers of both parties ready to receive it; it seldom touches the ground, but is sometimes kept in the air for hours before either party can gain victory. In the game I witnessed, the Sioux were victorious, more I believe from the superiority of their skill in throwing the ball, than by their swiftest runners."

What Pike also began to notice was that lacrosse games were occurring as Nations came together for trade or other gatherings. Lacrosse or ball-play was central to community life and was not a side show; it was a part of tradition of gatherings.

In 1851 at the Treaty of Traverse des Sioux, near what is today the town of St. Peter, the Wahpeton and Sisseton bands ceded their lands in southern and western Minnesota Territory.

The Wahpeton and Sisseton bands of the Dakota had been slow to trade away so much land, but older members of the tribes believed that the results of the 1825 Treaty of Prairie du Chien, and the Dakota defeat in the Black Hawk War, was a sign of change that could not be stopped.

Dakota chief Little Crow compared the white settlers to locust who covered and consumed the land. During the time leading up to the treaty, fur traders had been encouraged to run up debts with the Dakota that were beyond what they could pay. At the treaty gathering, the territorial leaders used this debt as leverage against the Dakota to help force them to cede land in exchange to pay off debts.

Territorial Governor Alexander Ramsey attended the treaty signing, and oversaw the negotiations with the Dakota. But Congress in Washington did not approve the giving of reservation land to the Dakota. Wanting to resolve the issue, Ramsey offered the Dakota reservation land along the Minnesota River, which he had no right to do. The treaty was signed anyway, and Ramsey was later investigated for fraud but not brought up on charges.

At the Treaty of Mendota just a couple of weeks later, on August 5, the Mdewakanton and Wahpekute bands of the Lower Sioux ceded their territory. The Lower Sioux had little choice after the other Dakota bands had sold their land.

This was an historic event in Minnesota history because in less than a decade of these two treaties the territory became a state and over 100,000 white settlers moved into the area. These treaties were broken and this led to the US-Dakota War in 1862.

One reason to mention these two treaties is an artist named Frank Mayer. Mayer was a resident of Baltimore, Maryland and had travelled to Minnesota and attended the Treaty of Traverse des Sioux.

> **SIDE WALL:**
> *The remains of the Dakota hung at Mankato following the US-Dakota War in 1862 were buried in a mass grave but dug up that night for anatomical studies.*
>
> *Dr. William Mayo, father of Will and Charlie Mayo who founded the Mayo clinic, received one of the bodies to study. Marpiya Okinajin or He Who Stands in Clouds' skull was on display at the Mayo clinic for many years, but has since been reburied with chief honors.* (61)

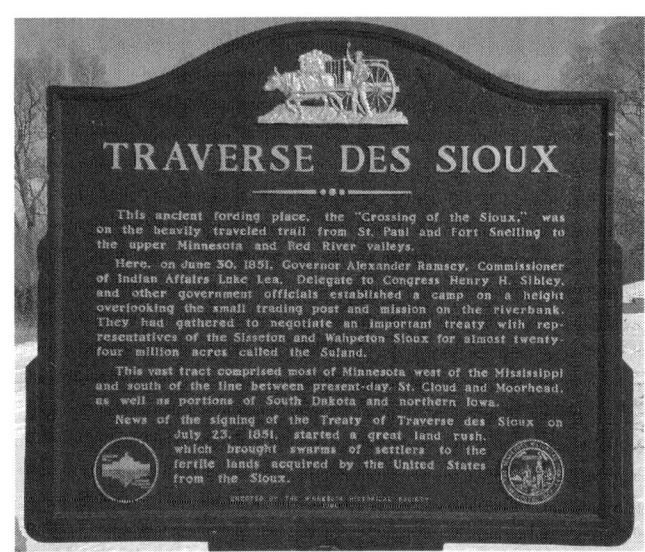

Chapter Five - Treaty, Trading, & Traditions of Lacrosse

Sign at the Traverse des Sioux Treaty Site History Center

The following year, 1852, the Dakota met again just before they were to move to the new reservation areas as defined in the two treaties. The Dakota met just south of the Gideon Pond house in Oak Grove (today's Bloomington, Minnesota). Along with his brother Samuel, missionary Gideon Pond worked in the area documenting the Dakota language. He authored a newspaper called the "The Dakota Friend," and in the August 1852 edition he wrote an account of this 3-day trade and lacrosse event:

From the August, 1852 edition of The Dakota Friend by Gideon Pond:

On Sunday, July 13th, 1852, SIX's band moved down to Oak Grove, previous arrangements having been made, to play against the three bands of GOOD ROAD, SKY MAN, and GREY IRON. The next day the game came off. The property bet was sixteen guns, six of which were double barrels; eight horses and blankets, calicoes, belts, garters, without number-worth at least $800. This was met by the same, or what was of equal value, by the other party-making the whole amount staked on the game $1,600.

Not far from two hundred and fifty men and boys joined in the play, and the spectators numbered between two and three hundred. Six's band won the prize. Two more games were played, both of which were also won by Six's band, but the amount of property staked on the last two games was much less than named above, say $1,000 for the two, which makes $2,600. And then they adjourned till the next day.

Tuesday, 15th – At 11 o'clock the ball was again set in motion, and the stake was taken by those who lost yesterday; and on the second game, that which was lost on the first game yesterday, was recovered by Good Road, Sky Man, and Grey Iron. The success to-day was attributed to the wakon virtues of the ball which was used. It was made long ago by the War-prophet, Ehakeku, formerly of the Wabashaw band; the same who fired the old, council-house at St. Peters, some years ago.

Near the close of play, Visible Mouth, a young "medicine-man", received a blow from a ball club on his side immediately over the place where the Medicine-God lies in him, which felled him to the earth. It was said that the god was stupefied by the blow; but was soon reanimated by the wakon applications of Medicine-men present. After the victors had challenged Six to play another game to-morrow, they adjourned to the lodges to dispatch a barrel of pork, two kegs of lard, and ten sacks of corn (which Sky Man's farmer had just arrived with from the Agency) and make up the stake for tomorrow.

Wednesday, 16th, 10 o'clock – Parties met. Present the same as yesterday, Six against Good Road, Sky Man, and Grey Iron. Guns, blankets, coats, calicoes, tomahawks, pipes, beads, garters, belts, to the value of $300 or $400 were tied up, and the ball started. Six lost and the stake was renewed. Six lost again; but while a new stake was being made up, a dispute arose between the parties concerning some of the property which have been won from Six's band, but which they kept back. They broke up in a row, as they usually do. Grey Iron's band leaving the ground first, *ostensibly for the reason above named, but really because Six's band had just been reinforced by the arrival if a company from Little Crow's band. Thus ended the ball play of three days continuance, during which time not less than $4,600 worth of property had been bet. How can Dakotas be otherwise than poor!*

Gideon Pond's account of the game clearly shows the gambling nature of the sport at the time and how tribes played games back and forth to regain winnings. Pond's comments about the Dakota being poor were a reflection of most missionaries and their view of lacrosse and gambling. This view led to policies and laws being passed to discourage and outright prevent lacrosse games from occurring at some events.

As the Ojibwe and Dakota received their payments, lacrosse games and gambling on those games were begun immediately. Traders who allowed Ojibwe and Dakota to buy items on credit became frustrated by the gambling because a years' worth of debt (real or inflated) was at risk of not being paid. Beginning in 1855 the US government banned lacrosse games at annuity payments.

These events and changes started to erode the frequency of lacrosse being played in the Great Lakes area. As bands were forced onto reservations, they lost the vital resource-rich areas where they hunted, fished, and harvested food.

All these losses added up to create an environment that led to the loss of culture. Soon, boarding schools brought a whole new level of cultural loss.

Minnesota Lacrosse: A History

Pond House in modern day Bloomington, MN
Photo by Author

SUGGESTED FURTHER READING

- *American Indian Lacrosse – Little Brother of War*, Thomas Vennum
- *Games of the North American Indians*, Stewart Culin
- *Lacrosse Legends of the First Americans*, Thomas Vennum

CHAPTER 6

FIRST RULES

The influence of the First Nations on the French settlers was evident in many ways, and this was very apparent as the First Nations played lacrosse games for the entertainment of the settlers. Unlike the English settlers who showed a distain for the First Nation culture, the French embraced many aspects of First Nation society. If the French had not done this we may have lost the game of lacrosse forever.

One of the first games to garner attention from the Canadians happened in 1834, when a game was arranged in Montreal at the St. Pierre race course. Teams from the Caughnawaga (Mohawk Nation) demonstrated the sport of lacrosse using the entire infield of the race course with seven players on each team. The Montreal Gazette reported on the game, calling it very athletic. (62)

Lacrosse games slowly continued over the years at St. Pierre race track. As the French settlers became comfortable with lacrosse, a team based in Montreal played against the Caughnawaga Nation. Lacrosse games started with five players for the Caughnawaga Nation, and seven players for the settlers. Once the settlers developed some skills, the Nations started to play seven players on each team. During this time it is said the settlers won only one game, and that was in 1851.

Minnesota Lacrosse: A History

These lacrosse games got rough at times and the First Nation players lamented about how violent the games could become. Reported in the Montreal Gazette:

```
"We are sorry to see one of the Montreal players
strike one of the Indians with his crosse. Doubtless
the gentlemen lost his temper in a rough tumble, but
nevertheless it was not the fault of the Indian." (63)
```

A GAME OF LACROSSE.

Canadian Illustrated News, September 6, 1879

The Montreal Lacrosse Club was formed in 1856 and along with other clubs began games in Montreal. On August 27, 1860 an historic match took place with the Prince of Wales as a spectator. The Montreal Lacrosse Club played with the Caughnawaga and St. Regis Nations with 25 players per side. The game ended in a 2-2 tie. A young man from the Montreal area had been selected to play goalie for Montreal. At age 17 William George Beers now took center stage as the "father of modern day lacrosse."

Shortly after this historic lacrosse game, George Beers, still doing a dental apprenticeship, wrote a pamphlet defining the rules and instructions for playing lacrosse. Beers described limiting the field to a ½ mile in length. Since

Chapter Six - First Rules

George Beers had seen the Mohawk games, the rules, sticks, and other parts of the Mohawk tradition are what he used to form the basis of the modern game of lacrosse.

Dr. William George Beers, US Lacrosse Museum

In July of 1867, Beers wrote an article published in the Montreal Gazette where he further defined the rules and team sizes. His idea was to limit the field to two hundred yards for twelve players a side and that the first one to score three goals won the match.

The Dominion of Canada was formed on July 1, 1867 and with the publishing of his article Beers declared that lacrosse was the National Game of Canada. He also claimed that Parliament passed such a proclamation; however, that was not the case. Over the decades, hockey eclipsed lacrosse in popularity, and Canadians assumed that hockey was their national sport. However, neither were officially proclaimed via Parliament. This error was uncovered in 1967 and sparked a major debate about sports in Canada between hockey and lacrosse. The dispute was finally settled and Canada officially has two national sports. On May 12, 1994, Parliament passed Bill C-212: "To recognize Hockey as Canada's National Winter Sport and Lacrosse as Canada's National Summer Sport."

Minnesota Lacrosse: A History

Dr. George Beers continued his work on lacrosse and in 1869 he published the book *"Lacrosse: The National Game of Canada."*

In the Beers' Appendix he published the approved rules from a year earlier, calling them the "Laws of Lacrosse." The book documented the origin of the game, giving credit to the First Nations as the true developers. He detailed how they played the game and the need to apply the scientific approach with rules and structure to grow adoption of the game. He included many details about how to face-off, pass, catch, shoot, and play goalie.

Beers was a true nationalist and loved Canada and its new game. Beers led tours overseas to England and Australia, demonstrating the game and creating more fans. His work led directly to the game being offered around the world.

While on a trip to England in 1876, his teams played before Queen Victoria who wrote in her diary that the game was "pretty to watch." This visit, along with others to Scotland, led to the first girls' lacrosse leagues being formed at St. Leonards School for Girls in St. Andrews, Scotland in the spring of 1890.

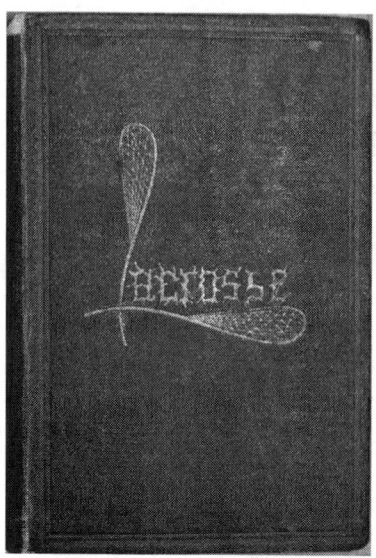

Lacrosse: National game of Canada by Dr. Beers 1869 – US Lacrosse Museum

Dr. Beers' book took a very scientific approach to the game as the world was adopting scientific reasoning. Charles Darwin's *"The Origin of Species"* was published only ten years prior in 1859.

Chapter Six - First Rules

Dr. Beers suggested that "Indian Wind" (the ability to run for long distances without getting tired) made the white settlers non-competitive. Therefore, he suggested that the game be modified into a passing game. Beers also slowly shrank the field length from his original ½ mile to 125 yards. After that, the white settlers could compete on equal ground with the First Nation men.

Here are a few drawings included in Dr. Beers' book on lacrosse.

Face-off

Scooping

Catching

Defense

In 1866, the lacrosse community crowned its first Canadian lacrosse championship. The Caughnawaga Nation defeated the Montreal Lacrosse Club to win Canada's first ever national championship.

The sport grew quickly in Canada. In the spring of 1867 there were a few clubs, but by the end of the same year there were over 80 clubs and 2,000 members.

67

96   POSTING AND DIRECTING THE PLAYERS.

C̄LUB versus

Match Played at   Date   "   18

	Names of Players.	Positions.	Foul Play Declared.	
			Against —— Club.	Against —— Club.
1		GOAL-KEEPER.	1st Game.	1st Game.
2		POINT.	2nd do.	2nd do.
3		COVER-POINT.	3rd do.	3rd do.
4		HOME.	4th d.	4th do.
5		CENTRE.	5th do.	5th do.
6		FIELDER.	SUSPENSIONS.	
7		Do.	Club.	Club.
8		Do.		
9		Do.	UMPIRES.	
10		Do.		
11		Do.	REFEREE.	
12		Do.		

RESULT.		REMARKS.
1st Game won by	Time,	
2nd do. do.	do	
3rd do. do.	do	
4th do. do.	do	
5th do. do.	do	

Sample score sheet from Dr. Beers Lacrosse book

Beers documented all aspects of the game from the origins of lacrosse (including the Mohawk and Algonquian versions of the stick) to how the games were managed and officiated. Beers wrote about skill development, tactical game plans, scoring, and even included sample score sheets on properly recording games.

Chapter Six - First Rules

At first, games were played as a Match. Best of 5 games won the match. A game was defined as a player scoring a goal. The amount of time it took to score a goal was recorded in most early newspaper accounts. Blowouts were defined as scoring goals in less than five minutes per game. Some games were played all afternoon with goals being scored hours apart.

Beers also named all twelve positions and how they should be set on the field. Many of these position names were copied in other sports, like hockey. When hockey first started, it used the Point and Cover Point position names. The term "In Home" is still used in lacrosse today and before each men's/boys' game a coach is required to declare who the In Home player is and that they will be required to serve any bench penalties.

	Goal	
	x	
Point x		o In Home
Cover-point x		o Out Home
Defence ⎰ x		o ⎱ Attack
Fielders ⎱ x		o ⎰ Fielders
x		o
Centre x		o Centre
Attack ⎰ x		o ⎱ Defence
Fielders ⎱ x		o ⎰ Fielders
x		o
Out Home x		o Cover-point
In Home x		o Point
	o	
	Goal	

Lacrosse fields positions as first defined by Dr. Beers.

The positions from the chart break down as follows:
- In Home is the closest offensive position to the opponent's goal. This often is the team's best goal scorer. He is covered by the strongest defensive player name the Point.
- Out Home is the offensive player next in line and he is covered by the Cover-Point defensive player.
- Next are three offensive Attack Fielders who are covered by the Defence Fielders.
- The Centre position was the player who faced off the ball.
- Goal was the goal keeper or goalie.

As seen in the previous drawing, the goals are flag posts. In the beginning there were no cages or nets. Beers defined a goal as passing a ball between two goal posts, and those posts were to be marked with flags.

By 1880 most lacrosse equipment was available commercially. A lacrosse stick sold for less than $1. (64)

Early Canadian Lacrosse game with flag goal posts

As Dr. Beers wrote the first rules of the game he included this rule:

Rule IX – Section 6 No Indian may play in a match unless otherwise agreed upon.

Chapter Six - First Rules

Rule 9 condemned the First Nation players to be left out of the new version of their sport, lacrosse.

Dr. Beers & H. Becket with Flagged Goal Posts - McCord Museum II-19570.1

Minnesota Lacrosse: A History

Canadians vs First Nation team – Courtesy of the Archives of Manitoba

SUGGESTED FURTHER READING

- *Our national game that never was*, Douglas Fisher. Canadian Geographic.
- *Lacrosse: The National Game of Canada*, Dr. George Beers

CHAPTER 7

EXPORTED TO THE UNITED STATES

After the Civil War ended, a movement of Canadians into the United States began. Canadians migrated from Ontario and other areas for many reasons, but a major factor was poor farming years and over-population in the rich fertile valleys, leading to high poverty rates. The United States industrial revolution had started and jobs with good wages were easy to come by. (65) The population of Canadians in the United States went from 250,000 in 1860 to 700,000 by 1880. This migration of Canadians had a major impact on the social and athletic scene all over the United States.

Many of these immigrants shared George Beers' ideals and brought with them their passion for lacrosse. One such person was Irish-Canadian John Flannery, who in 1867 played as a sixteen-year-old with the Shamrock Lacrosse Club of Montreal. While in Canada Flannery played for several world championships with the Shamrock Lacrosse Club.

Flannery moved to Boston for work and together with Sam McDonald, they started the Union Lacrosse Club. Union went on to become the first official United States National Championship team in 1879. Flannery, who worked for Standard Oil, moved to New York and formed teams on Long Island. Flannery founded the United States National Amateur Lacrosse Association on June 20, 1879 and promoted competition around the United States. He also promoted and trained many lacrosse players, helping to establish the game in America. Today he is fondly referred to as the "Father of American Lacrosse."

Before John Flannery moved to the United States, the Mohawk from Caughnawaga and St. Regis helped generate interest in lacrosse through a series of traveling shows that included dancing and lacrosse contests. Starting in 1863, their first visit was to Brooklyn. But the game did not catch on from these Mohawk promotions alone. (66)

Shamrock Lacrosse Club - World Champs, Montreal October 14, 1871

John R. Flannery, Sr. was the father of American Lacrosse First Player in center row reading left to right

John Flannery's 1871 Shamrock Lacrosse Club

By 1878 there were seven clubs in the United States, mostly in the Boston and New York areas. By 1885 the middle class Canadian populations in the United States had developed over 150 clubs including San Francisco, Milwaukee, Louisville, Chicago, Detroit, St. Paul, and even La Crosse, Wisconsin. (67) One common joke at the time was that white settlers played lacrosse in every city except La Crosse, Wisconsin, whose town was named after the game. But evidence shows Badger Lacrosse was formed in the city of La Crosse in 1882.

Baseball, which was very established at this time, tried to curb the fast growing sport of lacrosse. In 1907 a blue ribbon panel of prominent Americans proclaimed that baseball was a Native American sport because it was invented in the United States. (68) This claim was proven false. The roots of baseball were found in a European girl's game called "rounders." Nevertheless, baseball had nothing to fear from the lacrosse community. Lacrosse soon died off for many reasons, and baseball became the National Pastime.

The first American college lacrosse game took place on November 22, 1877 in New York. The game was played in Central Park between New York University (NYU) and Manhattan College. The written accounts of the game are limited, but we know that NYU scored first after 8 minutes, and again after 2 minutes. Lacrosse games, as defined by George Beers' rules, was that the best 3 out of 5 games won a match. Each goal scored was considered a completed game. For the next 85 minutes no more goals were scored, and the game was called because of darkness. NYU was declared the winner of the match 2-0.

In 1878, before a National Association was formed for lacrosse, the City of Boston donated a silver cup and invited the New York Ravenswood Club to play the local Union Club for the "Championship of United States." Ravenswood accepted and in Boston Commons on July 4, 1878 the local newspaper account bragged that 40,000 people saw Boston's own Union Lacrosse Club defeat Ravenswood 3 games to 0.

Seeing the success of this game the Westchester Polo Club invited the lacrosse teams to play again in Newport, Rhode Island. On August 23, 1878 before a "large and brilliant assembly" the Ravenswood team got their revenge and defeated Union by the same score, 3 games to 0. The first goal took 51 minutes to complete. (69)

From these two events, word spread and clubs began to spring up around the country. Baltimore did their first exhibition game on November 23, 1878, then club activity was reported in Buffalo, Detroit, and even San Francisco, which held a city championship.

With clubs formed around the country, John Flannery was able to found the United States National Amateur Lacrosse Association on June 20, 1879. Hermann Oelrichs became the First President of the Association and John Flannery became secretary and treasurer. Oelrichs was the treasurer of the Westchester Polo Club, secured the grounds to play on, and obtained funds to pay for the first national championship trophy.

The first three championship games for the United States Amateur Lacrosse Association were played in Newport, Rhode Island. At the time,

Newport was the "cradle of sports" in America. The game of polo was established in 1876, US Open Tennis in 1881, and US Open Golf in 1895. All have roots in Newport. Lacrosse was established during the same time frame as these sports, in the same place, and the same organization structure.

As was customary at the time, the winning club became the owners of the trophy. Other clubs then had to challenge the owners of the cup to get a chance to win the championship. The most famous of all challenge-based professional trophies in sports, Lord Stanley of Preston's Cup, was not awarded until 1892.

The National Lacrosse Association was formed in 1879 with the following clubs:
- Ravenswood – New York
- Brooklyn – New York
- Westchester – New York
- Bay Ridge – New York
- Osceola – New York
- Elmira – New York
- New York – New York
- Union – Boston, Massachusetts
- Bradford – Pennsylvania

Included with the nine clubs were two university teams, Harvard and NYU.

While Baltimore had clubs available, they did not join the National Lacrosse Association until 1880, along with Manhattan Lacrosse Club in New York.

1880 saw the Boston Union Lacrosse team do something no other US lacrosse club had done—they defeated a Canadian team on US soil. On August 5, 1880 at Boston Commons they defeated the Independent Club of Montreal by a score of 3-1.

In 1881, clubs began to appear in Louisville, Chicago, and Detroit. In 1882 La Crosse Wisconsin fielded a team under the name Badger Lacrosse.

The July 5, 1882 Republican Leader newspaper in La Crosse, Wisconsin included an article describing the development of lacrosse in 1882:

Chapter Seven - Exported to the United States

"The field is cleared and the flags set, and each player with a lacrosse in hand is at their station. Reader have you ever seen the game? No. Well we are not going to describe it. You will gain a much clearer idea of it by attending the practicings of the club, and your presence will help encourage the boys. A rubber of five games were played, the following being the contestants:

BLUES - E. Leprohon, Fayette Goodland, Dr. G.W. Waltz, Carl Jenks, Mark Wachenheimer.
REDS - Dr. R.E. Leprohon, Dr. C.A. Smith, J.V. Le Claire, W. Coulson, J. Danchertson.
Umpires - E.F. Doane and E. Kribbs.

The first game, which was keenly contested, was won by the Blues, and the second game more easily by the same color. The Reds scored the third and fourth games, but the Blues scooped them on the fifth game winning the match. Their success however opened their hearts and they proposed to give the Reds a chance by extending the number to seven games. The Reds again won, which made them feel pretty good, but victory was predestined for the Blues, who ran them out, making the score, Blues 4, Reds 3."

The Badger Lacrosse Club was formed by Edward Leprohon and his brother, a physician, who moved to the La Crosse area from Canada. They boasted of having played the game of lacrosse since they were young, and of its history with the First Nations. They formed the club with the above exhibition game on July 4, 1882.

Charlie Seymour, a local resident and editor of the La Crosse Republican Leader, fell in love with the game, promoted it and raised the interest of young men to attend practices. Uniforms consisted of red jerseys, red stockings, and a red skull cap.

Soon the Badger Lacrosse Club accepted an invitation to play at Chicago in October. The players returned with black and blue marks all over their bodies, which before long turned green and yellow. The team had lost to Chicago, and the wives and girlfriends of the players were disgusted with the new body colors of their players.

Minnesota Lacrosse: A History

The Leprohon brothers were disappointed in the reaction of the players and the town, and moved to Iowa. Most likely they moved to LeMars, Iowa where the St Paul Lacrosse Club played one of their first games in 1883. Lacrosse did not return to La Crosse until 2010 when a team of 18 players formed the La Crosse Lightening team. (70)

Lacrosse statue in downtown La Crosse, Wisconsin. The statue was built in the 1980s as the town began to embrace lacrosse and its history in the area. Photo by author

The stage was now set. Lacrosse had been established in the United States (including the midwest), and the only thing left was for Minnesota to join the Lacrosse League.

SUGGESTED FURTHER READING

- *Lacrosse: A history of the game*, Donald Fisher
- *Annals of American Sport*, John Allen Krout

CHAPTER 8

MINNESOTA SPORTS SCENE

To help understand how lacrosse came to be played so early in Minnesota's history, it is helpful to learn about the sports culture at the time. Lacrosse was hardly the only sport being played, and since hockey had not yet been invented, Minnesota was trying all sorts of new games.

Baseball

Baseball, introduced in England in 1744, was first played in the United States in 1845 with the Knickerbocker rules. As early as 1857, Minnesota formed a baseball team in Nininger near modern day Hastings. Nininger as a city did not take off after the "Panic of 1857" (the panic was a run on the banks in the Great Lakes Region). But Nininger put baseball clubs on the map, which then sprouted up all over the state, including some at Fort Snelling.

The University of Minnesota (UMN) played their first baseball game in 1876 against the Crescents from Hastings. (71) The UMN was defeated badly and did not field another team until 1883 when it played Hamline and Carleton Universities.

Professional vs Amateur

Professional baseball first appeared in St. Paul in 1877 with a team named the St. Paul Red Caps, playing in "League Alliance." At the time, there was a great debate across the country in all sports: should athletes be paid to play sports?

Sports like football, lacrosse, and cricket were amateur events and very against paying athletes. Baseball was the first to cross this line and openly pay players. Lacrosse and other sports struggled with this conflict in their organizations for decades, causing slow growth. Towns cheated by offering players easy jobs and paying them to work, but not paying them to play. Most clubs felt sports were played for the love of the game. This same debate is still going on in the National Collegiate Athletic Association (NCAA) sports as of the publication of this book.

Soccer, Rugby, and American Football

Soccer has its roots in China around 2,500 B.C. In 1815 there was a great divide in Britain. One side of the debate wanted players to continue touching the ball with their hands and having physical contact, including hitting an opponent who was carrying the ball. The other side wanted to limit ball movement to feet only. The first group left the soccer associations to begin Rugby.

In 1815, the first official rules of soccer limited physical contact and did not allow hands to touch the ball. In 1862 the first soccer club was formed in the United States called the Oneida Club in Boston.

Rugby formed a league called the Rugby Football Union in England in 1871. The first United States Rugby game was hosted by Harvard, who played Montreal's McGill University on May 14, 1874.

American football started when a divide in the rugby community began in 1880 and a "line of scrimmage" concept was introduced. Walter Camp at Yale proposed the rule changes in the United States, but they were not adopted in other countries. Walter Camp is now considered the father of American football. The first Minnesota college football game was held on September 30, 1882 between the University of Minnesota and Hamline University.

Hurley, Shinty, Bandy, Field Hockey, and Cricket

Many other stick sports existed in the European world as lacrosse was being "discovered" by the French. These sports developed along very different means and timelines.

Bandy was developed in Russia in early 10th and 11th centuries. Shakespeare even wrote about it in Romeo and Juliet. (72) Bandy rules were formally published and organized in 1882 by the Bury Fen Bandy Club in England.

Hurley was developed in Ireland, where it is still played today. Minnesota currently has a local Hurley Club in Eagan. Hurley rules were first published by the Irish in 1884.

Shinty was developed in Scotland and is played on grass, like hurley and field hockey. Shinty seems to have the smallest following today compared to other stick sports mentioned, but it is still played in Scotland. Formal rules were published in 1893.

Field hockey's roots trace back to ancient Egypt and has been played on many continents. The Blackheath Hockey Club was the first to organize in England in 1840. Next, the Teddington Cricket Club was looking for a winter sport and took to the outfield of one of the cricket pitches, using a cricket ball to play hockey. In 1874 they started to draw up formal rules to play the game. Field hockey grew in popularity in Europe and was introduced to the United States at Harvard in 1901.

The history of cricket can be traced to southern England in the 15th century. It was spread throughout the British Empire, and in 1728 the Duke of Richmond drew up the first set of rules.

Other sports in Minnesota – Golf, Boxing, Curling, and Basketball

There were many other sports also starting up in this era of industry and settlement in Minnesota.

Golf was established in Minnesota with the opening of the St. Paul Town and Country Club on June 1, 1893.

For boxing, Winona hosted its first major event in 1871 when Dan Carr knocked out Jim Taylor in 18 rounds. (73)

Curling was established with the St. Paul Curling Club on November 16, 1885.

Basketball started in 1895, and again the first contest was between the University of Minnesota and Hamline University.

History of the Cricket Bat

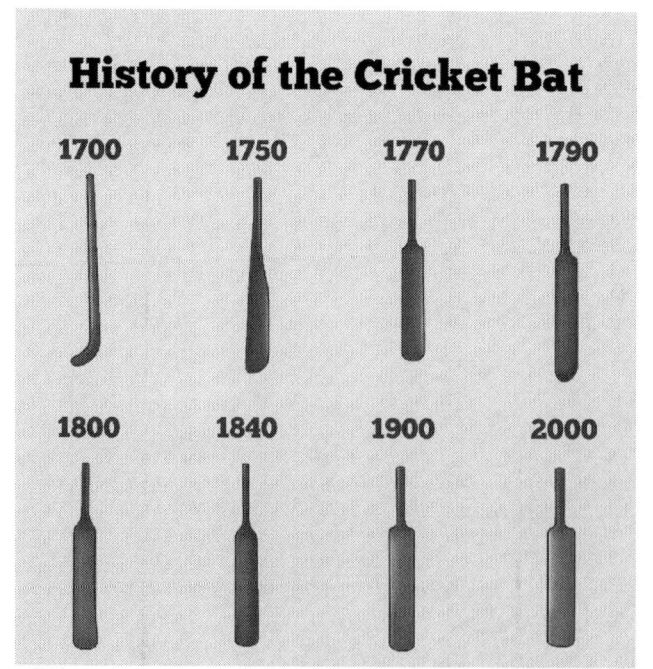

| 1700 | 1750 | 1770 | 1790 |
| 1800 | 1840 | 1900 | 2000 |

Of interesting note is that the first cricket bat looks very similar to Bandy and Field hockey sticks.

Roller Polo and Ice Hockey

To understand the origins of hockey, and to see why players moved to play lacrosse, the evolution of polo must be understood, including why it started with the name "polo."

The roller skate was invented in Europe in 1700s, but the skates were limited in their ability to change direction.

In 1863, American James L. Plimpton introduced a roller skate that offered balance, speed, and maneuverability. The roller skating craze began in New England and spread throughout the country. It wasn't long after roller rinks were built that skating lap after lap got boring.

Fancy skating started with tricks and maneuvers to keep the rinks filled with patrons paying to maintain them. But again, this phase soon faded.

The next idea was to promote folk games of the time to the roller rinks. Games like hurley, shinty, bandy, lacrosse, and field hockey were combined to a new game on roller skates called "polo."

Chapter Eight – Minnesota Sports Scene

The natural question is why it was called "polo." During the 1860s, British commanders brought back from India a new sport: polo on horses. In an effort to create something new, fun and exciting, roller rink owners latched onto the name "polo" as a way to define the new sport of roller polo. It worked. Polo (or sometimes called roller polo) now brought the patrons back to the rink to learn this new game, either as participants or spectators.

Roller Polo on cover of Harper's Weekly September 8, 1882

Minnesota Lacrosse: A History

1885 Wichita Roller Polo Team

In 1885, the Pioneer Press reported 11 roller rinks in Minneapolis and 4 in St. Paul. This was a lot of opportunity for patrons to skate and play polo.

The organizers of the game adopted rules very close to Dr. George Beers' lacrosse rules, with a match being the best three of five games and a game defined as scoring a goal. They used a ball similar to a lacrosse ball and started with flagged goal posts. However, they soon developed a net to catch the ball as it went across the goal line.

About this same time, in 1883, a promoter by the name of Frank Barron developed roller polo leagues during the heyday of the roller rinks.

Barron saw the opportunity to go outside to play on the ice, and he named the game ice polo. He kept most of the same rules as roller polo, including the names of positions like Point and Cover Point. He also continued to use a ball on the ice. (74)

Chapter Eight – Minnesota Sports Scene

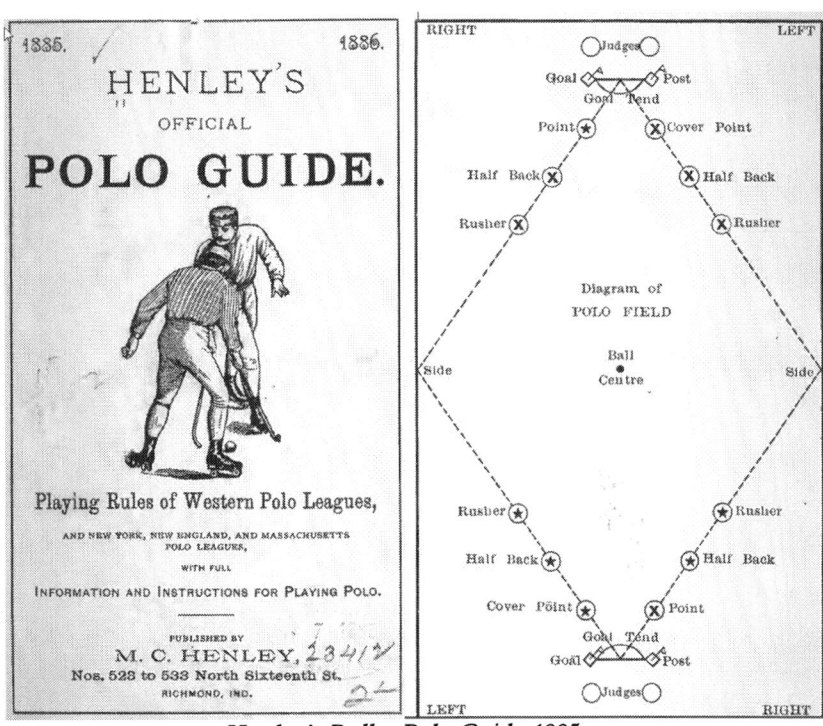

Henley's Roller Polo Guide 1885

A fun story was that in October of 1894 a touring group of ladies from Boston were on their way to San Francisco. They stopped in Minneapolis to play a game of roller polo. Match scoring was used and soon the game was tied two games/goals apiece. The next goal won the match.

Frank Barron played goalie for the ladies team, who played a local men's team. Barron saw one of ladies lose her skate and need repair, so he left the net and skated down and scored the game winning goal. Ladies won 3-2 over the local men. The men demanded a rematch the next night which they won 3-0.

Frank Barron was a great athlete in his time, competing in 100-yard dash events, mile events, and many skating events. He once raced J.T. Hirst of the St. Paul Bicycling Club on his skates; he lost in a mile-long race but proved how fast he could go.

Minnesota Lacrosse: A History

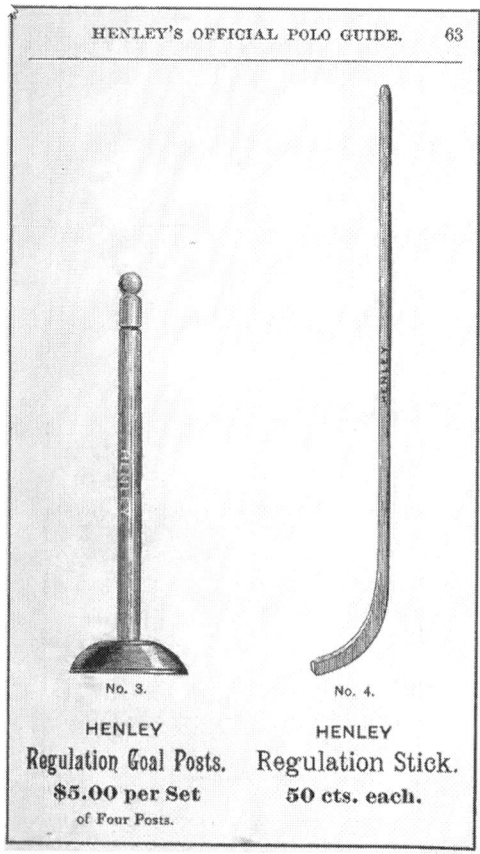

```
        HENLEY'S OFFICIAL POLO GUIDE.        63



              No. 3.              No. 4.
              HENLEY             HENLEY
        Regulation Goal Posts.  Regulation Stick.
           $5.00 per Set          50 cts. each.
            of Four Posts.
```

Roller Polo Stick and Goal Posts for Sale in Henley's Guide

In 1886, Barron tried to organize the first ice polo event with the St. Paul Winter Carnival. It was a warm winter and no ice could be made. However, the next winter they were able to play on January 22-23, 1887 at the Winter Carnival ice palace grounds.

Three teams competed in the tournament:
Royal Route Club
Junior Carnival Club
Carnival Skating Club

Chapter Eight – Minnesota Sports Scene

St. Paul Globe Sketch of Frank Barron in 1894

The first recorded hockey game in Minnesota was played in 1895 between the University of Minnesota (including "foot ball" and " ice polo" players) and a team from Winnipeg named the Victorias. The game was played at Athletic Park in Minneapolis near the corner of First Avenue North and Sixth Street. This was about the same time that Canada was introducing the game in New York and Boston.

Back east a big event was held with two games of American hockey (ice polo) and two games of Canadian hockey (ice hockey). The United States won both ice polo games and the Canadians won both ice hockey games.

As with the players from the University of Minnesota, the players from the American team agreed the game of hockey was more fun, and started to use a puck instead of ball, a smaller ice surface that required more agile skating and not just speed, and required the skill of dodging like the game of

Minnesota Lacrosse: A History

lacrosse. The next year ice polo began a decline and ice hockey became the skating game of choice for America.

The Minneapolis Hockey Club was formed the following year, and a great tournament of four ice hockey teams (two from St. Paul, one from Minneapolis, and one from Winnipeg) returned. They held what is believed to be the first tournament of international ice hockey. The games were played during the Winter Ice Carnival at the Aurora Rink in St Paul.

First Round
Winnipeg 13   St. Paul Team One 2
Minneapolis 4   St. Paul Team Two 1

Finals
Winnipeg 7   Minneapolis 3

Ice polo did not die all at once, but the last State Championship was played in 1899 and was won by the Duluth Zeniths.

Ice Polo Minnesota State Champions
1887 St. Paul Carnival Club
1888 St. Paul St. George
1893 St. Paul Henriettes
1894 Duluth Ice Polo Club
1897 St. Paul NP
1898 St. Paul Summits
1899 Duluth Zeniths

Chapter Eight - Minnesota Sports Scene

Duluth Ice Polo Team - 1899 State Champions

A partial list has been compiled (see next page) for a quick overview of the sports and the dates those sports organized with published formal rules. The sports are listed in order of first-published rules.

In reviewing the dates, notice the amazing growth and interest of sports around the world in the late 1800s. In the United States, the Civil War had ended and the industrial revolution was creating a middle class that could afford to play sports. Universities were starting up and educating a new society and the scientific technique was being applied to all areas, including sports. Dr. Beers used a scientific approach to document the game of lacrosse, create rules, and taught the world how to play the game.

By 1880, over 3,100 miles of railroads existed in Minnesota. Steamboats carried freight and passengers up and down the Mississippi River, and transportation was easier and more convenient for the new middle class. So now that they had science, industry, jobs, and railroads, what did Minnesotans do?

They played lacrosse.

Sport First Rules and Organizations

Sport	Rules Published	Minnesota First
Curling	Scotland, 1716	St. Paul, 1885
Cricket	England, 1740	?
Boxing	England, 1743	Winona, 1871
Baseball	England, 1744 Knickerbocker Rules, 1845	City of Nininger, 1857
Golf	Scotland, 1744	St. Paul, 1893
Soccer	Boston, 1862	?
Lacrosse	Montreal, 1867	St. Paul Lacrosse Club 1883
Rugby	England, 1871	?
Field Hockey	England, 1874	?
Ice Hockey	McGill University Montreal, 1875	UMN vs Winnipeg Victorias 1895
Roller Polo	London, 1878	St. Paul, 1882
American Football	New Haven, 1880 (Yale)	UMN vs Hamline, 1882
Bandy	England, 1882	?
Ice Polo	St. Paul, 1883	St. Paul, 1883
Hurley	Ireland, 1884	?
Shinty	Scotland, 1893	?
Basketball	Springfield, Mass, 1891	UMN vs Hamline 1895

SUGGESTED FURTHER READING

- *Before the Stars – Early major league hockey and the St. Paul Athletic Club Team*, Roger Godin
- *Four Centuries of Sport in America (1490-1890)*, Herbert Manchester
- *"Polo at the Rinks": Shaping Markets for Ice Hockey in America 1880-1900*, Stephen Hardy
- For more information on the development of ice hockey, the works from Donald Clark and the US Hockey Hall of Fame located in Eveleth, Minnesota are recommended.

CHAPTER 9

FIRST MINNESOTA LACROSSE TEAM

To review, the game of lacrosse was first brought to Minnesota by the Ojibwe Nation, and the Dakota Nation played the game with the Ojibwe. The modern rules of the game were developed from the Mohawk version by Canadian Dr. George Beers.

The game was first played by US teams in the 1870s when Canadians like John Flannery crossed the border. By 1882 the following events had occurred:

- United States National Amateur Lacrosse Association was formed in June, 1879
- 1879 league teams were from New York, Boston, and Pennsylvania, along with two colleges (Harvard and NYU)
- Baltimore joined the league 1880
- Teams from the midwest joined the league in 1881, including Chicago, Detroit, and Louisville
- Badger Lacrosse started in La Crosse, Wisconsin in 1882

The following national champions had been crowned in lacrosse the first few years:

- 1879 Boston Union Team – Defeated New York Ravenswood
- 1880 Boston Union Team – Defeated Manhattan Team
- 1881 New York Team – Defeated Baltimore Team
- 1882 Louisville Team – Defeated New York Team

In 1882, the Garry Lacrosse Club of Winnipeg and the Montreal Lacrosse Club visited Chicago and St. Paul to promote the game of lacrosse. Their visit appears to have succeeded in planting a seed in St. Paul, and the very next year St. Paul formed its first lacrosse team.

The phrase "Lacrosse Club" is mentioned in the St. Paul newspapers several times before 1883, but never actual games or team rosters—mostly only in conjunction with fundraising events. It appears that the club promoted athletic events like running and jumping. The lacrosse club was also used to raise funds for local charities in the area.

The first mention of a lacrosse club being formally organized was on May 17, 1883 at the Merchants Hotel in St. Paul.

St. Paul Globe Newspaper May 18, 1883

"The St. Paul Lacrosse Club was organized at a meeting held at the Merchants hotel last evening with thirty odd members, and the following officers: Dr. MacDonald President; Thomas McCann Vice President; G.W. Purdy Secretary; F. Conaughton Treasurer; and A.A. Dennie Captain.

The organization is a result of A.A. Dennie, the general agent of John Endres and liquors and importers of wines and liquors, and one of the most noted lacrosse players in the country, having won himself the reputation of being the best 'point' in this country, if not the world."

The newspaper went on to define the game of lacrosse as being of Native origin, that it used a bent stick and rubber ball, and required 12 players per team. Many newspaper articles had details wrong and tended to exaggerate the points being made. For instance, the article said that while lacrosse had only started three years ago, there were already over 250 teams in the United States.

The club was made up of young men who, as the Globe put it, had gone into it for the "outdoor exercise it gives." Dr. MacDonald's St. Paul office at 3rd and Wabasha acted as headquarters for the club, and practices and scrimmages were held in local parks.

Chapter Nine - First Minnesota Lacrosse Team

Not to be outdone by their sister city, Minneapolis organized a lacrosse club that same year, on June 19, 1883.

St. Paul Globe Newspaper June 20, 1883

"The organization of a Lacrosse Club in Minneapolis has been perfected with the following officers: President, J.T. Lee; Vice President, S. Freedlander; Secretary and Treasurer, R.M. Jaffray; General Committee, D. Messers, E.R. Shepard, John Woods, H. Chapin, L. Fournie, J. Biser, Frank Conway, and E.G. Jaffray. Monday, Wednesday, and Friday evenings were set apart for practice, and regular weekly meeting will be held on Wednesday evenings. Sticks will be ordered immediately, and the first practice will be held tonight."

The first year of lacrosse clubs in Minnesota, 1883, saw only two clubs formed—one each in St. Paul and Minneapolis. The clubs acquired sticks from back east and began to practice.

On June 30, 1883 the very first game of lacrosse played by a white settler club, not a First Nation like the Ojibwe or Dakota who had been playing for centuries, occurred. The game took place at 4pm in Minneapolis, on the corner of Fourth Avenue and Tenth Street South.

The only roster published for the game was by the St Paul Lacrosse Club:

```
Goal           - Warwick
Point          - Giberton, A.
Cover Point    - Dowell
First Field    - Walsh
Second Field   - Wight
Third Field    - Giberton, E.
Centre Field   - Dennie
Fourth Field   - Whitcomb
Fifth Field    - Chivreli
Home           - Devine, Fry, Smith
Field Captain  - J.A. McShane
```

The field captain was not a player on the field, but played the role of coach and reviewed the rules agreed upon with the officials. The Minneapolis field captain was listed as R.M. Jaffray, but no other team members were mentioned in the newspaper account.

A lacrosse match was defined by the Canadian rules of Dr. Beers—as a best-of-five-games series, and with a game being a single goal scored. The statistic that was tracked consisted of how long it took for a goal to be scored. The quicker the goal, the more dominant the team. First team to score three goals won the match.

Here are the stats from the first lacrosse club game between St. Paul and Minneapolis:

Goal – St. Paul – Frye – 4 ½ minutes
Goal – St. Paul – Smith – 31 ½ minutes
Goal – St. Paul – Devine – 6 minutes
Results St. Paul Lacrosse Club 3 - Minneapolis 0

Minneapolis challenged St. Paul to another game on July 28, 1883 at Brown Stocking Park in Minneapolis. For this game, Minneapolis was more prepared.

Rosters

St. Paul	Position	Minneapolis
A B Wallace	Goalie	McWalters
H Warwick	Point	Dafoe
S Chivrell	Cover Point	Donahue
A Giberton	1st Field	Wood
W Frye	2nd Field	Hollowell
Peters	3rd Field	Bicer
E F Walsh	Center Field	O'Connor
E Giberton	1st Home	Jaffrey
Whitcomb	2nd Home	Moore
Geo Smith	3rd Home	Thompson
Punch Lovell	4th Home	George Wilson
A.A. Devine	Home	J.I. Brown

Here is the account of the game from the St. Paul Globe July 19, 1883:

"The game of lacrosse played yesterday afternoon on the base ball grounds at Minneapolis results in the favor of St. Paul by 3 to 2.
The first game was put through by J.I. Brown, of Minneapolis; time 45 minutes. The second game was put through by Devine of St. Paul; time 5 minutes. The third game was put through by W. Thompson, of Minneapolis; time 25 minutes. The fourth game was put through by Devine, of St.

Chapter Nine - First Minnesota Lacrosse Team

Paul; 13 minutes. The fifth game was put through by Devine, of St. Paul; time 16 minutes. The match being the best of 5, was accordingly declared in favor of St. Paul."

THE ST. PAUL LACROSSE TEAM OF 1883

Left to right, standing—Devine, Wernick, Martin, Lovell, McAuly, Try, Smith, Gibberton. Sitting—Main, Stark, Auty, G. Gibberton, Warner, Dr. A. Macdonald, president of team, in center of group.

St. Paul Globe May 22, 1904 History of Lacrosse Article

Another game between St. Paul and Minneapolis was recorded on August 11, 1883, with St. Paul beating Minneapolis 3-1.

The first team photo of the St. Paul Lacrosse Club shows that they did not adopt the sticks of the local Ojibwe or Dakota players. Instead, they purchased sticks from the same place as the rest of the league, using a style of stick from the Mohawk. Dr. Beers had based his rules for the game on the Mohawk version.

After St. Paul's success against its neighbors, the St. Paul Lacrosse Club challenged the closest team in the National Lacrosse League, the Calumets of Chicago. The Calumets had beaten Louisville for the national championship earlier that year (1883).

Minnesota Lacrosse: A History

The Calumet team held the National Lacrosse Championship Cup when St. Paul challenged them. Since the protocol was that any team could challenge for the cup, St. Paul was allowed to make this offer for a game and it must be accepted by the championship team or the cup would be forfeited to the challenger. However, the holder of the cup was allowed to dictate the location of the game and when the game would be played.

The name Calumet comes from a Norman/French word used to describe the "peace pipe" they found among the First Nation people they encountered. The Chicago-based team used the name Calumet to honor the origin of the game of lacrosse.

The Calumets accepted the offer from St. Paul to play a game on their field in Chicago on September 15, 1883. Since this was the Calumet's first defense of the National Championship Cup after beating the Louisville team, Chicago heavily promoted the game.

Both teams bought new uniforms for the game and made quite a spectacle in their outfits. This is the first mention that the colors of St. Paul were blue and white, and the first mention of the team being called the St. Paul Athletics.

> Special Telegram to the Globe
>
> "A highly interesting game of lacrosse was played here today at the base ball park between the St. Paul club and the Calumet Club of Chicago. The St. Paul team arrived here this morning and presented a fine appearance.
>
> The St. Paul boys were attired in blue hats, white knit shirt, gray knee breeches with blue stockings and rubber soled lawn tennis shoes. The costume was picturesque, and the young men were in fine form. The Chicagos were costumed in white hats, striped shirts, yellow breeches, and blue stockings.
>
> James Shay, captain of the St. Pauls, was constantly on the field coaching his men, although he was not in the game. The game was called and first ball passed at 3:30pm and in seven minutes the St. Pauls, by a brilliant series of maneuvers, drove the ball through the Chicago's goal and won the first game, amid

Chapter Nine – First Minnesota Lacrosse Team

vociferous cheers from the audience, Devine casting the ball which won the game.

The second goal was won by the Chicagos after a hard struggle for forty minutes. For the third game the St. Paul Athletics came up smiling and fresh, while the Chicagos were considerably winded. However the home team showed the benefit of their summer practice.

The third was also won by the Chicagos after a most exciting contest of nearly half an hour. The fourth goal and the match was won by the Chicagos in thirty minutes, they being entirely exhausted at the close.

The score stood St Paul 1, Chicago 3, the contest being the best 3 in 5. The Calumets won the contest and still remained the Champions of the United States."

Rosters

St. Paul	Position	Chicago Calumets
A B Wallace	Goalie	HH Graham
H Warwick	Point	J A Stuart
Donahue	C Point	J Ferron
A Giberton	D Field	H Larkin
W Frye	D Field	J Carlton
E Giberton	D Field	M Malone
E F Walsh	Center	W H Comstock
Peters	Home field	A C Way
Whitcomb	Home field	A G Goldsmith
Chivell	Home field	B Dickinson
Lovell	Home	L Murphy
A A Devine	Home	C Mather

As the game was depicted, another detail about sports at the time is defined. The players wore hats for the color of their team. This was a long time before helmets, and it helped the players to quickly recognize their teammates.

Another detail is that there were no jersey numbers or ways to tell who was who on the field; one team wore shirts of solid colors and the other wore stripes.

Minnesota Lacrosse: A History

Solid color vs Stripes

Book of Athletics Face-off Drawing 1900

Another game was recorded in the Minneapolis Tribune on Sunday, September 18, 1883, after the St. Paul team played a club from Le Mars, Iowa.

"The St. Paul Lacrosse Club was badly defeated on Saturday by the club of Le Mars, Iowa."

No score or location was recorded about the game. It was very typical of a hometown newspaper to not record many details about a loss. (If you think the local press are "homers" now, you should read the guys back in this era.)

After the Calumet game in Chicago, one of the founding members of the St. Paul Lacrosse Club, A.A. Dennie, was offered a job to start an athletic club in St. Louis. He left St. Paul in late September in 1883. Once in St. Louis, he was responsible for forming teams for lawn tennis, cricket, and a lacrosse club at a new athletic complex.

Book of Athletics, 1900
Ground ball scrum with two striped players and one solid color player

Chapter Nine - First Minnesota Lacrosse Team

The first year of club lacrosse came to an end with only a few games being played in St. Paul and Minneapolis. But this was just a start of what was to come. Lacrosse had taken root in the Twin Cities and now the promise of joining the National Lacrosse League was upon them.

St. Paul Globe Cartoon showing interest in the new sport of lacrosse.

Minnesota Lacrosse: A History

St. Paul Globe cartoon

CHAPTER 10

FIRST CHAMPIONSHIP

In 1884 the Minneapolis Lacrosse Club petitioned the United States National Amateur Lacrosse Association to join the league. Along with Minneapolis, teams from Philadelphia and St. Louis were also accepted. St. Paul was considered a part of the league in 1883 because of their challenge for the championship against the Calumets.

The Minneapolis and St. Paul clubs met and made plans for summer lacrosse. To kick things off they helped organize the St. Paul Athletic Club events on Decoration Day.

Decoration Day was established to decorate the graves of soldiers who lost their lives during the recent Civil War. Decoration Day was held at the end of May because flowers would be in bloom in all states in the union. In 1967 Decoration Day was formally renamed Memorial Day, and now honors all military branches from all wars.

Early in lacrosse history there was a favorite contest for lacrosse players: the longest throw contest. This was popular in Canada and the United States. Yes, it's as simple as it sounds—throwing the lacrosse ball the farthest. On May 30, Decoration Day, the athletic events included many contests such as the 100 yard dash, hurdles, tug of war, the sack race, and the infamous fat man race. And in 1884 the Decoration Day contests included the lacrosse longest throw contest.

S.W. Chevrell won the lacrosse ball throwing contest with a mark of 104 yards. The Decoration Day events were scheduled to include a "Grand game of Lacrosse" between St. Paul and Minneapolis, but Minneapolis was unable to field a team and the game was cancelled.

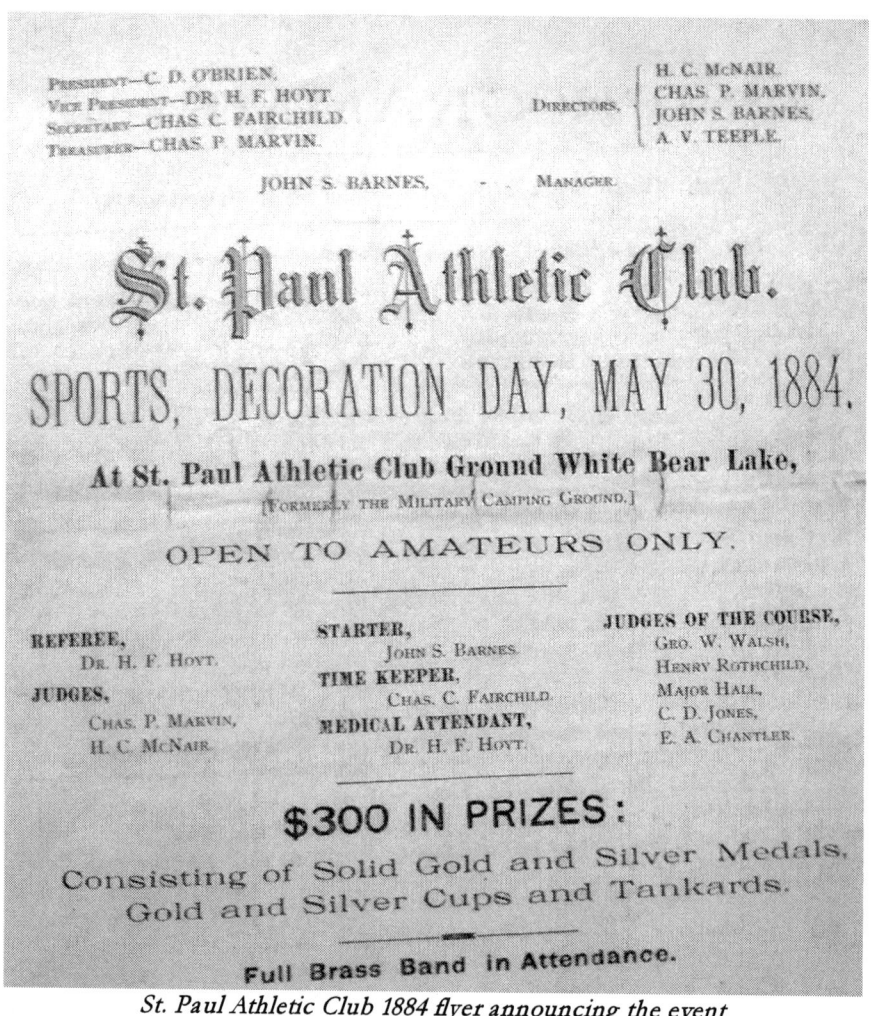

> **St. Paul Athletic Club.**
>
> PRESIDENT—C. D. O'BRIEN.
> VICE PRESIDENT—DR. H. F. HOYT.
> SECRETARY—CHAS. C. FAIRCHILD.
> TREASURER—CHAS. P. MARVIN.
>
> DIRECTORS, { H. C. McNAIR, CHAS. P. MARVIN, JOHN S. BARNES, A. V. TEEPLE.
>
> JOHN S. BARNES, - - MANAGER.
>
> **SPORTS, DECORATION DAY, MAY 30, 1884.**
>
> At St. Paul Athletic Club Ground White Bear Lake,
> [FORMERLY THE MILITARY CAMPING GROUND.]
>
> **OPEN TO AMATEURS ONLY.**
>
> REFEREE,
> DR. H. F. HOYT.
> JUDGES,
> CHAS. P. MARVIN,
> H. C. McNAIR.
>
> STARTER,
> JOHN S. BARNES.
> TIME KEEPER,
> CHAS. C. FAIRCHILD.
> MEDICAL ATTENDANT,
> DR. H. F. HOYT.
>
> JUDGES OF THE COURSE,
> GEO. W. WALSH,
> HENRY ROTHCHILD,
> MAJOR HALL,
> C. D. JONES,
> E. A. CHANTLER.
>
> **$300 IN PRIZES:**
> Consisting of Solid Gold and Silver Medals, Gold and Silver Cups and Tankards.
>
> **Full Brass Band in Attendance.**

St. Paul Athletic Club 1884 flyer announcing the event

Over the next few years Minneapolis struggled to consistently field lacrosse teams, while on the other side of the Mississippi River St. Paul built a strong program. To grow participation, St. Paul knew they had to be at community events and hold special contests so that people could see this fun game.

Chapter Ten – First Championship

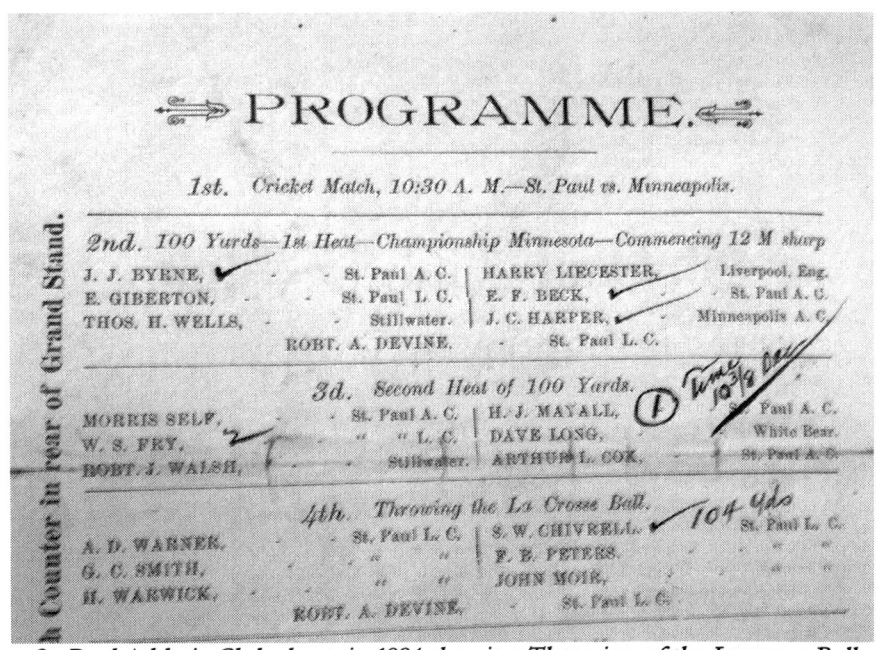

St. Paul Athletic Club sheet in 1884 showing Throwing of the Lacrosse Ball

The St. Paul Lacrosse Club staged contests between club members to gain interest in the new sport. On May 17, 1884 the club created two teams: "Commercial" and "Railroad." Employees of the railroads played on the "Railroad" team and those employed in any other business were "Commercial."

Here is the roster as published in the St. Paul Globe:

```
Commercial          Railroad
Warwick             Frye
Smith               Wallace
Giberton, A.        Giberton, E.
Shea                Lovell
Walsh               Ritchett
Keogh               Wight
Whitcomb            Hirst
Cavanagh            Stark
Myran               Brady
Joseph              Chivrell
Peters              Moir
Warner              Devine

Commercial defeated Railroad 3-2.
```

Minnesota Lacrosse: A History

In June of 1884 the St. Paul Lacrosse Club met with the newly-formed St. Paul Saints baseball team and made arrangements to use the new Fort Street Grounds for lacrosse practices and games. The Fort Street Grounds were located near Fort Street (now known as West 7th Street) and W. Jefferson Ave. in St Paul. This version of the St. Paul Saints played only one season in the Union Association League, and played only nine games, going 2-6-1 for the season.

The St. Paul and Minneapolis lacrosse clubs met together and came up with the "Minnesota Cup" trophy, which was contested each year to determine who was the best lacrosse team in Minnesota. On July 4, 1884 the first meeting to compete for the cup occurred in White Bear Lake on the St. Paul Athletic Club grounds.

Rosters

St. Paul	Position	Minneapolis
Sam W Chivrell	Goalie	JJ Gethen
H Warwick	Point	A Harrington
GC Smith	C Point	WH Patton
W Frye	D Field	GE Wilson
AD Warner	D Field	FF Whiting
FB Peters	D Field	AJ Harrington
EF Walsh	Center	C Esplin
LL Martin	Home field	J Gilkison
GJ Lovell	Home field	WC Wilson
E Giberton	Home field	C Gray
A Giberton	Home	WJ Thompson
Jno Moir	Home	JS Thompson
James Shea	Captain	J Gray

The St. Paul Globe reported that the game began at 3:40pm and the teams were suited up as follows: the St. Paul Club dressed in white shirts, white pants, blue stockings and brown caps while the Minneapolis club wore pink shirts, navy pants, and gray caps.

Here is an excerpt from the newspaper account:

> "Minneapolis securing the ball first, quick as a flash it was thrown down on the home team's goals, but Warwick, the point, with a quick dodge, sent it back again to center field, where Harrington, of the Minneapolis team, made a good catch and sent it down again to Thompson, who made a shot on the St. Paul goal, but was too

Chapter Ten – First Championship

wide; Chiverell got behind the flags and sent it up to Lowell, who had a four minutes tussle with Wilson; finally Peters came to the rescue and threw it up to Gibberton, he dropping it to Moir, who made a quick shot on the flags and the ball went through the Minneapolis goals, winning the first game for the St. Paul team. Time, 22 minutes."

The next goal happened when a too-aggressive goalie for St. Paul left his position.

"At 4:30 the ball was faced again, Walsh securing it first and dropping it to Lovell, who gave it to Peters, but Wilson, for the Minneapolis, gave him a good check and got the ball away from him and drove it down to Harrington, who passed it to Thompson, then Fry, of the home team, just came down the field in time and took it back again, making some exceedingly fine play.

Cheer after cheer went up from the audience at his remarkable playing. Down came the ball again on the home team's flags. Thompson of the Minneapolis team, securing it, made a quick shot on the goal, but was stopped by Chiverell, who passed it to Warrick, who threw it up to center, when a scuffle took place between Moir and Harrington, the latter securing it threw it to the left of the home team's flags.

Chiverell ran out after it but by having too many men checking him he lost it, when the ball was knocked through the home team's goal, winning the first game for Minneapolis. Time, 18 minutes."

The score was now tied 1-1 and Minneapolis had seized on a mistake by the St. Paul goalie, Chiverell. The game was now 40 minutes old. Typical rest periods were 5 to 10 minutes after each goal.

Game Three

"At 5:10 the ball was faced again. Harrington for the Minneapolis team getting it first passed it to Gray, who gave it to Esplin, but by a good check Fry got it and sent it upon the Minneapolis flags, where Moir, the two Gibbertons and Lovell

Minnesota Lacrosse: A History

of the home team, kept for fully 5 minutes, but G.E. Wilson came to the rescue and drove it down to center field.

Walsh, Peters and Warner were pushed hard for a few minutes, but finally lost it to Esplin, who gave it to Thompson, but G.C. Smith came in with a good check and at this point showed himself to be a very quick and neat player, the ball came down again on the flags of the home team and a shot was made on the goals but proved to be too wide, Chiverell ran out of goals and quick as a flash threw it up to Lovell, who gave it to A. Gibberton, who passed it to his brother, when Wilson came in on him from behind and gave him a good check, but he held the ball and quick as a thought, made a drop shot at the Minneapolis flags, which Moir very neatly caught and threw it through the Minneapolis goals on a bounce, winning the second game for the St. Paul team. Time, 20 minutes.

St. Paul now had a lead of 2-1, but rain clouds were rolling in.

Game Four

"At 5:40 time was called for the fourth game, but owing to the rain the Minneapolis team refused to play any more. The St. Paul team took their positions on the field and as the Minneapolis team did not come out the referee decided the match in favor of the St. Paul team, which entitles them to the championship challenge cup of Minnesota. We think St. Paul should give the lacrosse club lots of encouragement, as they expect to rank as No. 1 in United States before the season is over and will redeem some of the honors lost by the base ball clubs."

As with all Minnesota sports, the weather played a role in many games. Unfortunately, the first contest for the Minnesota Lacrosse Cup ended when the game was called due to bad weather.

Chapter Ten – First Championship

> **LACROSSE.**
> **CHAMPIONSHIP**
> **LACROSSE MATCH,**
> **Owatonna vs. Saint Paul,**
> AT
> **SEVENTH STREET BASE BALL PARK,**
> **This (Saturday) Afternoon.**
> Ball Faced at 4 P. M.
> Ladies free.

St. Paul Globe in 1884

The next game was later that summer, and included the first mention of a lacrosse team in Owatonna. St. Paul now called themselves the "champions of Minnesota."

```
July 30, 1884 St. Paul Globe article announcing
the Owatonna game:

Those who have never witnessed a game of lacrosse
should not fail to see Saturday's game between
the Owatonna club and the St. Paul club
(champions of this state.) The game is becoming
immensely popular all through the east, and is
fast making a place for itself in the west.

We have here in this city a number of players who
would not be out of place in any team in the
United States, and it behooves the people of St.
Paul to encourage them, as we feel sure that had
they one-quarter the patronage the people of St.
Paul gave base ball, they will this year be able
to take the championship of the United States."
```

The St. Paul Lacrosse Club accepted the challenge for the Minnesota Cup from Owatonna, and the game was played at the Fort Street grounds.

Rosters

St. Paul	Position	Owatonna
Sam W Chivrell	Goalie	Foster
H Warwick	Point	Racy
GC Smith	C Point	Hoffman
McCauley	D Field	Leick
LL Martin	D Field	Austin
Warner	D Field	Gramps
W Frye	Center	Misgen
FB Peters	Home field	Potter
A Giberton	Home field	McClintock
E Giberton	Home field	Chesley
J Moir	Home	Scott
Devine	Home	Schunaann
James Shea	Captain	R White

The St. Paul players were not challenged by Owatonna, and scored one minute into the game. A second goal was scored 15 minutes later, and after that the St. Paul team, to keep the game going longer, played around in the mid-field and, without attempting to shoot or score, held the ball for 30 minutes. Owatonna stole the ball and scored a goal. The St. Paul Lacrosse Club finished the match with the final goal in 10 minutes.

```
St. Paul 3 - Owatonna 1
```

St. Paul won and retained the Minnesota Cup and the title of State Champions.

After this victory the St. Paul Lacrosse Club sent a telegram to the Calumets of Chicago to challenge for the Championship of the United States. The Calumets had managed to hold onto the cup since the previous year when they defeated St. Paul. On August 22, 1884 the Calumets accepted the challenge for the Championship of the United States and set a date of Saturday, August 30. The game was played on the grounds of the Chicago base ball grounds.

The St. Paul Lacrosse Club left for Chicago at 2pm on August 29, via the railroad, to meet the Calumets. Accounts of the game are very sketchy; the local press did not travel with the team and Chicago did not report much about the game.

Chapter Ten - First Championship

First published was a telegram in the St. Paul Globe from Chicago.

```
The Calumets Downed.

Chicago, Aug. 30. — The game of Lacrosse between
the Calumets, of Chicago, and the St. Paul
Lacrosse club here this afternoon resulted in
favor of the St. Pauls, three games straight. The
playing of the St. Paul team was admired by all.
The Calumets played a strong game, but could not
cope with the team play of the St. Pauls. As all
played well, no mention may be made of
individuals. E. Gilberton took the first two
goals and Moir the third goal in 8, 40 and 6
minutes respectively.
```

The only roster published of the game were those who traveled from St. Paul to Chicago.

```
L. Martin        Goal
H. Warwick       Point
G. Hall          Cover point
W. M. Fry        Defense Field
A. Giberton      Defense field
J . Stark        Defense field
U. Caulcy        Center Held
E. Giberton      Home field
G. Lovell        Home field
A. Ault          Home field
J. Mair          Home field
R. Devine        Home field
James Shea       Captain
```

```
"S.W. Chivrell, St. Paul's regular goal keeper
was unable to go with the team on account of his
intended trip east next week. The cup which
accompanies the championship of the United States
is said to be valued at $500."
```

Upon their return to St. Paul, the team was greeted with great fanfare and excitement as the Champions of America.

SIDE WALL: *There were only 38 states in the Union when St. Paul won the Lacrosse National Championship.*

111

SUNDAY MORNING, AUGUST 31, 1884.

CHAMPIONS OF AMERICA.

The St. Paul Lacrosse Club Take the Trophy from the Calumet Club of Chicago.

St. Paul Globe August 31, 1884

Now that the United States championship resided in the city of St. Paul, they could dictate the time and place of its defense. Not long after St. Paul returned to the Twin Cities, Minneapolis asked to play for the cup.

Rosters

St. Paul	Position	Minneapolis
L. Martin	Goalie	J.J. Gethin
H. Warwick	Point	C.A. Harrington
J. Shea	Cover Point	W.H. Patton
W. Frye	Defense Field	F.E. Whiting
A. Giberton, Jr.	Defense Field	C. Esplin
J.B. Stock	Defense Field	Andy Grant
G.E. McCauley	Center	A.W. Stone
A.D. Warner	Home field	R.M. Jaffray
G.J. Lovell	Home field	W. Thompson
E. Giberton	Home field	G.E. Wilson
A. Ault	Home field	J.S. Gilkinson
J. Moir	Home field	J.S. Thompson

The game was held at the Fort Street Grounds and this time was hotly contested. St. Paul won and retained the cup, but it was a close call at 3-2.

Scoring was as follows:
   First Game - Minneapolis by J.S. Thompson, 40 minutes
   Second Game - St. Paul by John Moir, 15 minutes
   Third Game - St. Paul by John Moir, 9 minutes
   Fourth Game - Minneapolis by St. Paul defense mistake, scored on their goal. 33 minutes.
   Fifth Game - St. Paul by E. Giberton, 8 minutes.

Chapter Ten – First Championship

VICTORS AT LACROSSE.

The St. Paul Team Downs Minneapolis in a Magnificent Game.

St. Paul Globe September 26, 1884

This brought the 1884 season to an end and now the St. Paul Lacrosse Club was at the forefront of national acclaim as the Champions of the United States. On December 31, 1884 the Lacrosse Club did a press release describing the club and its players.

```
Captain James Shea
    Field captain, was born in Montreal and came to St.
Paul in April, 1883. Mr. Shea was captain of the Garry
Lacrosse Club, of Winnipeg, Champions of Manitoba. It
was through his and Dr. MacDonald's united efforts that
the twelve were in such good shape and claimed victory
at Chicago.

GOAL KEEPER
    Lewis Martin, the goal keeper, is the only American
on the team, and was born in Brooklyn, N. Y. He is
twenty-one years of age, and did not handle a lacrosse
stick until the beginning of the past season. Mr.
Martin, who works in the Omaha railroad office, is one
of the finest built young men of St. Paul. He came here
last May and fell in with the Canadians, having
attended the Jesuit College, in Montreal.

POINT
    Henry H. Warwick, the stone-wall point player, is
twenty-nine years of age, was born in Kingston,
Ontario, and moved to St. Paul in 1880. Mr. Warwick is
of the firm of Warwick & Costello, lithographers etc.,
and also publishers of the Portrayer, the St. Paul
```

"pictorial" Journal. He is without a doubt the best player the champions have.

COVER POINT.

Adrian Giberton, cover point, was born in St. Paul, but when very young his parents removed to Canada, where he took to the game, and joined the Victorias, of Montreal. Giberton is the ladles' man of the team, and although small in stature is a very hard player to run against. He is twenty-five years of age, and, as mentioned before, is the best "looker"' in the twelve. He returned to his native city in 1881, and is salesman at P. R. L. Hardenburgh's, on Third street.

FIRST DEFENCE FIELDER.

A. Dixon Warner, the noted Jackson street newsdealer, was born in Cornwall, Ontario, and came to St. Paul in the spring of 1883. He played in the Cornwall club for many seasons, and was always a "hustler" with the crosse. Mr. Warner is twenty-six years of age, and was at one time the best running broad-Jumper of Canada, having covered over twenty two feet at the Caledonian games in Montreal, July 1, 1880.

SECOND DEFENCE FIELDER.

John B. Stark, fielder, is the "kid" of the team; was born in Montreal and was a member of the Montreal Juniors, junior champions of that city. Master Stark, although very light, is one of the best fielders of the club, and played a magnificent game at Chicago, when the boys won the championship. He came to this city last summer, and is engaged In the Northern Pacific office.

THIRD DEFENCE FIELDER.

George E. Macauley, fielder, was also born in Montreal, and belonged to the "Vies", of that city. "Mac' is a fast runner, but excels more on the ice on the "steels," as he was the champion ten mile amateur of Lower Canada. Mr. Macauley is a commercial traveler, and although on the road all the time, is in elegant condition for every match; he is twenty-one years of age.

CENTER FIELDER.
William Fry, the "facer," is the sprinter of the champions, and probably one of the best 100 yards amateur runners in Minnesota, having deflated all comers at the sports at White Bear, July 4. He is only nineteen years of age, and promises to be a flyer, Prof. Barnes timing him at 10 ¾. He was born in Montreal, and belonged to the Victorias, spoken of before, and came here in the fall of 1882. Mr. Fry is employed in the Manitoba offices.

THIRD HOME FIELDER.
George J. Lovell, age twenty-two, was born in Toronto, Ontario, and came to St. Paul in 1881. He Is a clerk in the Manitoba offices. "Punch" is the heaviest man in the club, and is a "tough" one to tackle. He played with the Ontarios of Toronto for about three years, and also sprang from champion honors, that club holding the Intermediate championship of Canada for a number of seasons.

SECOND HOME FIELDER.
John Moir, fielder, has resided In St. Paul the past two years. He was born in Cornwall, Ontario, and played with the club of that city since a lad. "Jack" is one of the best players, and is exceedingly quick in the field. Mr. Moir is twenty-six years of age, and is bookkeeper at McMillan's pork packing establishment.

FIRST HOME FIELDER.
Arthur A. Ault came to St. Paul in June last, and works at Yanz & Howes, wholesale grocers. He is twenty-three years old, and is considered the best "home" player in the champions. Mr. Ault is lightening in a game and is always the right man in the right place. He was born in Aultsville, Ontario, and played with the Cornwall team. Arthur is small, but a stayer.

SECOND HOME FIELDER

Eugene Gibberton is also from Montreal and came to St. Paul some three years ago. "Gene" was successful in scoring the three goals last September when the team won the trophy. He is twenty-one years of age, and a fast man to catch on the field; he in very light but is always fast enough to make up in speed. He has a record of fifty-eight seconds for a quarter of a mile. Mr. Gibberton is a commercial traveler.

FIRST HOME FIELDER

Robert A Devine, inside home, plays one of the most responsible places in the field, and has filled it to the queen's taste. He too is a native of Montreal, and played with the Independents of that city. Bob is a "husky"' one, and when he goes for the rubber, is bound to get there.

NOTES.

In order to hold the championship the team must keep in constant practice. It is understood the Minneapolis club has imported some new material, and the champions will require to be wide awake to hold the trophy. Dr. MacDonald and Mr. John Smith, of St. Louis Jackson street, managers of the club, are negotiating for grounds in West St. Paul, and it is hoped they may be successful, as the boys are bound to hold the championship against all comers.

The above account was published in the December 31, 1884 edition of the St. Paul Globe.

CHAPTER 11

FIRST EAST COAST TRIP

When a team wins the cup for the lacrosse championship of America, it could take one of two approaches to defend it. The team could gain home field advantage by making the competition come to them. Or, the team could carry the cup on the road and taunt the other teams in the league, daring them to take it. The St. Paul Lacrosse Club met on March 26, 1885 and decided to take their new-found success back east to test if they were really worthy of being the United States champions of lacrosse.

Like every good travel team, they had to do some fundraising. One event notable of mention was on April 8, 1885 when they hosted a masquerade ball. The lacrosse club board members all dressed as monks and paraded around the party, judging the most eloquent costumes.

Next the St. Paul Club invited the Minneapolis Lacrosse Club to a game of indoor lacrosse. One the great trends noted earlier in the book was the rise of roller rinks. One of the biggest rinks ever built was the Washington Rink in Minneapolis. The Washington Roller Rink was built in 1884 at the corner of Washington and Tenth Avenue North. After the roller craze subsided, many events were held there including roller polo, concerts, boxing matches, bicycle races, and indoor lacrosse games. In future winters, the rinks were flooded for ice polo and ice hockey games.

The Washington rink which had a hardwood skating surface 80 by 325 feet—the largest in the world.

Minneapolis Tribune June 30, 1912

Since most of the lacrosse players also played ice polo, there was not much indoor lacrosse played during the winter months. But in the early spring, after the ice had melted, the indoor rinks were used to host lacrosse practices and scrimmages.

The scrimmage between Minneapolis and St. Paul was held at the indoor Washington rink on April 14, and was played to a tie. Neither team scored and the game was called after 45 minutes of play. Since the game was indoors the number of players was reduced to 8 players per team.

Rosters

St. Paul	Position	Minneapolis
L. Martin	Goalie	B. Dickinson
Warwick	Point	G. Wilson
J. Hughes	Cover Point	W.H. Patton
A. Gibberton	Defense Field	W. Thompson
W. Fry	Center	C. Eshlin
A.D. Warner	Home field	R.M. Jaffray
E. Gibberton	Home field	J. Thompson
J. Moir	Home field	J.S. Gilkinson

The Washington Rink was lost to a fire in 1898.

Chapter Eleven - First East Coast Trip

The interior of the Washington rink. The people seated in chairs are E. J. Canary, champion trick and fancy bicycle rider of America; Carrie A. Gilmore, champion woman skater and Will E. Livesey, champion trick and roller skater of England.

Minneapolis Tribune June 30, 1912

On April 27, the St. Paul Lacrosse Club held another exhibition game to raise money. All players from the club participated. This time they broke into two teams, the "Democrats" and the "Republicans." Since the 1884 election was the first time a Democrat had been elected President of the United States in 28 years (by just over 1,000 votes), the theme seemed to resonate with the locals. No score was recorded.

New clubs joined the United States Amateur Lacrosse Association including Stevens Institute, Boston, and Williamsburg, PA. A local team in St. Paul called the Independents requested but were denied membership in the league.

> **SIDE WALL:**
> *Stevens Institute holds the distinct honor of having the longest continually-run college lacrosse team. They have fielded a team every year since 1884.* (75)

Dr. Angus MacDonald, founder of the St. Paul Lacrosse Club, was appointed Vice President of the United States Amateur Lacrosse Association in 1885.

There does not appear to be a photo of the trophy, but the Globe published this account on May 25, 1885:

Minnesota Lacrosse: A History

```
The Champion Cup, which is now on exhibition at a
Third Street store, is a massive and elegant
emblem. It is of solid silver, hammered and
appropriately decorated in gold and copper with
lacrosse rackets and other devices, cost $500. It
is about ten inches high and stands upon an ebony
pedestal on which is an inscription "Lacrosse
Challenge Cup for the Championship of the United
States, Presented by the Westchester Polo Club."
```

As discussed earlier in the book, the Westchester Polo Club donated the cup used as the Lacrosse Championship Trophy for the United States. The trophy was the property of the winning club until they lost it in competition. Any one of the member league teams could challenge for a chance to win the cup.

St. Paul Globe Sketch of John F. Smith

John F. Smith of the St. Paul Lacrosse Club was the treasurer and organizer who made the arrangements for all team activities in 1885, including the trip back east. The trip was taken by train to Chicago, Detroit, Paris Ontario, Windsor Ontario, Toronto, Montreal, Boston, New York, and Brooklyn.

Chapter Eleven – First East Coast Trip

St. Paul and Minneapolis continued their new Decoration Day tradition by playing lacrosse on May 30, 1885. Minneapolis was unable to field a full 12 man team, so a 9 man team was agreed upon.

Rosters

St. Paul	Position	Minneapolis
L. Martin	Goalie	B. Dickinson
H. Warwick	Point	G. Wilson
A. Gibberton	Cover Point	Orr
W. Fry	Defense Field	W. Thompson
J. Moir	Center	Stewart
E. Gibberton	Home field	Lawrence
J. Hughes	Home field	Grant
D. Mahoney	Home field	Gilkinson
G. Warwick	Home	Carroll

```
First goal   St. Paul - 20 minutes
Second goal  St. Paul - 10 minutes
Third goal   St. Paul - 6 minutes
St Paul Lacrosse Club won 3 - 0
```

On June 10, the St. Paul Lacrosse Club went to Stillwater to help generate interest in the sport and played a scrimmage with local players mixed in with the club. It appears that this was the start of the Stillwater Lacrosse Club.

The St. Paul Lacrosse Club also worked in scrimmages with the Independents, who were denied membership in the National Lacrosse League. They saw that the local Independent Club was gaining players and improving.

In June of 1885, Fort Snelling staff documented that the National Guard entertained themselves with football and lacrosse games at the "Fair Grounds" at Camp Hubbard in Faribault.

Before the St. Paul team could make final plans for a back east tour, the Calumets of Chicago challenged for the cup. St. Paul was anxious to prove that winning the cup the previous year was no fluke, and accepted the challenge to play on July 4. Meanwhile, the Stillwater lacrosse team also wanted to challenge St. Paul for the Minnesota Cup as champions of the state on July 4.

St. Paul, which had been practicing and scrimmaging between themselves, decided to field two teams on July 4, one to defend the state championship against Stillwater and one to defend the United States Championship against the Calumets.

The St. Paul Lacrosse Club listed the following players as the "Junior Lacrosse Team" to play Stillwater:

```
C. Dufrene          F.B. Peters
B. Shea             R. Martin
A. Stark            A.P. Keough
F.R. Keough         P.H. Scanlon
J. Mann             A. Kerr
E. Murphy           J. Kenny
F.A. Woods          Captain James Shea
```

This was the first time that Ed Murphy was listed on a roster. There were three different Ed Murphy's mentioned in various sports including ice polo, ice hockey, and lacrosse. This particular Ed Murphy went on to lead the lacrosse club and play hockey for the next two decades.

The account of the Stillwater game is limited, mentioning only that the game was played at South Hill in Stillwater and witnessed by over 500 people. The game started slowly with no goals for the first hour. But shortly after that, Dr. Cowan scored for the home team of Stillwater. Within the next 40 minutes St. Paul scored three times in a row, winning the match 3-1. No final roster was given for Stillwater, and the only player mentioned was the goal scorer, Dr. Cowan.

For the other game on July 4, the Calumets had scheduled a special train to St. Paul from Chicago and brought 200 of their fans along. The team from Chicago arrived and the game was played at Leip's Grounds in White Bear Lake.

Rosters

St. Paul Saints	Position	Chicago Calumets
L.J. Martin	Goalie	N.J. Shannon
H. Warwick	Point	A.C. Way
A. Giberton	Cover Point	A. Baker
J. Moir	Defense Field	J. Dowell
W. Fry	Defense Field	T. Roe
R. Warner	Defense Field	S.C. Niel
H. Beasley	Center	J. Murphy
E. Giberton	Home field	M. Meehan

Chapter Eleven – First East Coast Trip

J. Stark	Home field	B. Crane
J. Hughes	Home field	J. Feron
D. Mahoney	Home field	M. Kelly
G. Warwick	Home field	R. McKee
G.J. Lovell	Captains	P. Enright

It is noted that neither of the captains played, but stood on the sidelines and coached.

St. Paul Globe, 1901

The Calumets had acquired new players, and a highly contested game was expected by both sides. However, the St. Paul team had been preparing for some tough games on their east coast trip, and were ready.

The game started with a face-off won by Murphy of the Calumets, but St. Paul did not allow a shot and turned the ball over. Hughes of St. Paul quickly scored the first goal in just one minute and thirty seconds. Just like that, the champions led 1-0.

After the next face-off, Warwick of St. Paul was called for a foul, but it was decided that his hit was an accident and could not be avoided. Hughes again found himself scoring the next goal, this time in 17 minutes and four seconds.

In the third game, St. Paul won the face-off, with Fry and Gibberton controlling the ball for a long time. Way of Chicago made a wonderful play and stole the ball from St. Paul, but in his attempt to dodge he dislocated his left knee. Time was called and Way could not continue. It was decided to remove a player from the St. Paul side to even up the teams and play continued. Being a gentlemen's sport, it was considered "good form" to remove a healthy player when a player from the other team could not continue. St. Paul continued to dominate the play and Hughes again found himself shooting the winning goal.

St. Paul 3 – Calumets 0 St. Paul held on to the United States Lacrosse Championship Cup.

St. Paul stayed focused on preparation for the trip back east. However, the Stillwater team wanted to play again and challenged the St. Paul team for the Minnesota Cup. Since the rule was that the holder of the cup could not refuse a challenge without sacrificing the cup, St. Paul was forced to accept the challenge. But rather than send the top players, who were practicing for the travel games, the St. Paul Lacrosse Club sent the junior team to Stillwater. For this game, Stillwater now had a formal roster of players.

The Stillwater Roster

Cushing (Captain)	Cowan
Kennedy	Butts
Belisle	Norris
Osborne	Birge
Welch	Merry
Grosvenor	

St. Paul Junior Lacrosse Roster

R. Martin	F. Duffy
A. Stark	W. McRobie
J. Kenny	C. Dufresne
R.A. Devine	F.A. Woods
E. Murphy	F. Barron
J. Kent	B. Shea
F.B. Peters	J. Hughes (Captain)

Chapter Eleven – First East Coast Trip

The game was played in Stillwater because the home field was being used for team practice by the St. Paul travel team. The Stillwater home team beat St. Paul by a score of 3-1 and took the Minnesota Cup.

The first mention of a team from Winona appeared in 1885. Winona challenged St. Paul to a game, but because the team was leaving for the back east trip they did not accept the challenge.

On the evening of August 15, 1885 the St. Paul Lacrosse Club left on the train to Detroit. In Detroit the St. Paul team faced a hand-picked all-star team with players from Chatham, Brantford, Tilsonburg, Windsor, and Detroit.

St. Paul Globe Newspaper

```
ST. PAUL BOYS WIN.
The    Champion    Lacrosse   Players   Knock   the
Detroiters Out After a Hard-Fought Battle.

Detroit, Mich., Aug. 17
The first game was won by the Detroits in twenty
one minutes, and the second by the champions in
forty-one   minutes,   scored   by   Warwick.   The
Detroits won the next game in fourteen minutes.

The champions showed fine form and won the next
two  games  in  seventeen  and  ten  minutes,  Mahoney
and  Hughes  having  the  honor  of  scoring.  The  game
was  the  hardest  ever  fought  in  Detroit.  The  boys
are  unhurt  barring  a  few  scratches  and  leave  for
New York at 7:30 o'clock.
```

The first road trip game was a win and the St. Paul team kept the championship cup and traveled on to the next city. Accounts of these games are very limited; home team newspapers rarely wrote much on losses and telegrams were the only way to tell Minnesotans of the successes.

Meanwhile, a group of Ojibwe was visiting St. Paul to make arrangements to participate in the State Fair. They heard about the white settlers playing lacrosse back east and offered to challenge the St. Paul Lacrosse Club to a game at the State Fair. The next day the St. Paul team accepted the challenge of the Ojibwe, via telegram, to play a game at the State Fair upon their return.

The St. Paul Lacrosse Club now faced a new team, the Williamsburg Lacrosse Club, on the road in Brooklyn. This was no ordinary lacrosse club.

This was John Flannery's team, famous on the east coast and considered one of the best teams in the world.

On August 21 a telegram was sent to the St. Paul Globe:

ST. PAUL CHAMPIONS. Our Crack Lacrosse Club
Defeats the Williamsburg Team
New York, Aug. 21.

The St Paul Lacrosse club, under the management of J. F. Smith, won their second victory against New York's crack club, the Williamsburgs, defeating them in three straight goals. Time, 23, 1, and 6 1/2 minutes. The visitors outplayed the home team all through and were enthusiastically cheered by the spectators for their magnificent team and individual playing. It is one of the finest clubs that ever visited the city. Had it not been for the bungling of the advance agent a much larger audience would have greeted them. The games were taken by Mahoney, Sherwood and Warwick.

Rosters

St. Paul Saints	Position	Williamsburg
L.J. Martin	Goalie	C. Crosbie
J. Burns	Point	F. Crosbie
H. Larkin	Cover Point	C.R. Roberts
W. Hughes	1st Defense	C. Brown
W. Orr	2nd Defense	C. Bush
J.B. Clark	3rd Defense	R.L. Brackett
C. Sherwood	Center	G.W. Gilmore
J. Hughes	2nd Home field	L.T. Smith
P. Costello	1st Home field	J.R. Flannery
D.J. Mahoney	Outside home	E. Titlon
G. Warwick	Inside home	F.W. Burns

Chip Sherwood broke his finger in the game and John Flannery was described as clearly the best player on the field. However, due to St. Paul's strong defense, Flannery did not manage to score a single goal.

Chapter Eleven – First East Coast Trip

Now the team was on a roll. It's one thing to win over another midwest team on the road at Detroit, but now they were in Long Island, New York and had beaten the best lacrosse team the east coast had to offer.

Chip Sherwood – St. Paul Globe Sketch 1885

Chip Sherwood had recently moved to St. Paul and joined the team. Chip hailed from Winnipeg and was considered one of the best players in Canada. Rumors said that Chip was recruited to an easy job in St. Paul to help the team. Chip did not stay in St. Paul long and moved back to Canada in less than a year.

On August 22, 1885 the St Paul Club finally suffered a defeat at the hands of the Montreal Lacrosse Club. Since this was an international game, St. Paul did not lose the crown as American Champions. Dr. Angus MacDonald noted in a telegram that the team was not expected to win against the great Montreal team. The score was 3-2.

Back home on August 23, the lacrosse team from Stillwater traveled to Duluth. Stillwater won 2-1. There seemed to be a trend in Minnesota that if games were going long, a match could be considered three games and not five games. This was the 1880s, and not many places had artificial lighting to hold games into the evening. Almost all games started around 3 or 3:30pm in this era. Thus, many games were called due to darkness.

Minnesota Lacrosse: A History

On August 26, another telegram from Dr. Angus MacDonald was received, this time announcing that the St. Paul Lacrosse Club had beaten the Ottawa team. He did not report a score. Instead Dr. MacDonald reported the first record of a complaint about an official, saying that the St. Paul team's loss to the Montreal Shamrocks was the official's fault. He wrote in his telegram that the official was "bulldozed into giving the game to Montreal."

On August 26, Stillwater played a new lacrosse club from Winona at Leip's Park in White Bear Lake. This was Winona's first game and Stillwater put up the Minnesota Cup as the prize for the winning team.

Winona Roster

T.E. Higgins(Captain)	J.R. Marfield	J.D. Miller
O.H. Webber	E.D. DeGroff	C. Forbush
F. Fenell	William Wells	George Gartside
Ed Porter	John Hollowell	George Booth
E.C. Smith		

Stillwater Roster

Bellister	Watier	Welsh
Merry	Cushing	Birge
Butts	Newberry	Roney
Osborn	William	McRobie

Stillwater wore their normal red and white uniforms, while Winona was eloquently dressed in grey flannel, black caps, a neck tie, and high stockings. The Winona team was very young and "light" in size compared to the Stillwater team. Stillwater won the game three goals to none.

```
First goal - Stillwater Cushing, 3 minutes
Second goal - Stillwater McRobie, 5 minutes
Third goal - Stillwater McRobie, 5 minutes
```

Stillwater agreed to stay and practice game skills with Winona. The Winona team also played the St. Paul Junior Lacrosse Club and lost 3-1.

Back on the road, the St. Paul team arrived in Toronto, who had beaten the Montreal Shamrocks earlier in the summer to become the Canadian Champions. Now with St. Paul still in possession of the United States Championship Cup, the local press titled this game as the "Championship of the Americas."

A large crowd watched a very fast-paced game, where goals came quickly and evenly, and both teams played aggressively.

Chapter Eleven – First East Coast Trip

The first goal was scored by Toronto in six minutes. St. Paul came right back and scored the second goal in four minutes. The game was 1-1 in less than 10 minutes. Toronto scored again, this time in five minutes. Again St. Paul countered with a match-tying goal in three minutes. At 18 minutes into the match it was tied 2-2. The next goal won the Championship of the Americas. This goal took the longest at eight minutes and Toronto won 3-2.

One can only imagine what would have happened if this game had been played under the new time-based rules. Surely this contest would have been a very high-scoring and entertaining game. As it was, the Championship of the Americas was over in less than 30 minutes and the Canadians continued their bragging rights as lacrosse champions.

St. Paul Globe headlining the return of the St. Paul Lacrosse Club

The St. Paul Lacrosse Club returned home without losing a single game to any American team, and thus retained the United States Championship Cup. Their record on the road trip was 6-1-0-1. Six wins, one loss, no ties, and one *jobbed* by the officials.

While the St. Paul Senior team was in Canada, the St. Paul Junior team lost the state championship to the team from Stillwater. Stillwater twice defended the cup against Duluth and Winona.

The St. Paul team wasted no time and traveled to Stillwater to recover the state championship. The St. Paul junior team were the primary players, but since some boys were unavailable to play in this game, their positions were filled by returning players from the east coast trip.

Rosters

St. Paul	Position	Stillwater
B. Shea	Goal	Joe Bellisle
Wm. Orr	Point	Dr. Watier
John Stark	Cover Point	Robert Welsh
E.H. Whitcomb	Defense Field	Charles Merry
F.J. Duffy	Defense Field	William Birge
C. Sherwood	Center	Ed Butts
A. Stark	Home field	?
Gene Giberton	Home field	W. Newberry
R.A. Devine	Home field	George Cushing
F.A. Peters	Home field	Nat Roney
W. McRobie	Inside Home	Ed Osborne

For St. Paul, the match did not start as expected. Stillwater won the first game with a goal from Roney in 22 minutes. St. Paul was down a goal, and it had taken almost as long as the entire Toronto game to get the first score. However, the next three goals went to the saintly boys dressed in blue and white.

Devine scored next for St. Paul in 11 minutes. This goal was disputed by the Stillwater team as having not completely crossed the goal line. Video had not yet been invented, so no replay was available. In addition, there were no nets on the lacrosse goals, just two poles with flags on them. After a "lengthy discussion" it was decided that the ball had crossed the goal posts and it counted for the St. Paul team. Chip Sherwood scored in 18 minutes, and lastly Gibberton scored in just 3 minutes.

```
St. Paul 3 - Stillwater 1.
```

CHAPTER 12

FIRST STATE FAIR LACROSSE GAME

The Minnesota State Fair began first as a territorial fair, having been founded prior to statehood. In 1854 the Minnesota Agricultural Society was formed to promote agriculture. The first annual Fair was held in Minneapolis in 1855. After Minnesota became a state in 1858, the first official State Fair began in 1859.

The State Fair moved around the first few years with many cities hosting the event, such as St. Paul, Rochester, Red Wing, Winona, and Owatonna. The Fair got its permanent location in 1885, the same year the Ojibwe and St. Paul Lacrosse Club decided to play lacrosse games at the State Fair.

As mentioned in the previous chapter, the Ojibwe had challenged the St. Paul Lacrosse Club for the Championship of the United States while they were in New York. A telegram from Dr. Angus MacDonald confirms that the club accepted the challenge upon their return. The Ojibwe had been invited to St. Paul to demonstrate dances and drums, show furs, and provide other entertainment at the State Fair.

BAND OF CHIPPEWA INDIANS in Lacrosse Games.
They Challenge the Championship of the United States.

St. Paul Globe August 23, 1885 State Fair Ad

Minnesota Lacrosse: A History

> **FROM THE FAIR GROUNDS.**
>
> An effort is being made to secure railroad rates at one-half regular fare for the round trip from points on lines in the state.
>
> Measurements were made of the grounds yesterday and the site found to be 2,425 feet east and west, and 3,025 north and south, an area of 7,335,625 feet.
>
> The St. Paul Lacrosse club has sent word that they will challenge the visiting Indians, who are said to be experts, to play a game, the Indians to fix the date.

St. Paul Globe August 21, 1885

Accounts of the great skill with which the Ojibwe played lacrosse may have been discussed when the St. Paul team came back. On September 1, the St. Paul team announced that playing the Ojibwe would be the same as playing a base ball team—it was a completely different game.

> Last evening the managers of the state fair accepted the proposition of the St. Paul Lacrosse club to give a match game on the grounds on Friday forenoon. The two twelves represent the champions of the United States and of Minnesota, and a warm and interesting contest may be expected. There will be no hippodroming. It was proposed to have a match between the white club and the Indians, but their games are so radically different that it would be impossible. In fact, it would be as sensible to match a base ball team with the Indians as the white lacrosse club.

St. Paul Globe September 2, 1885

The article above tries to justify not playing the Ojibwe as "no hippodroming." This phrase refers to a fixed game where gambling is involved and the outcome of the game has already been determined.

The St. Paul team knew that lacrosse played by the Ojibwe involved heavy gambling at times. If St. Paul believed they could not win the game, then the

Chapter Twelve – First State Fair Lacrosse Game

gambling would be fixed and the State Fair would not have allowed the game to be played. We cannot know for sure why St. Paul recanted and refused to play the Ojibwe at the State Fair, but had the event occurred it most likely would have been a major event. (One account in the newspaper that year referenced a game that was played by the Ojibwe, while the St. Paul team was still back east, against the junior lacrosse team. The account was a 17-0 score in just a matter of minutes.)

St. Paul had another excuse not to play the Ojibwe: they were not part of the United States Amateur Lacrosse League and therefore could not challenge for the championship without first being accepted into the league.

The league required that a team be amateur only, and First Nation teams often charged a gate or ticket price to help cover their travel costs. The St. Paul team did fundraising instead of selling tickets, thus could retain amateur status.

One of the main reasons the league adopted amateur teams was to keep First Nation teams out of the league. Why? Because they had dominated white teams in the past. The white settlers did not want a First Nation dominated league.

The State Fair program was changed and the Ojibwe and St. Paul lacrosse games were listed separately and played on separate days. The disappointed Ojibwe (also referred to as Chippewa) still came and played their own games, performed dances and entertained the State Fair crowd.

> A BAND OF CHIPPEWA INDIANS Monday, Tuesday and Wednesday forenoons in Lacrosse Games and exciting War Dances, with war clubs, drums, feathers, paints and furs.
> GRAND SHOOTING TOURNAMENT under the auspices of the St. Paul Gun Club Wednesday, Thursday and Friday. Over 100 Sportsmen entered. A splendid GOLD MEDAL offered by citizens of St. Paul; $1,000 in money prizes and the STATE BADGE to be competed for.
> THE ST. PAUL LACROSSE CLUB, champions of the United States, and the Champions of Minnesota, in a grand contest on Friday.
> Many other Novel Miscellaneous Attractions.

St. Paul Globe September 6, 1885

No rosters, scores, or play information was recorded about the Ojibwe games. It was normal to not record the Ojibwe lacrosse events, compared to the detailed accounts that were offered to the St. Paul Lacrosse Club games.

The St. Paul Lacrosse Club divided into two teams at the Fair, with twelve players being on the United States Champion team and another twelve being called the Minnesota State Champions.

Rosters

State Champions	Position	U.S. Champions
H.T. Martin	Goal	Joe Bellisle
H. Warwick	Point	George Warwick
A.D. Warner	Cover Point	W. Orr
J. Kinney	Defense Field	Dr. Whitcomb
R. Martin	Defense Field	E. Walsh
E. Murphy	Defense Field	B. Shea
J. Stark	Center	Chip Sherwood
Coglon	Home field	Scanian
E. Giberton	Home field	A. Stark
J. Mann	Home field	D.J. Mahoney
A. Giberton	Home field	R.A. Devine
Ehle Allen	Captain	Dr. A. MacDonald

Game Summary:
First Goal – Minnesota Champions, 17 minutes
Second Goal – Minnesota Champions, 12 minutes
Third Goal – U.S. Champions, 10 minutes
Fourth Goal – U.S Champions, 12 minutes
Fifth Goal – Minnesota Champions, 8 minutes

Minnesota Champions 3 – United States Champions 2

The grounds at the State Fair were not well suited for lacrosse. Players complained of holes in the fields and very long grass that made it difficult to secure the ball off the ground.

Lacrosse games continued to be played by the Ojibwe at future State Fairs, but it appears these were the only games played by the St. Paul Lacrosse Club on the Fair grounds.

Chapter Twelve - First State Fair Lacrosse Game

ST. PAUL'S DAY
STATE FAIR,
A Magnificent Program.
FRIDAY, SEPT. 11!
SPORTS ALL DAY!
SPORTS FOR THE MULTITUDE!
The Great Day of the Fair!

At 11:30 A. M.

Grand Games of Lacrosse, between the Champions of the United States and the Champions of Minnesota.

St. Paul Globe, 1885

THIS IS SAINT PAUL DAY
Minnesota State Fair!

Hamline, Midway Between St. Paul and Minneapolis. Take Interurban Street Cars.

Products of Minnesota, North and South Dakota, Montana, Idaho, Oregon and Washington.

GREAT RACES TODAY! W. W. P. to pace against the track record; Marion Mills to pace against her record without harness, sulky or driver. Trotting, Pacing and Running Races. Game of Lacrosse between Winnebago and Chippewa Indians. Balloon Ascension, Trick Bicycle Riding, etc.

1896 St. Paul Globe Minnesota State Fair Winnebago vs Chippewa

Minnesota Lacrosse: A History

Lacrosse game in rough grass similar to the State Fair Grounds
Minnesota Historical Society GV3.14 p8

CHAPTER 13

FIRST ST. PAUL WINTER CARNIVAL

In 1886, St. Paul was preparing for the first Winter Carnival. St. Paul was considered the fastest growing city in the nation, going from 39,000 residents in 1880 to over 120,000 by 1886. Motivated by this growth and a need to respond to a New York article calling St. Paul the Siberia of the United States, the leaders of St. Paul worked on creating a great winter carnival similar to one held in Montreal.

One of the city leaders was Dr. Angus MacDonald, President of the St. Paul Lacrosse Club. He was elected President of the St. George's Snowshoeing Club that ran a great snowshoeing event at the first St. Paul Winter Carnival.

Minnesota Lacrosse: A History

the snowshoe clubs of Canada. He is also a crack lacrosse player and is the president of the St. Paul Lacrosse club.

Sketch of Dr. MacDonald in St. Paul Globe January 7, 1886

Dr. MacDonald had a successful medical practice in St. Paul and participated in many of St. Paul's activities. The doctor's office was located at Third Street and Wabasha.

The reason to mention the carnival is to show the activities of the lacrosse club and their involvement in many parts of society. This included pride in arts, commercial businesses, railroads, medicine, and of course the city itself.

CHAPTER 14

LOST CHAMPIONSHIP 1886

1886 started with the Stillwater Lacrosse Club trying to start a tradition of playing on New Year's Day. Remember that hockey had yet to be played in Minnesota, so the NHL Tradition of hockey games on New Year's was still decades away. But due to what the St. Paul Globe described as a "large snowfall" on New Year's Day, the Stillwater lacrosse game was cancelled.

Lacrosse clubs typically formed in April of each year after the winter activities such a curling and skating had ended. Stillwater, Winona, and St. Paul formed teams in April, 1886. Where did these teams get their lacrosse equipment? In 1886 there were not many sports stores, and lacrosse sticks were handmade, almost exclusively in Canada.

Lally Lacrosse Stick Catalog

Minnesota Lacrosse: A History

The St. Paul Lacrosse Club ordered their lacrosse sticks from Lally's of Cornwall, Canada. Lally's was *the* stick maker in the 1880s.

St. Paul Lacrosse Club John Stark's "Lallys Special" Lacrosse Stick
Minnesota Historical Society (9079.1)

St. Paul Lacrosse Club George Kervin's "Duke's Special" Lacrosse Stick
Minnesota Historical Society (9079.2)

When Joe Lally retired, he sold his lacrosse equipment business to Chisholm Lacrosse Manufacturing, which was owned and operated by the First Nations on the St. Regis Reservation in Ontario.

Chisholm became "*the* wooden stick maker" until 1968 when the company warehouse burned down and created a massive stick shortage across Canada and the United States. It was this event that opened the door for the synthetic-head stick makers to step in and offer a new stick for the mass market of new lacrosse players.

Chapter Fourteen - Lost Championship 1886

This report of the fire appeared in the June 17, 1968 issue of Sports Illustrated:

> "Lacrosse enthusiasts like to boast that theirs is the fastest-growing sport around. But last week the lacrosse boom came to a sizzling stop. The factory that makes 97% of the lacrosse sticks in the world burned down. Until the fire, the Chisholm Lacrosse Manufacturing Company near Cornwall, Ontario had been doing a rush business, with production this year slated for a record 72,000 sticks, 22,000 more than last year.
>
> Not everyone can make lacrosse sticks, which retail at from $5 to $17.50. The Chisholm company's 75 employees are all Mohawk Indians, mostly descendants of stickmakers. The sticks are made from select hickory, so select indeed that Colin Chisholm, the company founder, travels 15,000 miles a year looking over wood. Back at the factory, the Mohawks set to with electric drills and sanders, but even with such modern gadgets it still took a year to cure and bend the sticks in proper fashion.
>
> There was a stick shortage before the fire. In Canada an estimated 25,000 youngsters took up lacrosse this spring, and many had been playing without sticks of their own. Unless the plant can get back into production soon—a highly unlikely event since it was uninsured—there will be a shortage of 3,000 to 4,000 sticks just in Ontario alone. Earlier this year a Canadian sent a stick to Japan with the hope that manufacturers there would come up with a plastic or fiber-glass substitute. So far nothing has come of this but, after all, the enterprising Japanese are famous for their sticktoitiveness."

The Japanese did not come up with the solution; STX and Brine, both U.S. companies, did. The NCAA then accepted synthetic sticks, relegating wooden sticks to a specialized niche.

Back to 1886, Stillwater joined the United States Amateur Lacrosse League. In June the St. Paul Lacrosse Club received two challenges for games:

one from New York to play for the Championship Cup, and one from Winnipeg who wanted to host the United States Champions.

New York made arrangements for the game and boasted in the papers that the lacrosse championship had been "in the west" for too long. New York had held the cup in 1882, but lost it to Louisville, who in turn lost it to Chicago, who in turn lost the cup to St. Paul. New York had its opportunity to take back the cup in 1885 when St. Paul toured the east coast, but no other American team was able to beat the US Champions that year. So far in 1886, New York had beaten all other lacrosse clubs in the area and felt confident that traveling to Minnesota would result in the national championship cup being returned to the east coast.

But before the New York team came to town, St. Paul traveled to Winnipeg. As previously discussed, when a team lost a game the write-up was often very brief and non-informative. Here is the St. Paul Globe account of the Winnipeg trip and game:

> **St. Paul Beaten.**
> Special to the Globe.
> WINNIPEG, July 2.—The St. Paul Lacrosse club was defeated by the Winnipegs in three straight games this afternoon.

St. Paul Globe July 3, 1886

Of course the next day the newspaper staff was already providing a reason for the loss.

> THERE is one explanation of the defeat of the St. Paul lacrosse team by the Winnipeggers which may not have occurred to the general public. They were saving themselves for to-morrow's game with the ambitious New Yorkers.

St. Paul Globe July 4, 1886

Chapter Fourteen - Lost Championship 1886

The New York Club and many fans arrived in Minnesota by rail on July 4, 1886. The accounts of the game say the New Yorkers were met by a large crowd and were treated well by the host city.

Since St. Paul was the holder of the championship cup, they chose the location of the game. St. Paul picked Leip's Park in White Bear Lake. The Globe reported that an "immense crowd" watched the game, but no formal numbers were documented.

Each team brought their own official. New York's was M. Squires, and St. Paul's was Wilson. Before the game even started, the New York team lodged a complaint, claiming that the St. Paul team had two illegal players who had not resided within the city of St. Paul for the prior 30 days. The St. Paul captain assured the New Yorkers that the players had been with the team for over a year. The New York captain, E. Clapp, insisted that St. Paul was cheating but agreed to play the game, under protest.

The teams agreed to a time limit of 90 minutes, and if the game was still tied it would be called a draw. The game was started at 4pm.

Rosters

St. Paul	Position	New York
G. Warwick	Goal	F.T. Wheeler
H. Warwick	Point	D. Brown
A. Giberton	Cover Point	A.D. Richey
G. Smith	Defense Field	J.A. Hodge
McGuire	Defense Field	?
R. Warner	Defense Field	H.J Wright
C. Sherwood	Center	J.C. Gerndt
R. Giberton	Home field	J.F. McClain
R.A. Devine	Home field	C. Flash
H. Quigley	Home field	W. Mahoney
D. Mahoney	Outside Home	G. Popham
Matthews	Inside Home	C. Lennox
J. Shea	Captain	E. Clapp

The St. Paul Globe reports the first game as:

> Sherwood got the ball and put it down to the enemies' goal, where a smart scrimmage took place; the ball did not long remain with the rack, however, but was sent spinning down to the home goal by Richey, and in a few seconds was

143

cleverly passed between the goals by third home field (Wright).

This put the champions down very quickly at 0-1.

The next game was the most controversial of the day. Remember that there were no goal nets to establish whether a ball passed between the goal posts. It was up to officials standing near the goal posts to call a ball good or wide. The next game had such a controversy.

St. Paul Globe reports the second game as:

> Second game was more hotly contested and some very clever play shown by Smith and Sherwood from the home team, and Popham, Lennox and McLain for the visitors. The latter with a good throw placed the ball plump into Umpire Squire's chest. After hesitating some time, he decided it a goal. Upon this a short rose from the grand stand and "outside" was yelled by a thousand throats, all on lookers and the St. Paul players near the goal contending that the ball did not go between the posts.

The *thousand throats* comment can easily be compared to today's parents yelling from the sidelines. But Squire, the New York Official, had called it a goal. St. Paul was down 0-2.

The St. Paul players were angry with the New York official, and played much more aggressively in the third game.

St. Paul Globe reports:

> Both teams had now become pretty well warmed up and the St. Paul boys pressed the playing pretty hotly keeping the ball dangerously near the enemies portals. A scrimmage ensued in which Warner pounced on the ball and sent it flying behind the goal. Captain Clapp of the New York team in a rage sprang upon Warner and struck him in the face. Warner seized Clapp and administered a pretty severe pummeling upon the mouth and nose drawing the claret freely. Four other New Yorkers then sprang upon Warner, and then the whole field made a rush and a bloody battle was imminent. In a few moments there was the wildest confusion;

Chapter Fourteen - Lost Championship 1886

```
men left the stand and rushed into the field, but
in a few moments the contestants were separated.
```

The New York field captain rushed the field and struck an opposing player (Warner) who then proceeded to return the hits until his nose bled. The New York players then jumped Warner and a brawl ensued between both teams. The fans emptied the stands and rushed the field to help their team.

Eventually, the fans returned to the stands and the game resumed. St. Paul wanted a penalty on the New York Captain for starting the fight, but the game continued at even strength.

At the restart of the third game, the newspaper reported that the players abandoned their positions and began to hit each other with sticks, clubbing each other on the shins, arms, and heads. The New York players again attacked Warner of the St. Paul team, "knocking him flat out." The official was forced to call a break and sat both teams down to cool off. The official again restarted the third game. This time St. Paul managed to steal the ball and Sherwood passed to Wright in front of the goal, and scored. The game was now 1-2.

The fourth game began and St. Paul again gained control. The New York center followed the St. Paul player "in a rage" and slashed him repeatedly in the shins and arms. The crowd called foul but the officials made no calls. New York regained control of the ball and McClain scored the winning goal.

After the game, Captain James Shea lodged a protest about the second goal, but New York was still awarded the Championship Cup. In fact there were three protests lodged to the league. The Calumets claimed that New York did not notify the league of the game and that the Calumets had planned to challenge for the cup again in late summer. New York complained that St. Paul had taken two players from the Winnipeg team they had just played the week before, and should be disqualified from the league.

In the end New York left Minnesota with the US Championship lacrosse cup. New York wanted to explain their position and to "state the facts of the game" so wrote an open letter in the New York Times:

New York Times July 14, 1886

"To those acquainted with the facts of the case, the Associated Press report of the recent match at St. Paul for the lacrosse championship of the United States looks like a gross and deliberate misrepresentation. Our team made up entirely of gentlemen amateurs went 1,400 miles to win a cup as they expected under fair play and gentlemanly treatment. Instead as soon as there were any signs of their success, some of the St. Paul players resorted to the most ferocious form of play, in which they were encouraged and abetted by the plaudits of a rowdy element among the spectators. Three of our players were soon disabled.

Our captain, however refused to yield to urgent protests against continuing the game, and it went on until a culminating assault of the most brutal and unsportsmanlike character was made on one of our players, upon which our Captain, justly indignant, lost his temper for a moment and rather vigorously defended his man. It was a hasty act, immediately apologized for.

The umpire of New York was treated with savage indecency and intimidation that a row of a really sanguinary character was only averted nu the cooler and clearer heads present. I have received a letter from a gentleman who saw the game, who describes the treatment of our men and their representative as outrageous in the extreme. I ask you to give this vindication of the New York Club publicly equal to that of the original report, and I ask it none the less because the truth puts the St. Paul players in the position of men who sought to avert by physical violence a defeat achieved at their expense by the superior skill and sportsmanlike behavior of our own club.
 T.M. MARSON, Secretary New York Lacrosse Club."

New York was clearly not happy with the way the original Associated Press article portrayed them and their captain. St. Paul and the Calumets lost their protests and New York retained the Championship Cup.

Back home it was reported that after the loss on July 5 to the New York team, the St. Paul players asked Dr. MacDonald to take them out for supper. However, the Doctor refused. This refusal brought on bad feelings and the

Chapter Fourteen - Lost Championship 1886

players asked the doctor and the entire board to resign from the club. They resigned and on July 20, 1886 the St. Paul Lacrosse Club had a new board.

The following officers were elected:
President - Lew Maxfield
First Vice President - D. R. Finch
Second Vice President - Harry Werrick
Secretary - Ralph Martin

The board promised to restore honor to the club and to challenge for the championship, and to travel back to New York in September. However this board was not as strong as the board that resigned, and no trip or challenge for the championship was made.

Instead, the remaining local teams of Stillwater and Hastings played games for the rest of the 1886 season. Reports of these games were very limited and lacrosse seemed to be headed for extinction. Nebraska challenged the Minnesota clubs to come and play lacrosse that summer, but again no reports of scores or accounts of games are found in the local newspapers.

Big Ed Murphy (in the hat) at a St. Paul Lacrosse Club practice

CHAPTER 15

UGLY ERA OF THE GAME

After the defeat of the St. Paul Lacrosse Club, the nation as a whole saw the game deteriorate into a state of uncontrolled games, violence, and cheating with paid players. This era spelled the end of the first national lacrosse league.

The president of the United States Amateur Lacrosse Association, Erastus Wiman, resigned at the end of the 1887 lacrosse season. Wiman believed the game had grown so fast that the Association, in his opinion, had no real control of the sport anymore, and he could no longer be involved with such an organization. (76)

One incident leading up to his decision was that New York, after winning the championship from St. Paul, went on a tour and won games against east coast and Canadian teams.

However, on October 22, 1886 they lost to a team named the Independent Lacrosse Club of Boston. The Independents were rumored to not be in the league, and New York refused to surrender the championship cup. After a meeting of the Lacrosse Association, the championship cup was awarded to the Calumets.

One can speculate that a possible reason for this was because the board might have upheld the Calumets claim that the game by New York over St. Paul was not properly managed.

The cup was not returned to St. Paul, and since the St. Paul players revolted and replaced their board, the Calumets only had to defend the cup once in 1887 and they did so against a local Chicago team. (77)

The east coast teams were in an uproar that the cup was given to a midwest team who never traveled back east in 1887. In 1888 the United States Amateur Lacrosse Association was gone. Teams met in the east and created what they called the Eastern Association and Western Association. The dividing line between the east and west was the Pittsburgh area. The concept was that an eastern winner and western winner would meet in a championship game every year to declare a national champion.

The violent nature of the game, along with bad blood with the east coast teams, caused a decline in lacrosse in the midwest. Because of this, no actual national championship game ever took place between these Eastern and Western organizations.

Coincidently the great powerhouse of college lacrosse, Johns Hopkins, began their great lacrosse tradition in 1888. Unfortunate timing for the game.

The Calumets of Chicago were the last team to be in possession of the original Championship Cup of the United States, as presented by the Westchester Polo Club. The interesting trivia is that they did not win, but were instead awarded the cup.

Back in St. Paul the clubs tried to develop interest in the game of lacrosse again. In February 1887 the St. Paul Globe ran a full page article describing the game and its origins. They included sketches of players and described the positions of the sports. These sketches are from a February 20, 1887 St. Paul Globe article.

Chapter Fifteen - Ugly Era of the Game

BAGATAWAY PLAYER.

A LONG THROW.
St. Paul Globe, 1887

This looks very much like a base ball pose from the era. There are long sleeves, pants to the knees, and long stockings. The teams normally used caps of different colors to differentiate the teams, and individual player numbers have yet to be introduced.

Minnesota Lacrosse: A History

HARD PRESSED.

COVER POINT.

St. Paul Globe, 1887

152

Chapter Fifteen – Ugly Era of the Game

GOAL IN DANGER.

St. Paul Globe, 1887

There are still no goal nets, just the flags as introduced by Dr. Beers in 1867. Since St. Paul lost the National Championship on a missed goal by an official not seeing the ball score, St. Paul and other teams wanted a solution where a ball crossing a goal line could be proven. That invention soon came as hockey developed cages for goals.

This 1887 promotion of lacrosse did see some players express interest in the St. Paul Club. But without a national league to join, St. Paul did not have any opponents to play.

Seeing that the United States Lacrosse Association failed, the Canadians invited the St. Paul Lacrosse Club to join their new Northwestern Lacrosse League. The league included the Ninetieth Battalion Club, Plum Creek, and Winnipeg Club teams.

Plum Creek, located east of Winnipeg, had developed a strong lacrosse club. In 1887, when St. Paul was offered a place in the Northwest Lacrosse League, Plum Creek were the champions of Manitoba.

Minnesota Lacrosse: A History

Plum Creek Lacrosse Team Photo
Archives of Manitoba – Sports, Lacrosse #9

Ninetieth Lacrosse Club
Archives of Manitoba – Sports, Lacrosse #6

Chapter Fifteen – Ugly Era of the Game

The Ninetieth Battalion Winnipeg Rifles, a military group in Manitoba, fielded a lacrosse team that competed in the Northwestern Lacrosse League.

Winnipeg Lacrosse Club
Archives of Manitoba – Sports, Lacrosse #7

This photo of the Winnipeg Lacrosse Club shows the continued popularity of hats and moustaches. One note on why moustaches were popular on lacrosse teams should be mentioned here. When lacrosse leagues were formed by the white settlers, they did not want First Nation players on the teams as "ringers." They banned them from the league and called them "professionals" since they charged gate fees to help cover travel costs. The settlers justified this rule by creating a lacrosse "amateur only" league.

The white settlers believed that First Nation people could not grow facial hair. Therefore, teams used moustaches to show they weren't cheating by using First Nation players. This was not true, and many First Nation players snuck onto teams by simply growing facial hair.

St. Paul did not join the Northwest Lacrosse League in 1887. In fact, in 1887 there was only one game mentioned and that was St. Paul versus Stillwater. St. Paul won 1-0 after two and a half hours of play. The Calumets, who had been awarded the United States Championship Cup, offered to host the St. Paul Lacrosse Club. The St. Paul Club tried to practice and get into

Minnesota Lacrosse: A History

shape, but according to club secretary Ralph Martin, the team was simply not fit to play.

The Ojibwe continued to play and appeared at the State Fair numerous times. Accounts of the games were not reported, nor were the scores. To show how inaccurate many newspapers were at the time, here is an example from the St. Paul Globe announcing lacrosse games at the State Fair.

```
August 23, 1896 St. Paul Globe

Three games of lacrosse are to be played by teams of
Winnebago and Chippewa Indians. Lacrosse has the
combined features of football, polo, shinney, base ball
and slugging. So it should be apt to please all lovers
of athletic sports, especially as the Indians play the
game very fiercely.

The Indians are to live in a village constructed of
their own tepees, with their squaws and papooses. A
number of noted chiefs come with them, among whom are
Black Hawk, who is nearly a hundred years old, Green
Cloud, Gray Wolf, Crazy Horse and Standing Bear; all of
whom are Indians of national reputation. Besides
playing lacrosse the Indians are to give horse races,
running races, exhibitions of horsemanship, hold bow
and arrow shooting contests, etc.
```

Promoting the lacrosse game with "noted chiefs" is fine, but Crazy Horse died in 1877, and Black Hawk was also dead. As to whether they were fans of lacrosse we cannot say, as there is no record about their interest or what might have been their own playing days.

In 1888 the game of lacrosse was tried again but lost momentum. The Eastern Association continued and so did the game in Manitoba, but the game in Minnesota had slowed among the white settlers. After this year the game seemed to be on hold for more than a decade. The St. Paul Athletic Club was created with former members of lacrosse teams but they played other sports now, including hockey starting in 1895.

As hockey grew in Minnesota, interest in lacrosse resumed as the hockey players wanted to play lacrosse in the summer. In 1899 the St. Paul Athletic Club announced it would attempt to bring back lacrosse.

Chapter Fifteen – Ugly Era of the Game

March 25, 1899 St. Paul Globe

"The St. Paul Athletic club Is making an earnest effort to receive the old-time interest in the game of lacrosse. Several members of former successful lacrosse teams are still members of the club, and are planning to organize a winning team for the coming season.

The matter has been talked over with all Interested, and the athletes have received the promise of liberal patronage If they will organize and get out. As soon as the weather permits a team will be named and practice commenced on the club's grounds at the corner of Tenth and Jackson streets.

Lacrosse is a game which has been very popular in St. Paul, and it is thought that it can be made so again. In 1884, a St. Paul team held the championship of the world, defeating the Shamrocks of Toronto. Ont., a club which at that time was looked upon as well nigh invincible."

St. Paul organized a lacrosse club and helped sponsor a team in Minneapolis again, this time teaming up with the YMCA.

May 11, 1899 St. Paul Globe

Lacrosse Practice.
The Lacrosse team will meet at Lexington Park this evening at 6:30 for a practice came. Capt. E. J. Murphy and Secretary J. Elliott, of the St. Paul Lacrosse club, visited Minneapolis last evening and perfected arrangements for a match game with the Y. M. C. A. club on Decoration day.

The St. Paul Lacrosse Club was in need of a place to play, and worked a deal with the St. Paul Saints baseball team, which had been formed again. They built a ball field called Lexington Park, located a couple miles from downtown in a residential area where the citizens didn't mind a Sunday afternoon game.

St. Paul Lacrosse Club at Lexington Park, circa 1910
Minnesota Historical Society (GV3 14 p14)

The St. Paul Lacrosse Club made arrangements to play on game days before or after the baseball games. The first of these games was played on May 30, 1899 just before the St. Paul versus Indianapolis baseball game. The game was between the two cities for bragging rights.

Rosters

Minneapolis	Position	St. Paul
Lalonde	Goal	McMilan
Best	Point	Murphy
Lawerence	Cover Point	Burdett
Taylor	Defense Field	J. Stark
Danz	Defense Field	Whyte
Deslauries	Defense Field	Bailey
Wilson	Center	Fry
Hall	Home field	Strahan
Wall	Home field	Webster
Baird	Home field	Colvin
Tate	Outside Home	Elliott
Miller	Inside Home	Howard
Webber	Captain	E.J. Murphy

Some new rules had been implemented by the Eastern Association but they appear not to be completely adopted yet. Gone was the *first one to score three goals* and it was replaced with halves. Halves were to be 30 minutes each. This game was won under the old scoring model of three goals.

Chapter Fifteen – Ugly Era of the Game

```
First goal  - Bailey, St. Paul    10 minutes 30 seconds
Second goal - Tate, Minneapolis   1 minute 30 seconds
Third goal  - Tate, Minneapolis   7 minutes
Fourth goal - Murphy, St. Paul    6 minutes
Fifth goal  - Howard, St. Paul    9 minutes

St. Paul 3 - Minneapolis 2
```

The next game was played in June and this time the game format had been switched to the new time-based game. St. Paul won again, this time 6 – 0.

The 4th of July game ended in a 2-2 tie when it became too dark to play. The next game on July 29 was the first win of the year for Minneapolis.

Rosters

Minneapolis	Position	St. Paul
Seller	Goal	Moore
Lalonde	Point	Fink
Baird	Cover Point	Hamilton
A. Raymond	Defense Field	Frye
Walls	Defense Field	Webster
Vance	Defense Field	Jones
Raines	Center	Strachan
Viall	Home field	Newson
Currie	Home field	Elliott
Tate	Outside Home	Whyte
S. Raymond	Inside Home	Agnew
Taylor	Captain	Stewart

Umpires: Woolover, Chinn, Russell
Referee: Harry Luxton

Goals Scored by Minneapolis – Tate(2), Raines, Currie(2), A. Raymond, Vance – St. Paul scored on themselves as their goalie Moore scored for Minneapolis. Minneapolis won 8 - 0

No other teams seem to have re-formed other than the Minneapolis and St. Paul teams in 1899. The 19th century came to an end with lacrosse again being played in Minnesota.

CHAPTER 16

20TH CENTURY LACROSSE BEGINS

As 1900 begins, so does a new era for lacrosse in Minnesota. The St. Paul Lacrosse Club asked to join the Western Canadian Lacrosse Association (WCLA) and was accepted on May 8, 1900. St. Paul was the first American team accepted into the league, and were given the opportunity to compete for any and all awards offered.

Minneapolis decided to form a team and asked to join the WCLA. Minneapolis was accepted and their first league game was against St. Paul. To help promote the game, the two teams agreed to play on neutral grounds at "Tonka," a western suburb,

St. Paul won the game 4-1. Game observers described the St. Paul players as too fast for the Minneapolis players.

Rosters

Minneapolis	Position	St. Paul
McBride	Goal	Brown
Best	Point	Fink
Sullivan	Cover Point	Murphy
Walls	Defense Field	Hartney
Seller	Defense Field	Hamilton
Baird	Defense Field	Ohme
A. Raymond	Center	Strachan
Raine	Home Field	Webster
S. Raymond	Home Field	Stewart
McLeod	Home Field	Elliott
Currie	Outside Home	Bailey
Webber	Inside Home	Whyte
F.E. Taylor	Captain	W.D. Stewart

During the 1900 season, the newspaper accounts in the St. Paul Globe describe the interest of youth players who came out to practices and stayed to

Minnesota Lacrosse: A History

play some lacrosse. Since lacrosse sticks were difficult to obtain, the youth players had to wait for the sticks of the St. Paul Lacrosse Club to become available after practice. Youth took to the game and developed skills very quickly, saying that lacrosse as fun and challenging.

The WCLA league model was to play many local games, such as St. Paul playing Minneapolis three times. At the end of the season there was a three way tie for first place between St. Paul, Winnipeg, and Fort William. St. Paul was invited to Winnipeg to participate in a playoff series to decide the championship of the WCLA.

To this point in lacrosse history no United States team had ever won a championship trophy from a Canadian league, though east coast teams had tried.

The trophy the WCLA played for was the Drewry Cup. The team that won the Drewry Cup then played the winner of the Eastern Canada League for the Hudson Bay Cup, the overall Championship of Lacrosse in Canada.

In mid-August the Canadian teams had second thoughts about allowing St. Paul to compete for the Drewry Cup. Some Canadian teams felt it was not right to allow a United States team to compete for a Canadian traditional lacrosse trophy like the Drewry Cup. After much debate and angst, the Western Canada Lacrosse Association decided to allow St. Paul to compete for the cup, but only after a Canadian winner was first decided. So Winnipeg and Fort William played first for the championship of Canada, and the winner of that game then played St. Paul.

St. Paul made the trip to Winnipeg on August 23, 1900. They arrived in time to see the Winnipeg team defeat Fort William 12-3. The St. Paul players commented that they liked the style of the Winnipeg team because they played hard, refrained from rough play, and were very skilled.

The St. Paul Globe carried a special article from Winnipeg describing the game as brilliant, fun, and exciting. The final score of the game was 8 to 3 in favor of the Winnipeg champions.

Chapter Sixteen – 20th Century Lacrosse Begins

*Drewry Cup – Championship Trophy of WCLA
(Western Canadian Lacrosse Association)
Archives of Manitoba, O'Dowda Collection #174*

BEATEN, NOT DISGRACED

ST. PAULS GAVE WINNIPEGS FASTEST GAME SEEN THERE IN YEARS

WHYTE THE STAR OF THE DAY

Others Right in It, Too—Visitors Applauded to the Echo and Commended on Every Hand.

WINNIPEG, Man., Aug. 25.—(Special.)— Although the score was 8 to 3 against the St. Paul team this afternoon in the finals for the Western lacrosse championship, it did not indicate inferior play on the part of the visitors. At the final championship match fully 3,000 persons were present.

St. Paul Globe, August 25, 1900

In this game the St. Paul team wore a visiting white uniform made especially for the championship. Winnipeg wore a purple uniform. The game was close in the beginning and observers described the strength of the St. Paul team as being great long distance passers and catchers, while the Winnipeg team excelled at the short game. This indoor lacrosse style observation of the Manitoba boys still holds true today - a great short game was evident even in 1900. For example, the Winnipeg players moved the ball quickly down the field with a series of short passes. The St. Paul team made just a couple of long passes clearing the ball down the field.

It is interesting to see this playing style difference make itself evident so early in the game. In reading Dr. Beers' scientific approach he praised the quick-pass game as a way to beat "Indian Wind." Dr. Beers pointed out that in order to beat the First Nation players, who were generally in much better

Chapter Sixteen – 20th Century Lacrosse Begins

shape than the white settlers, the ball needed to be passed more in order to create scoring opportunities.

St. Paul took the lead 1-0 with a goal by Hartney in 13 minutes. Robertson for Winnipeg soon tied the game with a goal, and scored again as Winnipeg took the lead away from St. Paul. Both teams played very fast, with players moving at a pace seldom seen in regular lacrosse.

The home team of Winnipeg was said to have an advantage on the prairie grass field that St. Paul players were not used to. Remember that the St. Paul team was practicing and playing at Lexington Park back in St. Paul. The first half came to an end with Winnipeg and St. Paul tied at 2-2.

A Canadian Lacrosse Club – Archives of Manitoba, O'Dowda Collection #176

After halftime the Winnipeggers took over with quick goals from Roach and Robertson. Cassidy scored for St. Paul, and soon Roach for Winnipeg was called for a penalty for striking McLeod of St. Paul over the head with his crosse "in a foul manner" and was sent off on a penalty.

From then on Whyte of St Paul was said to have taken over the game with his speed at center. But even though he outran, skillfully dodged, and beat the

Winnipeg defensive players, after he passed to his teammate they could not score on the Winnipeg goalie. Again and again, Whyte controlled the play for St. Paul, but his team could not score. The reporters describe St. Paul as owning the middle of the field, but the area in front of each net was owned by Winnipeg due to their masterful short passing game.

Fans and players complimented the fast and gentlemanly play of both teams. There was only one penalty in the game and no one was injured. Winnipeg was so impressed by the St. Paul team they offered to come to St. Paul to play games in the future. In fact, on the trip back, several Winnipeg team members joined them on the train to attend the Minnesota State Fair.

The St. Paul team returned home and the stories of their great play in the championship was heard around the city. The St. Paul Globe reported the following headline on August 28, 1900:

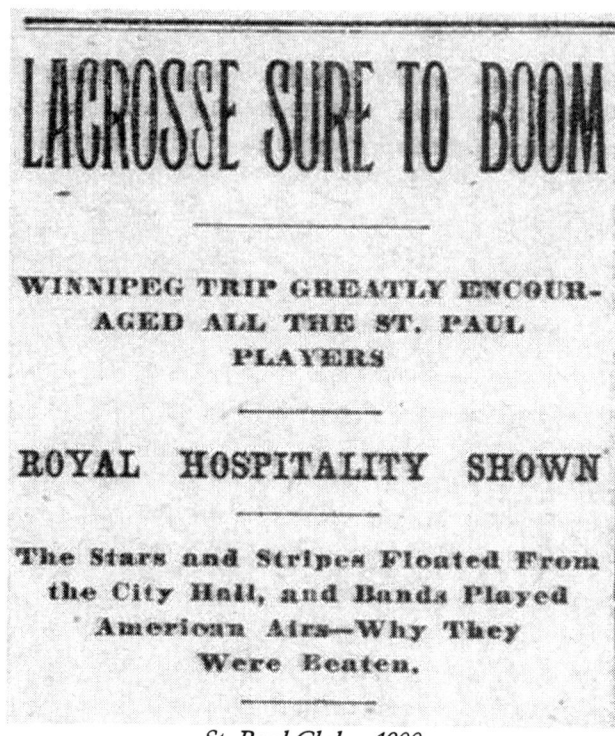

LACROSSE SURE TO BOOM

WINNIPEG TRIP GREATLY ENCOURAGED ALL THE ST. PAUL PLAYERS

ROYAL HOSPITALITY SHOWN

The Stars and Stripes Floated From the City Hall, and Bands Played American Airs—Why They Were Beaten.

St. Paul Globe, 1900

Chapter Sixteen - 20th Century Lacrosse Begins

As the year 1900 came to an end, tragedy struck the St. Paul fire department. The St. Paul Globe reported:

"Whereas, on the morning of Oct. 21, 1900, at and during the progress of a disastrous fire at the Minnesota Transfer, and while in the performance of the duties imposed upon them by their respective positions, William H. Irvine, the second assistant chief of this department; Francis M. Edey, a lieutenant, on duty with engine company No. 13; Bertram P. Irish, a second pipeman, and Louis Wagner, a driver, member of that-same company, lost their lives."

What is significant about this event is the role the local lacrosse clubs played. They took the lead in coordinating, with other groups in St. Paul, fundraisers for the firefighters and their families. Shows, smokers, and of course lacrosse games were held to raise money for the families of the brave men who lost their lives. In the same spirit that the creators of the game used lacrosse as a healing game, the white settlers had found a cause to use the game to help heal their own community. In many lacrosse circles throughout the country today, lacrosse is used to help raise funds.

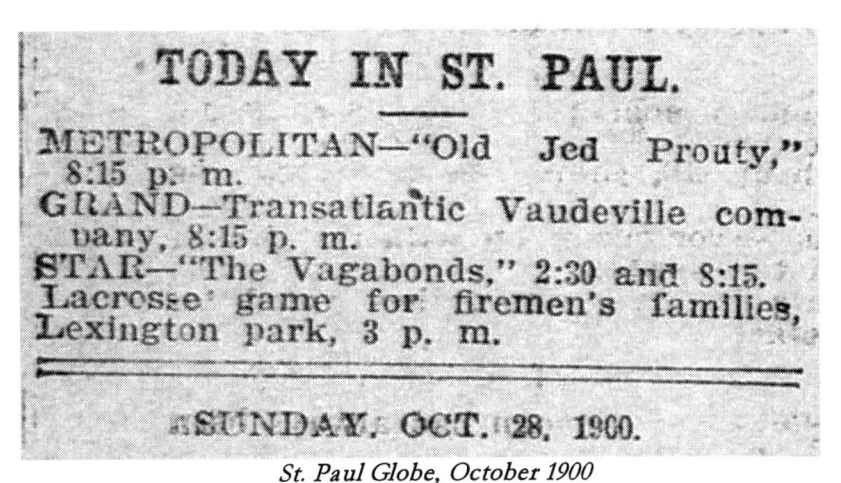

TODAY IN ST. PAUL.

METROPOLITAN—"Old Jed Prouty," 8:15 p. m.
GRAND—Transatlantic Vaudeville company, 8:15 p. m.
STAR—"The Vagabonds," 2:30 and 8:15.
Lacrosse game for firemen's families, Lexington park, 3 p. m.

SUNDAY, OCT. 28, 1900.

St. Paul Globe, October 1900

The fundraiser game was played with no set teams. The names of the clubs were called Minneapolis and St. Paul, but members from both clubs were split between the two teams. No real score was kept and when the game was nearing the last two minutes Ed Murphy called out that the game was tied

5 to 5. The newspaper wanted to report a score, and they did as 14-4, but the team members made it clear that this game was not about winning or losing.

St. Paul Lacrosse Club, 1900 - Minnesota Historical Society (GV3 14 p6)

The St. Paul Hockey Club formed in 1898. The Minneapolis Hockey club was formed in 1900 with the help of McLeod, Chipman and Miller. Lacrosse players, looking for a winter activity, joined the new club. Hockey was now an established club sport in the Twin Cities.

Together St. Paul, the Mechanic Arts High School, and two Minneapolis teams formed the first Twin Cities Hockey League (TCHL) for the 1900-1901 season. (78) Minnesota now had its first hockey league, encouraged by the lacrosse players at the time.

The year 1900 ended on a very sad note for the lacrosse community as a whole. The St. Paul Globe ran the following announcement from Montreal on December 31, 1900.

Chapter Sixteen – 20th Century Lacrosse Begins

FATHER OF LACROSSE DEAD.

Dr. Beers Reduced Game to a System From Indian Sport.

Dr. W. G. Beers died at Montreal Saturday. He was the father of the modern game of lacrosse, which, originating in Montreal, has spread all over Anglo-Saxondom.

St. Paul Globe, December 31, 1900

Dr. Beers, the father of modern day lacrosse, died of heart disease on December 26, 1900 at age 59.

CHAPTER 17

NORTHWEST LACROSSE LEAGUE

The lacrosse players in the Twin Cities were active in many sports. Many players worked for the railroad or other manual labor jobs. In addition to starting the hockey clubs, the lacrosse players also participated in curling. Curling began in St Paul in 1895. On March 11, 1901 the players of the St. Paul curling team visited the Minneapolis boys and defeated them 19-5, with the St. Paul team skipped by Ed J. Murphy, captain of the St. Paul Lacrosse Club.

On April 17, 1901 the St. Paul Lacrosse Club formed for the season and a new board was announced. The club also decided to start a Junior Lacrosse Club to meet the needs of teenage and youth players who attended practices the previous season and wanted to play.

St. Paul Lacrosse Club Board Members
Honorary President – Lem Defiel
President – J.B. Stark
Vice President – D.P. Whyte
Secretary – W. J. Bailey
Captain – E.J. Murphy
Minneapolis formed their lacrosse club on April 21.

Minneapolis Lacrosse Club Board Members
President – T.W. Hall
First Vice President – Dr. T. Russell
Second Vice President – J. Lalonde
Secretary and Treasurer – J.M. Best
Manager – R.W. McLeod

Minnesota Lacrosse: A History

The St. Paul Globe began to carry some announcements of First Nation lacrosse games up north. These reports were very general and had no mention of player names or game outcomes. But they are mentioned here to show that the game was strong at this time, even though boarding schools were in full swing moving the First Nation children away from Ojibwe and Dakota traditions. (See chapter 22 for further information).

Tribal elders were trying to hold on to traditions and held lacrosse games like the one announced in the Minneapolis Journal on May 21, 1901.

> **Lacrosse and Baseball.**
> Special to The Journal.
> Cass Lake, Minn., May 21.—In addition to the baseball game which will be played here Sunday next, a lacrosse team, picked from among the Cass Lake Indians, will play a game of lacrosse with the Indian team from Leech Lake. It is expected that Flatmouth, the chief of the Chippewa Indians, will witness the game.

Minneapolis Journal, May 21, 1901

St. Paul and Minneapolis both played in the Western Canada Lacrosse Association (WCLA). In 1901, the league claimed 34 lacrosse teams from the Great Lakes area to the Rocky Mountains. The teams participating were not listed, but it can be assumed that most were from Canada.

In July the town of Buffalo, New York hosted the Canadian-American lacrosse championship. The event included east coast teams and First Nation teams. The Crescents of Brooklyn, Rangers of Rochester, Toronto, Ottawa, Seneca Nation, and Cattaraugus were among those playing. The Crescents made the finals but the Capitals of Ottawa prevailed with a score of 7-3 for the championship of lacrosse.

At the event in Buffalo, the St. Paul and Minneapolis lacrosse clubs played an exhibition game.

The lacrosse accounts are sketchy at best for the year 1901. Discussions about going to Winnipeg, Chicago, and other places have no details that the games were actually played. But on December 1, 1901 the St. Paul Globe published the following photo of the St. Paul Lacrosse Club with no story.

Chapter Seventeen – Northwest Lacrosse League

ST. PAUL LACROSSE CLUB, CHAMPIONS OF THE NORTHWEST.
Geo. Seaborn, Trainer. P. Radney. F. Ohms. J. Elliott. Ed Murphy, Captain. J. Start. J. Shepperd. W. Stuart, President.
J. Jones. B. Armstrong. Dr. Burdette.
T. White. J. Bailey. Frank Thompson.

1901 St. Paul Lacrosse Club (St. Paul Globe December 1, 1901)

Can it be assumed that in 1901 St. Paul beat the Canadians in their league? The archives in Manitoba are also silent on the lacrosse championship in 1901.

The 1902 lacrosse season began with the clubs ready to compete in the Western Canada League. Teams this time sought out the St. Paul team, visiting Minnesota to set up lacrosse games. A couple of new rules were introduced in the midwest this season, including that the goal posts must have a "top bar" or "crossbar." No more shooting over the goal posts and it still being good. A net was introduced but not yet mandated. The playing length of the field was now required to be between 110 yards and 125 yards, and the goal crease was reduced to 12 x 12 feet. From the beginning, the goal has been a square or rectangle area of 12 x 12 or 12 x 18.

173

Below is a drawing of the recommended new goal and goal crease.

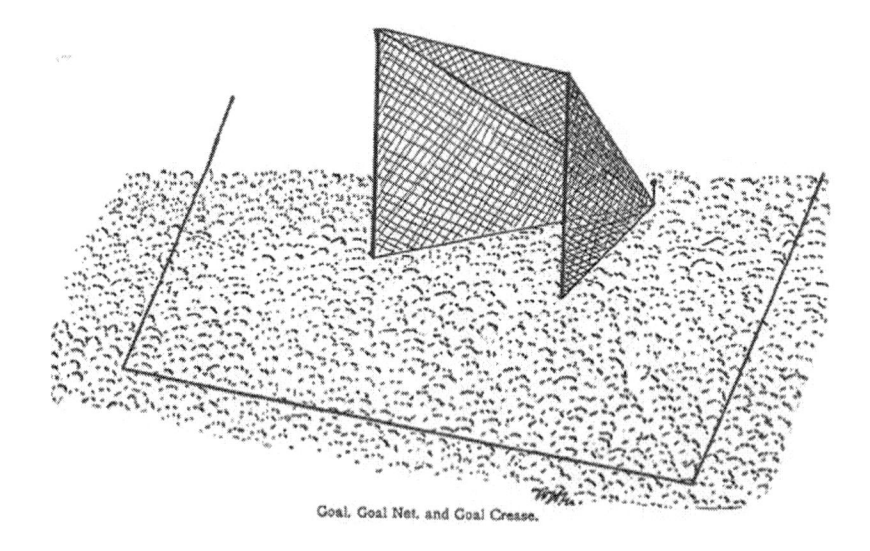

Goal, Goal Net, and Goal Crease.

The first of the competitors in 1902 were the Calumet Lacrosse Club players from Chicago. Upon arriving in St. Paul the Globe gave an overview of the game for new fans.

St. Paul Globe June 29, 1902

"A match game of lacrosse is played with twelve men on each side. The lacrosse grounds are 125 yards long, with goals at each end as in football.

Goal posts six feet apart and six feet high. The ball must go between, the goal posts to score a goal. The object of the player is to pass the ball between their opponents' goals and prevent it from being passed through their own. The playing time Is 90 minutes, the team scoring the largest number of goals in that time to win the match. The teams will change ends every 20 minutes. Ten minutes rest at half time."

For the first time, the newspaper published a photo of the official for the game, R.H. Dunbar. Dunbar was a famous curler in the Twin Cities, and was the person who donated the Dunbar Cup to the Twin Cities Hockey League. A competition for this cup was held annually from 1902 – 1910.

Chapter Seventeen – Northwest Lacrosse League

The St. Paul Lacrosse Club wore its signature blue and white uniforms, while the Calumets were dressed in red and white. The game was held in Lexington Park, home of the St. Paul Saints baseball team.

The game preview in the Globe contained observations from the Calumets' practice the day before, saying they were a smaller and quicker team with great passing skills.

Game time arrived and the two teams took the field. The stadium was full at 1,800 paid spectators and more could be seen at the fences. This was a major event for the city.

The game started quickly as the St. Paul team went right to work and Elliot scored the first goal. But the Calumets had not traveled so far to let the game get away from them. The red and white of the Calumets switched their style to the short passing game, Canadian style, and Donnelly scored the next two goals. The Calumets took the lead 2-1.

R. H. DUNBAR,
Referee in Today's Lacrosse Game.

After this explosion by the Calumets to take the lead, Jack Elliot of the St. Paul Club took over the game. The observers said he was everywhere on the defensive side of the field, the middle, and the offense. It is still a decade away from having any offsides rule, so players from both teams can cover the whole field.

A long time passed and the Calumets started to get tired. St. Paul then took their opportunity and Raymond for St. Paul tied the game right before halftime, 2-2. The halftime could not come soon enough for the exhausted Calumet players.

As the second half began, observers noted that the red and white team slashed the St. Paul players on the legs from behind because they could not keep up. They also noted that the St. Paul players were generous in returning blows with their sticks to the ribs and backs of the Calumets. It was a long time before the next goal. Play continued up and down the field with neither team able to shoot the ball into the net.

Finally the Calumets broke free as a blue and white player fell to the ground and Calumets' Rubridge broke for the goal and slipped the ball by Burdette. The Calumets were now up 3-2.

The St. Paul team knew that if they wanted another opportunity at the Winnipeggers, they needed to win this game. Elliot and Slattery rallied the team and soon Armstrong tied the game. Through the mastery between Elliot and Slattery they scored to take the lead. Before the Calumets realized it, the score was 6-3 and the final whistle had blown. St. Paul was victorious over the visitors from Chicago.

Rosters

Calumets	Position	St. Paul
Woods	Goal	Burdett
Morrow	Point	Sheppard
Cameron	Cover Point	Slattery
Collins	Defense Field	Murphy
Mulligan	Defense Field	Wadsworth
Beaton	Defense Field	Raymond
Barker	Center	Oehme
Rubridge	Home Field	Best
Guy	Home Field	Mossop
Fogg	Home Field	Armstrong
Donnelly	Outside Home	Elliott
Carney	Inside Home	Whyte
Gillespie	Spare Man	Newson
Martin	Field Captain	Stewart

Upon hearing the news of the win, the Western Canadian Lacrosse Association sent word that they would first determine a winner on their side of the border and after that was decided would send the winner to St. Paul to compete for the league championship. But before St. Paul could respond, the Calumets asked for another chance to play and redeem themselves. The generous St. Paul Club accepted the offer.

On August 17, 1902 the Calumets returned to St. Paul for a rematch. Again the St. Paul Lacrosse Club defeated the Calumets, only this time the score was 9-4. St. Paul never trailed in the game and Calumets returned to Illinois licking their wounds.

```
Goals Scored:
St. Paul  - Elliot (2), Whyte (5), Armstrong, Oehme
Calumets - Fogg, Beaton, Carney (2)
```

Chapter Seventeen – Northwest Lacrosse League

LACROSSE TEAMS MEET THIS AFTERNOON

Otto Oehme.   W. D. Stewart, Field Captain.   Jack Elliott, by a Staff Photographer.

SOME OF THE PLAYERS ON THE ST. PAUL LACROSSE TEAM.

St. Paul Globe, 1902, Oehme, Stewart, and Elliott

Previously the game between St. Paul and Winnipeg was for the Drewry Cup or WCLA championship. This year the commissioner of the WCLA donated a new International Trophy for the Canadian and United States teams to play for. The commissioner was C.C. Chipman and the trophy was named the Chipman Cup.

The teams initially agreed to play in St. Paul on September 28, 1902 for the International Championship and Chipman Cup. However, September 28 was a Sunday. After much complaining by the Winnipeggers, the game was moved up to Saturday the 27th, and this was approved on Friday, the 26th. This did not go over well with the home team, which had sold over 5,000 tickets for the championship game on Sunday.

The league had spoken and the game was moved to Saturday because the Canadians refused to play for the championship cup on a Sunday.

Rosters

Shamrocks	Position	St. Paul
West	Goal	Sheppard
Cattanack	Point	Murphy
Full	Cover Point	Jones
Reynolds	Defense Field	Raymond
Buetz	Defense Field	Macauley
Laidlow	Defense Field	Wadsworth
Innis	Center	Clarke
Pentland	Home Field	Oehme
Burns	Home Field	Armstrong
Laidlaw	Home Field	Mossop
O'Brien	Outside Home	Elliot
Hennessy	Inside Home	Whyte

The game was a battle and the score went back and forth. The Shamrocks scored the first goal with a shot by Hennesay, but St. Paul answered right back with a goal from Whyte. O'Brien scored for the Shamrocks who took the lead again. Then St. Paul dug in and got the next two goals from Macauley and Whyte, taking the lead 3-2 before halftime. Whyte's goal was recorded as a shot 140 feet away from the goal as time ran out in the first half.

Elliot from St. Paul was not feeling well and reports say he became winded. The Shamrocks matched O'Brien on him, who scored the next goal tying the game at 3-3. St. Paul answered with Macauley scoring his second goal and taking the lead. But the Shamrocks, using their fast passing style, worked the St. Paul defense hard and Pentland scored the game's tying goal with little time left. The Shamrocks again pressed and Hennesay, who scored the first goal of the game, now scored its last goal with less than one minute remaining. The Shamrocks won.

```
Shamrocks 5 - St. Paul 4
```

The first championship for the Chipman trophy went to the Canadians.

On Sunday, the two teams played again—not for the Cup but for what they called the Western Canadian League Championship. Since it was Sunday, the Canadians were not allowed to play for the Cup. However, since both teams wanted to play again, they agreed to play for the title of Western Canadian Lacrosse Champions.

This game went well for the blue and white of St. Paul. Observers said St. Paul out-played and out-shot the Winnipeggers, but the score showed a 12-2

Chapter Seventeen - Northwest Lacrosse League

loss. The game was lost mostly in the midfield, as St. Paul could not keep up with the speed and quick passing of the Shamrocks.

Not long after the loss to the Winnipeg Shamrocks, the St. Paul Lacrosse Club received a telegram from the Shamrocks of Montreal, who were in Seattle. Upon hearing about the great game played for the Chipman Cup trophy, they asked to play the St. Paul team on their trip home.

Excited to play the legendary and World Champion Montreal Shamrock Lacrosse Club, St. Paul accepted. The Montreal team arrived as promised on October 12, 1902. Then rains came. All afternoon it rained, and since Montreal had to catch the evening train, they decided to play in the rough conditions. The rains kept the audience down but the teams kept playing. St. Paul's Armstrong scored first for an early lead, making some viewers believe the St. Paul team might possibly win the game.

Montreal proved why they were the World Champions by pressing and checking very hard and taking the ball away from St. Paul at every turn. St. Paul fell behind the brightly clad green Shamrocks 7-1. The observers noted that the teamwork of the Shamrocks was impeccable and that they were truly a championship team. Now with the lead, the Montreal players relaxed. This emboldened St. Paul to score five goals in a row, making the score 7-6 with only a few minutes remaining. The Montreal Club scored one more time and won the game 8-6.

Given the rainy conditions, the St. Paul and Montreal teams agreed to change from two halves to four quarters, with the teams switching sides each quarter. After this game, the midwest teams began playing quarters in 1902. The formal rule in the east did not change until 1932.

Rosters

Montreal Shamrocks	Position	St. Paul Saints
McKoewn	Goal	Burdett
Riley	Point	Murphy
McIlwane	Cover Point	Flett
Howard	Defense Field	Clark
Cananaugh	Defense Field	Bretz
Smith	Defense Field	Sheppard
Currie	Center	Oehme
Nolan	Home Field	Armstrong
Hoovin	Home Field	Slattery
Robinson	Home Field	O'Brien

```
J. Brennan          Outside Home     Mossop
P. Brennan          Inside Home      Whyte
```

Members of Montreal Shamrocks, Champion Lacrosse Team of the World.

St. Paul Globe, 1902

With the 1902 season coming to the end, this was truly a memorable experience for the state playing the Canadian Champions of the West and the East. Although St. Paul did not win the games, the spectacle of high-level lacrosse was in town and the sport was starting to again develop support in the community. Youth teams had developed and interest in playing lacrosse was growing.

In 1903, the Minneapolis Journal lamented on the mysteries of crowds not following lacrosse. The discussion included the decline in activities such as croquet, and how such a fever had developed for the new game of hockey in town. It discussed how hockey had exploded on the scene while interest in lacrosse was stagnating, and that the imported American baseball was "utterly unattractive." Even then, lacrosse could not draw the crowds that hockey, football, and baseball drew, despite the visits of WCLA and World champion

Chapter Seventeen – Northwest Lacrosse League

teams the previous year. The sport was certainly enjoyed by those who played lacrosse, and youth were interested in playing, but audiences did not follow the interest.

1903 started with St. Paul traveling to Duluth to play a game at Oneota Park on May 30. No rosters were published but the score was reported as 5-3 in favor of the St. Paul Lacrosse Club.

Duluth returned the favor by traveling to St. Paul, playing at Lexington Park on June 8, 1903. Duluth wore blue and red colors while the St. Paul Club wore its traditional blue and white. The excitement of the day surrounded a young man named Mr. Towers from Duluth, who played a vigorous game mixing in every scrum for the ball. For his troubles, Towers received a bloody nose, bruised shins, sprained knee, and several body bruises. The crowd of over 1,100 fans cheered as Towers kept coming back to play more.

Rosters

Duluth	Position	St. Paul
Fauble	Goal	Murphy
Grant	Point	Armstrong
Trask	Cover Point	Cowie
Gillson	Defense Field	Gaiseford
Cargill	Defense Field	McAuley
McDonald	Defense Field	Raymond
McMullen	Center	Oehme
Towers	Home Field	Allen
Saunders	Home Field	Mossop
Wink	Home Field	Elliott
Grimes	Outside Home	Brown
Prouix	Inside Home	Whyte
Foreman	Field Captain	Bailey

The home team did well against the visitors from Duluth, playing very fast and striking first with a goal by Allen. But Duluth answered right back with a goal by Cargill. With the game tied 1-1 the St. Paul team discussed a new strategy to handle the new players Duluth had acquired since the last meeting. St. Paul went on a streak, scoring four goals in a row by Elliot, Brown, Allen, and Brown again.

Duluth answered with two goals by McMullen and Cargill. The score was now 5-3 and again the teams traded goals with Duluth's McDonald and St.

Paul's Whyte. After that Duluth did not score again and the final was 11-5 in favor of the home squad. Duluth had built a good team of players and certainly entertained the St. Paul crowd.

LACROSSE TEAMS READY FOR BATTLE

St. Paul Club and Calumets of Chicago to Clash This Afternoon.

Game announcement for August 2, 1903 – St. Paul Globe

On June 14, 1903 the Calumets traveled to St. Paul with a new goalie named Baker. This game put St. Paul dangerously close to their first loss to an American team in this century.

Baker proved to be an excellent lacrosse goalie. The blue and white started the game and scored first with a goal by Raymond. But the next goal didn't come until much later in the game. Baker was turning St. Paul shots away, again and again. The Calumets scored and at the end of the third quarter the Calumets led the game by a score of 3-1. During the last break before the fourth quarter St. Paul knew they needed to change tactics to get the ball past Baker.

The Calumets had a lead, and with no offside rule in place, started putting all their players in front of the net to make getting a shot through the defense almost impossible. St. Paul decided to abandon their defensive positions and moved all players to offense, leaving Murphy alone in the goal.

St. Paul dominated the play, with the red and white occasionally scooping the ball and throwing it the length of the field to clear it. All the St. Paul players took turns to see who could get a shot past the goalie, but attempt after attempt was denied by Baker.

Chapter Seventeen – Northwest Lacrosse League

After fourteen minutes of play Kervin was standing on the crease and got the ball past Baker. One minute remained in the game and St. Paul was still down by one goal, 3-2. The Calumets won the face-off and ran to the St. Paul end trying to kill the last minute off the clock.

The St. Paul players surrounded Morrison and he was forced to shoot the ball towards the goal. McCarthy stuck his stick in the air, stole the ball and started to run towards Baker on the other end of the field. McCarthy's teammates joined him. Quick passes from McCarthy to Elliott to Armstrong to Brown—as they had learned from the Canadians—took place in front of the net.

Seeing that time was about to end, the referee put the whistle to his mouth and took a breath to blow his whistle. But just then, a roar from the crowd came as Brown scored. St. Paul tied the game with no time left. Final score 3-3. No overtime was played.

Rosters

Calumets	Position	St. Paul
Baker	Goal	Murphy
Clewes	Point	Armstrong
Collins	Cover Point	Cowie
Slattery	Defense Field	McCarthy
Woods	Defense Field	Gaiseford
Beaton	Defense Field	Raymond
Barker	Center	Oehme
Kearney	Home Field	McAuley
Donnelly	Home Field	Allen
Rubridge	Home Field	Elliott
McFadden	Outside Home	Brown
Morrison	Inside Home	Kervin
Tudhope	Field Captain	Bailey

Reported in the St. Paul Globe this same month was a treaty celebration. It had been 35 years since the White Earth Reservation had been established. There was a large celebration at White Earth, and other Ojibwe and Dakota Bands were invited. Band members from Red Lake, Leech Lake, and Mille Lacs attended the celebration. The Globe shared that there were many activities including a dramatic reenactment of Hiawatha, dances, the burying of hatchets, smoking the peace pipe, and lacrosse games. No accounts of these games survive nor are there photographs to share; however, lacrosse games were very common at treaty signings and other celebrations.

Towards the end of summer the Calumets and St. Paul were the best northwest teams in the United States and met again to decide who would face the winner from Canada. The newspapers continued to promote the games and publish the results for the local teams. In this game the St. Paul team was better prepared and won the game 7-3. It must also be noted that the famed Dr. Baker, who played goalie in the first game for the Calumets, was unable to make the trip to St. Paul. Most observers felt he was the reason that St. Paul struggled to earn a tie earlier in the summer.

The St. Paul Globe defined the Calumets now as "rivals" in the league and they had certainly become that. St. Paul, however, seemed to win the majority of the contests between the two cities over the years. The sports rivalry that now exists in many sports between the two cities began with the game of lacrosse.

LOCAL LACROSSE MEN DEFEAT THEIR OLD TIME RIVALS

St. Paul Globe, August, 1903

Rosters

Calumets	Position	St. Paul
Booth	Goal	Wadsworth
C.J. Donnelly	Point	Armstrong
Black	Cover Point	Cowie
Collins	Defense Field	Barclay
Beaton	Defense Field	Raymond
Allen	Defense Field	Wood
Sadler	Center	Oehme
M. Donnelly	Home Field	Mossop
P. Rubridge	Home Field	Elliott
Morrison	Home Field	Kervin
G. Woods	Outside Home	Brown
Gaugean	Inside Home	Whyte
F. Rubridge	Field Captain	Monkman

```
Gilles              Umpire          Stark
Wright              TimeKeeper      McDonald
Attendance: 2,571

Goals for St. Paul - Elliot (2), Whyte(2), Brown(3)
Goals for Calumets - G. Woods(2), Gaugean
```

A feature began to be reported in the newspaper—an injury report. Or, as the Globe called it, "casualties" of the game. The game was violent at times and this was a draw for the spectators.

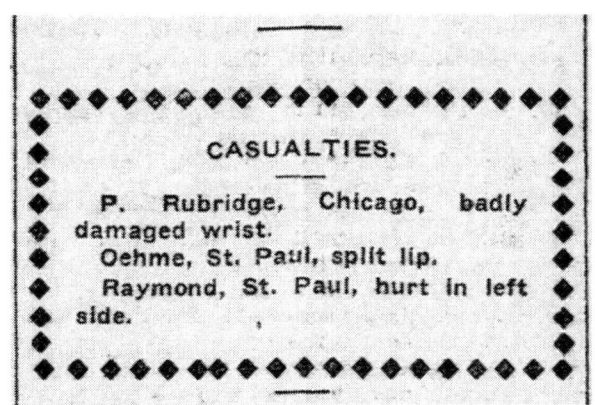

> **CASUALTIES.**
>
> P. Rubridge, Chicago, badly damaged wrist.
> Oehme, St. Paul, split lip.
> Raymond, St. Paul, hurt in left side.

St. Paul Globe – August 3, 1903 Lacrosse Game Casualty Report

The St. Paul Globe mentions a few other teams south of the Canadian border who were in the league, including St Paul, Duluth, Houghton, Ishpeming, Marquette, and Chicago.

In September 1903, the Olympic committee announced sporting events to be held in St. Louis the following year. This marked several firsts for the Olympics, including the first time the games were held on the American continent, first time in the United States, and the first time lacrosse was a featured sport in the games.

The St Paul Lacrosse Club began discussions with the lacrosse Western and Eastern Associations on how the teams would be selected to represent the United States. The initial response was a playoff series to be held in spring, with the winner having the privilege to represent the United States at the Olympics. (This will be discussed more in the 1904 chapter.)

Having traveled twice to St. Paul, the Calumets now insisted that they be allowed to host a game before the championship in 1903. St. Paul traveled to Chicago on August 17 to face the Calumets on their home field. This time the result did not favor the St. Paul Saints. The Calumets won 11-2 but the game was stopped in the second quarter after St. Paul players left the field and refused to play until the referee was replaced. They claimed the official was so bad that he was costing them the game.

Baker was again in goal for the Calumets and he turned the St. Paul shots away again and again. Since this was a loss, there was little reported on the game in the home newspaper. This is the entire article reporting the game.

ST. PAUL LACROSSE TEAM IS DEFEATED

Calumets Win at Chicago by the Score 11 to 2—Referee Blamed.

August 17, 1903 – St. Paul Globe

The teams in Manitoba had played off, and Winnipeg defeated Souris for the Canadian championship. Since St. Paul had defeated the Calumets prior to the playoff series, they had already made plans to travel to St. Paul for the International Championship on Labor Day, September 5.

Because the Calumets had defeated St. Paul on August 17, the Calumets claimed that they had won the US side of the league and asked the league to award them the championship opportunity. By the time the league answered, the Winnipeg players were on their way to St. Paul. The league ruled that the Calumets could not do math. The series tally for the summer was 1 win, 1 loss, and 1 tie for both teams. The series was tied, and the teams needed to play one more game to decide the US winner of the league.

Winnipeg arrived on September 5 and played games with St. Paul that did not count for the International Championship. This was unfortunate since it seemed like every new year meant a new trophy to be played for. The Hudson Bay Cup for the International Championship was now added. But since the US could not decide which team would play, by default it was given to Winnipeg.

Winnipeg did offer to play two games while in town. The games were held at Lexington Park in St. Paul.

Rosters

Winnipeg	Position	St. Paul
Percy Quinn	Goal	Barclay
Clark	Point	Armstrong
Winkler	Cover Point	Murphy
Tooke	Defense Field	Gaiseford
McLeod	Defense Field	Raymond
Hendron	Defense Field	Allen
Murphy	Center	Oehme
Kirk	Home Field	Mossop
Cameron	Home Field	Elliott
Winkler	Home Field	Kervin
C. Quinn	Outside Home	Brown
Cassidy	Inside Home	Whyte
R.H. Smith	Field Captain	Monkman

Goals for St. Paul - Kervin, Elliot, Whyte(4), Brown(2)

Goals for Winnipeg - Kirk(5), Hendron, Quinn(4), Cassidy

Winnipeg won the first game 11-8 in a high scoring competition. A crowd of about 1,500 watched. Hendron from Winnipeg ended up being a crowd favorite as the tiny 115-pounder took a beating and kept getting up to return to play. The crowd affectionately called out "Little No. 7" as he again and again successfully scrummed for the ball.

The two teams played again the next day on September 6 and this time the St. Paul team took it to the Winnipeggers 10-8. It was another high scoring game and would have been higher if not for the brilliant play of the legendary goalie Percy Quinn. Quinn was an amazing talent; the crowd said his stops were brilliant and amazing to watch. Observers also noted that Quinn sacrificed his body and took amazing abuse by shots from St. Paul's Wyte and others, and it never phased him. He continued to jump in front of the goal to protect it. But the St. Paul players were able to score and managed to defeat the Winnipeggers and split the series.

For International Lacrosse

The Hudson's Bay Cup
St. Paul Globe, 1903

Chapter Seventeen – Northwest Lacrosse League

One trend that began this year was that newspapers started calling the team the St. Paul "Stickers." The nickname was used during baseball season to reduce confusion due to both teams being named the "Saints." Lacrosse game headlines usually included Stickers, Saints or sometimes both.

CALUMETS ARE COMING TO TRIM THE SAINTS

Chicago Lacrosse Team Will Play St. Paul Stickers at Lexington Park.

October 1, 1903 – St. Paul Globe

Remember that the St. Paul team had to watch the Winnipeggers receive the new famed Hudson Bay trophy and could not compete for it. The Calumets series was tied at 1-1-1, and no US Western Championship was awarded. The St. Paul Club, specifically the President of the club, W.D. Stewart, invited the Calumets back to settle the score. This game would officially settle who was the US Western Lacrosse Champion. The game was played on October 4, 1903.

The newspapers carried the trash talk between the clubs. The Calumets talked about "trimming the Saints" and St. Paul commented that the "Windy City Boys have nothing on us."

Both clubs wanted to prove themselves winners. Why? Because the Olympics were coming to this continent the following year. And the Eastern Association was planning a large playoff series to see who would earn the right to represent the United States in the first Olympics on US soil. This also meant that the first lacrosse gold medal would be awarded. St. Paul wanted to send a message to the back east teams that they should be the lead club in the west to be considered for the Olympics.

The St. Paul players practiced and met to discuss the big game with the boys from Chicago. Much of the discussion focused on Dr. Baker, the goalie for the Calumets. Players discussed how to shoot on Baker with a high shot, low shot, side shot, and bounce shot. Players commented that all of these shots looked the same to Baker, and his goalie skills were second to none. The St. Paul players worked up plays to confuse Baker, designing hard-to-see shots in hopes of scoring enough goals to win.

W. D. STEWART,
President of the St. Paul Lacrosse Club.

W.D. Stewart - St. Paul Globe October 3, 1903

The Calumet players arrived from Chicago and a large crowd assembled to watch the game at Lexington Park. The newspaper told the story of the largest audience ever assembled for a lacrosse game in St. Paul, but no attendance number was reported. What is surprising is that Dr. Baker, whom the St. Paul lacrosse team had been preparing for, did not make the trip.

The game took seventy minutes to complete, and the result was in doubt right up to the last whistle, despite a final score of 9-5.

The Calumets came out playing a rough game and St. Paul did not back down. Ed Murphy of St. Paul was applauded for his generous body checks.

Chapter Seventeen – Northwest Lacrosse League

Elliott of St. Paul appeared to be the marked man, and was slashed, bruised, then finally knocked out. He recovered, the team put him in at the goalie position, and moved Brown to the midfield. Mossop took a gash to his face, while Oehme and Whyte joined Ed Murphy on the body checking committee.

The paper reported these as non-serious injuries and that the players all finished the game without incident. And the rapid ball passing of the St. Paul players that had been practiced for Dr. Baker? It worked well in front of the net for Kerwin and Whyte.

George Kerwin – St. Paul Globe October 4, 1903

Minnesota Lacrosse: A History

Rosters

Calumets	Position	St. Paul
Morrill	Goal	Brown
Gaugun	Point	Armstrong
Collins	Cover Point	Murphy
Black	Defense Field	Gaiseford
Beaton	Defense Field	Raymond
Mulligan	Defense Field	Mossop
Goulett	Center	Oehme
C. Morrison	Home Field	Elliott
Rubridge	Home Field	Allen
Donnelly	Home Field	Kirk
Sadler	Outside Home	Kerwin
Labatt	Inside Home	Whyte
F. Rubridge	Field Captain	Monkman

Official A. A. Smith from Minneapolis Lacrosse Club
Scorekeepers MacDonald and Mulligan

Goals for St. Paul - Kerwin(2), Whyte(3), Kirk, Brown(2), Elliott
Goals for Winnipeg - Rubridge(3), Labatt, Morrison

The 1903 lacrosse season came to an end with St. Paul being the Western United States Champions, but not formally competing for the International Championship. This was due to the earlier loss to the Calumets and the confusion of naming a US champion in time to compete over the border.

With winter now approaching, the lacrosse players took an even larger role in the developing Twin Cities Hockey League. The following players joined the St. Paul Hockey Club: [79]

```
W.D. Stewart - Honorary President
Ed. J. Murphy - President
Jack Elliott - First Vice President
R. Bell - Second Vice President
A.L. Kirk - Secretary and Treasurer
George Kerwin - Manager
"Jimmie" Monkman - Trainer
Haines, Kirk, Allen, Brown, and Gaiseford as hockey players
```

Chapter Seventeen – Northwest Lacrosse League

ROBERT BELL,
Auditor of the St. Paul Lacrosse Club.

Side wall:
Perhaps one of the most odd pictures to appear in the timing of this final game was the photo of Robert Bell. Bell was not player, a coach, nor had even picked up a stick.

He was the Auditor of the St. Paul Lacrosse Club. Why his picture is in the paper is a mystery. The article promotes the game to take place in October, along with the location and time to be there, but Robert Bell is not mentioned and is just pictured next to the article.

St. Paul Globe October 4, 1903

Newspaper advertisement showing popularity of lacrosse to sell cigarettes

CHAPTER 18

1904, THE FIRST AMERICAN OLYMPICS

The modern era Olympic Games returned in 1896 at Athens, Greece. The next Olympics took place in Paris, France in 1900. The Olympics at that time were very small and did not have the coverage it enjoys today. The 1904 Olympics were held in St. Louis and, since it was the first Olympics on US soil, the Americans wanted to show the world their love for sports.

The games had originally been awarded to Chicago, not St. Louis. St. Louis was organizing a 100th anniversary celebration of the Louisiana Purchase, to be held in 1903. However, planning fell behind and they delayed the celebration until 1904. Fearing that attendance would be split with Chicago hosting the Olympics, St. Louis threatened to hold their own athletic games. The Olympic Committee gave in and took the games away from Chicago and awarded them to St. Louis.

Back in the fall of 1903 the Eastern Lacrosse Association was in charge of selecting a team to play in the Olympics. Since the host country chose the sports to be involved in the games, lacrosse was a natural choice because of its popularity as an amateur sport. But as the time drew near, the east coast teams became involved in accusations of using professional athletes, which derailed bids from east coast teams that planned to attend.

The St. Paul Lacrosse Club had requested to be part of the selection process, after having won the Western United States Lacrosse Championship. The Eastern Lacrosse Association had decided to exclude college lacrosse teams from the Olympics. Other teams being considered for a chance to play in the Olympics were the Brooklyn Crescents, the Bison of Buffalo, and Detroit.

EDWARD J. MURPHY,
New President of the St. Paul Lacrosse Club.

Ed Murphy, St. Paul Globe February 20, 1904

The St. Paul Lacrosse Club gathered earlier than usual in 1904, expecting to hear if they would be selected for the Olympics. They wanted to be prepared to play games early in the season regardless of the selection process. On February 20, 1904 the club elected Ed Murphy President. The club had generated great interest from the Victoria Hockey team, a group of mostly high school players who had won the Twin Cities Hockey championship the last two seasons. With so many new players, it was going to be tough for some older players to keep their spots.

By Decoration Day, the Eastern Lacrosse Association had narrowed the selection of lacrosse team for the Olympics to three teams: St. Paul, the Brooklyn Crescents, and St. Louis. St. Louis was a newer team, but because they were the host city they were allowed to be considered.

Chapter Eighteen - 1904, The First American Olympics

To prepare for the upcoming Olympic games, the St. Paul Club challenged the Chicago Calumets to a game on Decoration Day. St. Paul traveled to Chicago, where St. Paul easily won 7-2. Kerwin and Allen both scored three goals, with the final goal by Towers. Sewell scored both goals for the Calumets, each coming late in the fourth quarter.

The Calumets decided to return the favor and traveled to St. Paul. This game turned into a brawl and was played to a tie of 5-5. Observers noted the rough play and two fights.

Next up for St. Paul was the Algonquin team from Port Arthur, Canada. The team came by boat to St. Paul and played at Lexington Park. The Canadian teams were considered to be faster and better skilled players, but St. Paul had been changing its style to play against the Canadians.

Rosters

Port Arthur	Position	St. Paul
Fauble	Goal	Haines
Bowell	Point	Armstrong
McCallum	Cover Point	Raymond
Lawrence	Defense Field	Gaiseford
H. Simons	Defense Field	Mossop
Ferguson	Defense Field	Sellers
McMullen	Center	Oehme
McClinsky	Home Field	Allen
Brennagh	Home Field	Elliott
Traer	Home Field	Kerwin
McKinstry	Outside Home	Brown
McNaughton	Inside Home	Whyte
Gordon	Field Captain	Monkman

The game started off slowly and the end of the first quarter had the St. Paul team holding on to a slim 2-1 lead. That all changed in the second quarter when St. Paul went on a six-goal run. The halftime score showed 8-1 in favor of the Saints. The game ended 10-2 and St. Paul had its biggest victory ever over a Canadian team.

Minnesota Lacrosse: A History

CRESCENT ATHLETIC CLUB OF BROOKLYN

C C MASON   M ROSE   J P CURRY   H L PARSONS
E H JEWELL   E MCLEAN
C DE CASANOVA   J S GARVIN   C F ROBERTS   L MOSES
           (CAPT)
H MCCONAGHY   CC MILLER
        J A LEIGHTON   G WHITING   T H DUNCAN

Crescent Lacrosse Team - US Lacrosse Museum

As the political battles waged back east, the Brooklyn Crescents were disqualified from the Olympics because they had used professional players in games during the season. So, the battle was between the two remaining teams, St. Paul and St. Louis. Since no east coast team was going, no travel funds were approved by the Lacrosse Association. Instead they simply selected the home team, St. Louis, to represent the United States.

This deeply frustrated St. Paul. They had prepared, practiced, and defeated Canadian teams, only to be denied a chance to play at the Olympics and represent their country. St. Paul pleaded but no appeal was heard. The local lacrosse team in St. Louis was then given the opportunity to play in the Olympics.

The team that was selected to represent Canada was the Shamrocks of Winnipeg, both because they were a great team and also because they were closer to the event. Since neither the Crescents nor St. Paul were going, the

Chapter Eighteen - 1904, The First American Olympics

Shamrocks of Montreal felt no need to travel, sensing that the Winnipeggers could represent Canada just fine against St. Louis. The gold medal would be assured.

The Canadians from Winnipeg reached out to the St. Paul Lacrosse Club and offered to play them on their way to the Olympics as a practice game to help them prepare. St. Paul gladly accepted the offer to host the Shamrocks of Winnipeg and play them on home turf.

St. Paul Globe, 1904, players Seller and Raymond

On July 4, 1904 the biggest game of the season (and most likely the 20th century, at least for St. Paul) was played. Word went out that the champions of Canada were visiting on their way to the Olympics to play the local team. The event was so big that seven people were arrested for forged tickets printed by the St. Paul Pioneer Press office.

The game was held at Lexington Park in St. Paul. The Shamrocks started the game with a quick 2-0 lead by the end of the first quarter. Actually it was a former St. Paul player, Billy O'Brien, who scored both of these goals for the Shamrocks.

During the second quarter, Whyte and Kerwin scored to tie the game at 2-2, but by halftime the Shamrocks again scored and now led 6-2. But something changed during halftime. Instead of being down, St. Paul came out confident and played like champions themselves. Whyte scored the only two goals in the third quarter and closed the gap to 6-4 with one quarter remaining.

The fourth quarter was a blur for both goaltenders, who turned away shot after shot as both teams tried feverishly to score. Finally with only a few minutes left St. Paul scored, this time by Elliott then Allen. The game was tied and the crowd threw their hats, umbrellas and anything else they had into the air and "yelled themselves hoarse." As game time ran down St. Paul was clearly in charge, taking shots again and again and again, but could not score before the clock ran out.

1904 league rules stated that overtime must be held to decide the game. But since Winnipeg said it was a practice/warm up game for the Olympics, they refused to play overtime. Captain Orris of Winnipeg called his team off the field and declared the game a tie.

The final score was 6-6 and St. Paul had managed to control much of the game against the soon-to-be gold medal champions of the Olympics.

Rosters

Winnipeg Shamrocks	Position	St. Paul
Cloutier	Goal	Haines
Cattnach	Point	Armstrong
Blanchard	Cover Point	Raymond
Flett	Defense Field	Murphy
Bretz	Defense Field	Mossop
Innis	Defense Field	Sellers
Laidlaw	Center	Oehme
Brennagh	Home Field	Allen
Lyle	Home Field	Elliott
Burns	Home Field	Kerwin
Cowan	Outside Home	Brown
Billy O'Brien	Inside Home	Whyte
Carper	Field Captain	Monkman

Winnipeg Goals: Billy O'Brien(2), Cowan(3), Lyle
St. Paul Goals: Whyte(3), Kerwin, Elliott, Allen

With this game ending in a tie, one can only imagine how the Olympics would have gone for the United States had St. Paul been allowed to represent and play. We only have this game to show how close Minnesota came to a gold medal opportunity in lacrosse.

Chapter Eighteen - 1904, The First American Olympics

1904 World's Fair Program

The Shamrocks stopped in Chicago and played the Calumets on their way to the Olympics, and this time the Shamrocks won easily 14-5.

The 1904 Olympics are often considered to be the worst Olympics ever held for many reasons that require some elaboration. Since the World's Fair and Olympics were merged during this year, the games were extended over a long period of time. The event ran from July 1 to November 23, compared to today's standard of 16-18 days.

Perhaps the worst part of the 1904 Olympics was a subset of the World's Fair in which *"human zoo"* exhibits were created for crowds to gawk at indigenous peoples from throughout the world. As that grew dull, the World's Fair Committee decided to have the indigenous people participate in athletic events. Accounts from the time list the *"human zoo members"* as having come from Africa, South America, the Middle East, the Philippines, Japan, and the First Nations.

Official Olympic Sports in 1904	**Exhibition Sports in 1904**
Aquatics (Diving, Swimming)	Basketball
Archery	Hurley
Boxing	Baseball
Cycling	Water Polo
Fencing	
Football (Soccer)	
Golf	
Gymnastics	
Lacrosse	
Roque (a form of Croquet)	
Rowing	
Tennis	
Track and Field events	
Tug of war	
Weightlifting	
Wrestling	

Chapter Eighteen - 1904, The First American Olympics

James E. Sullivan, the head of the 1904 Fair's Department of Physical Culture, decided to have the Olympians compete against the Indigenous People. Sullivan called it the "Special Olympics," but it was officially dubbed the 1904 Anthropology Days because Sullivan brought William McGee, of the Fair's Department of Anthropology, to supervisor the event.

SIDE WALL:
The 1904 Olympics were the first to award medals in the standard we are familiar with today: gold, silver, and bronze. In the first Athens games in 1896 the winners received a silver medal and an olive branch, while the runners-up received a bronze medal and laurel branch.

In the 1900 Paris games the winners were awarded cups and trophies. So America began the tradition of gold, silver, and bronze medals we know today.

McGee, founding president of the American Anthropological Association, planned to collect data from the events to try to prove the indigenous people's athletic inferiority, but the event was a farce. Pitting trained athletes against competitors who didn't know the rules or understand them when they were explained in English—a foreign tongue—wasn't exactly a fair scientific experiment.

To give an example of how badly it went, the indigenous competitors didn't understand the concept of breaking through the tape at the finish line of the foot races: Some stopped short of the tape, others ran under it.

Other events included the high and long jump, tree climbing, archery, shot put, fighting demonstrations, mud throwing, and a Mohawk vs. Seneca lacrosse match.

Against this backdrop, let's review the two lacrosse games in the 1904 Olympics.

SIDE WALL:
The 1904 Olympics featured cheating that could not even be imagined by today's standards. In the marathon, Fred Lorz had started the run but grew tired and was picked up by a car. Near the stadium the car got a flat tire and Fred got out and started walking to the stadium. As Fred entered the stadium the crowd cheered, assuming he was winning the race.

Fred "went with it" and was even awarded the gold medal. Later it was discovered that he cheated and they awarded the medal to the next finisher, Thomas Hicks. Hicks had in fact been helped over the finish line with what is now the worst time in Olympic Marathon history with a time of three hours and twenty eight minutes.

Minnesota Lacrosse: A History

With three teams in the Lacrosse program, the Olympic Committee decided to seed the teams and have only two games. St. Louis and the Mohawk team from Canada played first and the winner faced the Shamrocks of Winnipeg for the championship.

The Mohawk Nation was from the area surrounding Brantford, Ontario. The Mohawk Lacrosse team also played in the Anthropology Days against the Seneca Nation. There is no mention of why the Seneca Nation did not play in the Olympic games and make a four-team pool. There is also no score of the games played between the Mohawk and Seneca.

The first game was played between the St. Louis and Mohawk Clubs on July 5, 1904. The score is recorded as 2-0 in favor of the St. Louis team and to date no description or photos of the contest can be found. The St. Louis team went on to the championship against the Shamrocks of Winnipeg.

On July 7, 1904 the gold medal game was played, with the Shamrocks easily defeating the St. Louis team 8-2. And just like that, the first lacrosse games at the Olympics were over. Winnipeg won the gold, St. Louis the silver, and Mohawk the bronze.

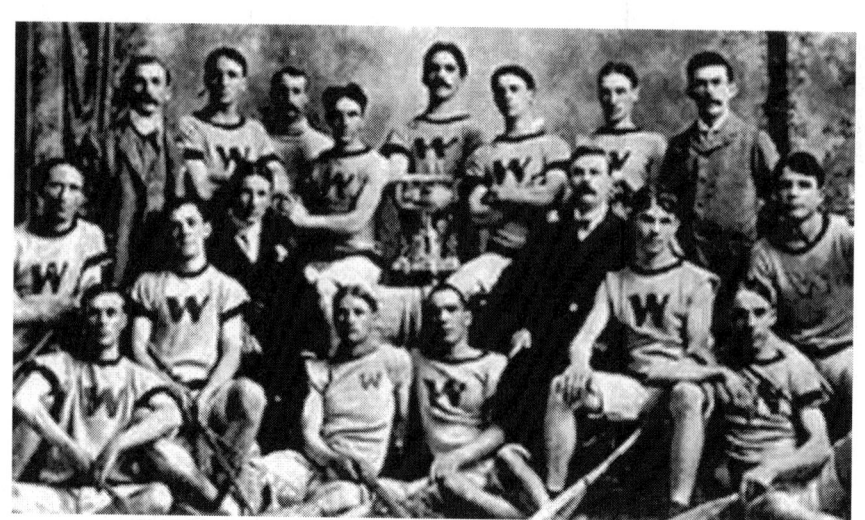

1904 Shamrocks of Winnipeg – Gold Medal Champions

Chapter Eighteen – 1904, The First American Olympics

1904 Olympic Lacrosse Rosters

Winnipeg Shamrock Lacrosse Team (Gold Medal)	
Élie Blanchard	Sandy Cowan
William Brennaugh	Jack Flett
George Bretz	Benjamin Jamieson
William Burns	Stuart Laidlaw
George Cattanach	Hilliard Lyle
George Cloutier	Lawrence Pentland

St. Louis Amateur Athletic Association Lacrosse Team (Silver Medal)	
J. W. Dowling	William Partridge
W. R. Gibson	George Passmore
Patrick Grogan	William T. Passmore
Tom Hunter	W. J. Ross
Albert Lehman	Jack Sullivan
W. A. Murphy	Albert Venn
	A. M. Woods

Mohawk Indians Lacrosse Team (Bronze Medal)	
Almighty Voice	Man Afraid Soap
Black Eagle	Night Hawk
Black Hawk	Rain in Face
Flat Iron	Red Jacket
Half Moon	Snake Eater
Lightfoot	Spotted Tail

The St. Paul Globe reported that the lacrosse played at the Olympics fizzled and failed to draw excitement because the Shamrocks were not challenged. Ed Murphy of the St. Paul Lacrosse Club invited the Winnipeggers to stop by and settle the tie on their way home.

Minnesota Lacrosse: A History

The Shamrocks accepted the invitation from Murphy and on July 9, the two teams squared off again. A storm rolled through and the field was wet and slick when the game started. St. Paul began the game strong and scored the first two goals, but by halftime the score was tied.

The green jerseys then took a lead in the third quarter, and the blue and white home team played desperately. Unfortunately, the home team forgot to pass the ball and took wild shots from the midfield in an attempt to get back in the game. The final score was close at 7-5, but the Shamrocks proved why they deserved the Olympic Championship.

The summer of 1904 saw several more games in the Minnesota area for the local teams. Soon after the Olympics, word spread about the powerhouse team in St. Paul. Detroit, St. Louis, and Michigan teams all sent invitations to the Saints. The Soo team, winners of the Ontario Lacrosse League, offered to come to Minnesota and play the blue and white. The Soo were from Sault Ste. Marie, Ontario. The Soo agreed to play two games, one in a downtown park in St. Paul and the second at Lexington Park.

The first game was played on Saturday, July 30 in a "down-town" park. The size of the park is smaller than a normal field so the rosters were brought down to 10 players aside to allow more room for passing.

Rosters

Soo	Position	St. Paul
McKinstry	Goal	Haines
Lewis	Point	Armstrong
Findlay	Cover Point	Raymond
Mole	Defense Field	Murphy
Hogarth	Defense Field	Gaiseford
McDonald	Defense Field	Seller
Hitchcock	Center	Oehme
Graham	Home Field	Allen
Cornell	Home Field	Elliott
Douglas	Home Field	Kerwin
Cowie	Outside Home	Brown
Baine	Inside Home	Whyte
Sutherland	Field Captain	Monkman

The game started slowly for the home team, falling behind 5–3 by the second quarter. But St. Paul figured out the Soo tactics, which involved a lot of slashes to the St. Paul players. Soon the home team started passing more

Chapter Eighteen – 1904, The First American Olympics

and created additional scoring chances, winning the game 11-8. The first game went to St. Paul.

On Sunday the full twelve-player roster was used at Lexington Park. The Soo team reworked their roster, moving players around. They decided to play man-to-man defense. The chant from their captain was "stick to your man." With that defense, they held St. Paul to only one goal in the game. The final was 4-1 in favor of the red team from Sault Ste. Marie.

Soo Lacrosse Team – St. Paul Globe, 1904

Just a week later the Calumets came to town to play their old-time rivals the St. Paul Lacrosse Club. The newspaper discussed the rivalry going back to 1883. While St. Paul had taken most of the games over the years, the recent pairings had been close, with the Calumets winning a couple of times.

On August 8, the teams played at Lexington Park with two new rules. The first rule change moved the distance between the nets from 125 yards apart to 95 yards. The second rule change reduced the number of players from 12 to 10 because of the smaller field. Both teams agreed to try these new rules that were being promoted back east.

Minnesota Lacrosse: A History

St. Paul won over the Calumets 9-6 in a close game where the superior passing of the Saints allowed them to tire the tough defense of the Calumets. The newspaper made reference to two players using left-handed sticks. It's not clear why this was pointed out, but the players listed were Sewell and Whyte. Most likely their right-handed sticks were broken and the only spares were left-handed sticks. Keep in mind these are still wooden sticks made by Lally and the head did not go all the way around. So the gut side determined if a stick was designed for the left or right handed player.

St. Paul Globe, 1904 St Paul Lacrosse Club

The Calumets wanted to play again and invited St Paul to return the favor and play a game in Chicago; St. Paul agreed and on August 21, 1904 they played a game in Chicago. This time the Calumets prevailed and won by a score of 9-5. Comments on the new ten-man roster said the game was rougher, and more injuries were occurring when compared to the twelve man game.

Chapter Eighteen - 1904, The First American Olympics

The game of lacrosse continued in other areas of Minnesota. Duluth played Canadian teams such as Port Arthur, Soo, Thunder Bay, and others. As the season was wrapping up, the Duluth team—which had played well up north—decided to travel to St. Paul for an end-of-season game on September 18. St. Paul had never lost to Duluth, and since the Calumets were delaying in order to get another game in this season, they accepted the challenge from the Zenith City (Duluth) club.

The Duluth team was now stronger because they had acquired players from the St. Paul Lacrosse Club and Canada. The game was held at Lexington Park on a beautiful fall day. St. Paul wore their famous blue and white colors, while Duluth countered with green jerseys. The game started with St Paul scoring the first two goals, but Duluth countered with a goal. Not long after Duluth scored, the Saints of St. Paul started to pull away from Duluth. The newspaper recorded that the Duluth team was very plucky and worked hard, but was just not in the same class as the Saints. The final score was 19-4.

Rosters

Duluth	Position	St. Paul
Malcolm	Goal	Haines
Hogarth	Point	Armstrong
Mcmullen	Cover Point	Murphy
Forman	Defense Field	Gaiseford
McKay	Defense Field	Raymond
Blaize	Defense Field	Sellers
Jimmy Murphy	Center	Mossop
Proulx	Home Field	Allen
Grimes	Home Field	Elliott
Grant	Home Field	Kervin
Cargill	Outside Home	Brown
Hunter	Inside Home	Whyte
Jefferson	Umpire	MacDonald
Ellert	TimeKeeper	Stewart

Dr. J. T. Christison was referee.

After this game the St. Paul Club assumed the season was over. Since they had defeated the most teams—including winning two games over the Calumets who beat them once—they thought they'd be awarded the Northwestern Championship trophy. But the Calumets, who after losing to St. Paul in August had gone undefeated with impressive wins over several Canadian teams, demanded a playoff game to settle who was truly the champion. Ed Murphy of the St. Paul Lacrosse Club agreed to a championship game in St. Paul.

The Calumets arrived in St. Paul on October 1, and the game was played on October 2, 1904. St. Paul was expecting a rough game and in advance practiced with their best Cover Point player, Murphy, at the In Home position—basically taking their biggest and best defensemen and moving him to the front of the crease on offense.

As expected, the Calumets came out swinging their sticks and bruising Big Ed Murphy again—on the head, shoulders, and everywhere they could reach. Murphy rebuffed the blows again and again, showing them that St. Paul was the toughest team in the league.

The Globe reported that the Calumets played hard, rough, and never gave an inch to St. Paul. But they had no answer for *"the Husky Minnesotan"* on crease, and the St. Paul team defeated the Calumets in convincing fashion 11-0. They shut out the Calumets and took home the Northwestern League Championship.

After this result, St. Paul reached out to their peers in Winnipeg, the Shamrocks, who had won the Olympic gold medal and defeated the Saints on July 8. St. Paul wanted to play for the Hudson Bay Cup. The Shamrocks declined the invitation however, citing a league rule that all challenges for cups had to be made before September 1 of each year.

CHAPTER 19

1905, INTERNATIONAL CHAMPIONS

1904 had been quite a year for lacrosse in the midwest. The Olympic games, in which St. Paul could have represented the United States; the amazing tied game between St. Paul and the Olympic gold medal winners, the Shamrocks of Winnipeg; and St. Paul winning the Northwestern Lacrosse League, but losing its bid for the Hudson Bay Cup trophy on a technicality. St. Paul recorded the attendance of these games at well over 3,000 spectators, and interest in the game was growing all over the country.

In 1905 the Junior Lacrosse Team of the St. Paul Club decided to move out from underneath the senior club and join the league on their own. These players were generally younger, but had experience playing hockey during the winter season. With such a strong club as the St. Paul Lacrosse team, it was tough for these younger players to find a spot on the senior squad. Games had been played between the two squads when they practiced before league games, but they were seldom able to play in the main games unless a player was ill or out of town.

Minnesota Lacrosse: A History

The senior team went under the name Saints, like the local baseball team, so the Junior teams decided to take names honoring the origins of lacrosse. The first junior club to form was called the Junior Chippewa Lacrosse Club of St. Paul.

JUNIOR LACROSSE TEAM WILL ENTER FIELD

W. D. BINGHAM
Captain

GEORGE A. BARTON
Secretary and Treasurer.

CLAUDE H. YOUNG
Vice President.

St. Paul Globe, 1905

On May 30, the Winnipeg Lacrosse Club came to Lexington Park for a game, and a fight broke out. The two heavyweight players, Murphy of St. Paul and McCarrey of Winnipeg, were said to have gone two rounds, with McCarrey becoming the sorely battered player.

The Minneapolis Journal mentions that many fights broke out in lacrosse games, and that most ended in a few minutes, except for this heavyweight match. It was official now—fighting had become a part of the sport of lacrosse. Winnipeg went on to win the game 6-5, but the spectators enjoyed the fights. Fans began to encourage more fighting.

After this game, the St. Paul team discussed having two officials at each game instead of one in order to cut down on the violence. This had already begun back east.

The first game of the series with the Calumets happened on June 18, at Lexington Park, to try and start St. Paul's season off with a win. The Saints were ready and the locals beat the Calumets 5-3.

Chapter Nineteen – 1905, International Champions

St. Paul Athletic Club, 1905 program

As had happened in St. Paul, Chicago was also attracting more talented players. A second team was added in Chicago to play in the league. They called themselves Chicago Lacrosse Club. The new Chicago team traveled to St. Paul to face the club at Lexington Park. It being their first lacrosse game, the St. Paul players were glad to welcome them to the league by defeating them 13-3.

Rosters

Chicago	Position	St. Paul
McCall	Goal	Haines
Grogan	Point	Armstrong
Ralph	Cover Point	Murphy
Morriston	Defense Field	Gaiseford
A. Wood	Defense Field	Raymond
Gougeon	Defense Field	Sellers
Fogg	Center	Mossop
Partridge	Home Field	Allen

```
Kearney          Home Field        Elliott
Sullivan         Home Field        Kervin
Elwood           Outside Home      Brown
Irwin            Inside Home       Whyte
Guy              Field Captain     MacDonald
```

Referee - George McDonald
Umpires - Sewall and W. McDonald
Timers - Wood and Crossen

The second game of the series with the Calumets was played in Chicago at the American League Park. This time the Calumets got the better of the St. Paul Club and won 10-4. The series was now tied for the season at one game each.

St. Paul Athletic Club, 1905

Chapter Nineteen - 1905, International Champions

Signs of increased violence in the game can be found with a game on July 31 between the Calumets and the new Chicago team. The game was played at American League Park and in the third quarter, with the Calumets leading 3-1, a number of players squared off in fights.

Charlie Comiskey, the owner of the White Sox baseball team, took to the field to stop the fighting. During the brawl Comiskey was slugged in the back of the head. Seeing Comiskey on the ground did not stop the fighting and it was some time before order was restored and the game resumed.

Soon after this game, St. Paul was headed to Chicago to play the Chicago Lacrosse Club again. On August 6, 1905, headlines warned police to be ready for the game. But instead of reports of fighting the day after the event, the following headline was printed:

MILLENNIUM MUST BE COMING FAST

Chicago Lacrosse Game Goes Thru Without a Single Fight.

Minneapolis Journal August 7, 1905

St. Paul won the game 10-5, but the locals seemed happy a lacrosse game could be played without bloodshed. The newspapers reported that the game was dominated by St. Paul because of their passing and hard work. On any given ground ball, St. Paul had three to four players versus Chicago's one.

The following week the Canadian Soo team came to Lexington Park. The St. Paul team was feeling good after the Chicago game, and wanted a challenge from a good Canadian team. St. Paul made a strong showing and won the game by a score of 5-0. Shutting out an opponent showed that St. Paul was working hard on their defensive game.

One item of note: the Shamrock team of Winnipeg—the team that beat St. Paul the previous year in 1904 and won the gold medal at the

Minnesota Lacrosse: A History

Olympics—disbanded as a team because of accusations of professional players. Instead a new team formed, called the Mintos of Winnipeg. When they heard the Soos had lost so badly to the Saints of St. Paul, they sent a telegram expressing interest in coming to St. Paul.

LAST GAME OF CUP SERIES

St. Paul and Chicago Lacrosse Teams Will Meet This Afternoon at Lexington Park.

THE CARLING CUP,
Trophy for which the St. Paul and the Chicago lacrosse teams will play to-day.

St. Paul Globe 1905 – Carling Cup

Chapter Nineteen - 1905, International Champions

The teams agreed to a two-day match, with teams playing on back-to-back days. The first game was played on September 3 at Lexington Park and was won by the Saints. The score was 11-4, but the newspapers reported that it was a much closer contest than the score revealed. Both teams were fast, strong, and played great defense until the end when St. Paul, which was the team in better shape, pulled ahead. The next day St. Paul was again victorious, this time with a score of 9-0. St. Paul had focused on defense, not allowing the Mintos much time in the offensive zone.

St. Paul Globe photo William Carling, sponsor of the Carling Cup

Now that St. Paul had beaten two Canadian teams in two weeks, they challenged again for the Chipman Cup. Since the Shamrocks were no more, the cup had been given to the Souris of Manitoba. The commissioner approved the challenge but did not require St. Paul to travel to Souris, which is remote and further west, located just past Brandon, Manitoba. The commissioner offered Souris two spots to host the game: Winnipegs or St. Paul.

St. Paul offered a guaranteed gate fee to the Souris team to help pay for expenses. Since it was late in the season, St. Paul felt it would be a tough draw to get attendance. They also had another distraction: Dan Patch.

In a strange twist, the Souris team chose not to defend the cup. Instead, they simply packed up the Chipman Cup and shipped it to St. Paul. The Souris offered to meet in Winnipeg for a "practice game," but the cup was going to St. Paul either way. The Souris Club, it appeared, did not like the commissioner deciding that Souris could not host the game.

> **SAINTS WILL ACCEPT**
>
> **Hate to Do It, but Take the Chipman Trophy.**
>
> The St. Paul lacrosse club at a meeting last night at the Windsor hotel in St. Paul decided to accept the Chipman International lacrosse cup which was awarded by the trustees thru the default of the other teams. The acceptance was with the proviso that the St. Paul club will be willing to defend the cup next year on neutral grounds.

Minnesota Journal October 3, 1905

The St. Paul Lacrosse Club was reluctant to accept the cup, not having won it outright. The one stipulation by the league was that St. Paul could not host the game to defend the cup and must play the game at a neutral site.

There were other rumors in town that the Calumets were upset about the cup and wanted a challenge, and about the other Chicago team also wanting to challenge. But it was now football season, and Dan Patch was running for a world record in Lexington, Kentucky. Dan Patch was a race horse born in Indiana but purchased and moved to Minnesota by Marion Savage. On October 7, 1905 Dan Patch set a world record for the mile at 1:55 ¼. The whole country was captivated by this horse.

How popular was Dan Patch? Think of it this way: Ty Cobb was the highest paid baseball player at $9,000 in 1910. Dan Patch earned over $1 million in prize money and endorsements every year during his peak racing career. The town of Savage, Minnesota is named after the owner of Dan Patch, and Dan Patch Days is held there annually in June.

At the end of 1905, the St. Paul Lacrosse Club had won the Carling Cup for the Northwestern Lacrosse League by beating the best United States teams. Now, by default, it was the first time in the history of Minnesota Lacrosse that a team became an International Lacrosse Champion by possessing the Chipman Cup. This was the case even though they did not have to win a single game against the previous holders, the Souris of Canada. Their wins over the other Canadian champion-caliber teams like the Soo and the Mintos did show how powerful the club was. Remember, too, that two of three games against Canadian teams were shutouts.

> **FIGHTING ON ICE**
>
> **Lacrosse Players Will Buckle On Their Skates.**
>
> Lacrosse is the next fall sport to buckle on its skates and announce that it will stick thru the winter. Following the lead of the football players the St. Paul Lacrosse club has announced that it will play the game on the ice. They say that the game is better adapted to the rink than football as it is more open. The idea of playing the game on ice is not entirely new as it is so played in Canada and several members of the St. Paul club have played it there. No effeort will be made to secure out-of-town games but the St. Paul Chippewas and the South St. Paul Mohawks will be invited to join in the sport.

Minneapolis Journal – December 19, 1905

Since Minnesota is the *land of 10,000 lakes*, and those lakes freeze over, skating sports were popular. Just as the Dakota were depicted playing lacrosse on the ice by Seth Eastman, the St. Paul Lacrosse Club decided to play lacrosse on the ice. The article above references football being played on the ice. It also refers to a second Junior Lacrosse Club that had started, named the South St. Paul Mohawks. This shows that the sport of lacrosse was still growing among the youth in 1905.

One of the biggest losses of 1905 was the St. Paul Globe. The newspaper quit publishing on April 30, 1905. Although we have the Minneapolis Tribune and Minneapolis Journal, neither covered the St. Paul lacrosse games in any detail like the Globe did. It became much more difficult to get details, rosters, and scores of games after the Globe stop printing.

Minnesota Lacrosse: A History

Lacrosse on the Ice, on the Tank at Montreal - **McCord Museum M975.62.159**

CHAPTER 20

1906, THE END OF MIDWEST LACROSSE

The first thing people ask when they hear that Minnesota once had National and International championship lacrosse teams is, "what happened to lacrosse in Minnesota?"

What happened indeed. Like most things that happen in a society, it was a combination of many events that led to lacrosse disappearing from the landscape. Many efforts were made to save the game over the years, but these failed.

The game had become too violent, leading to the shutdown of the Northwestern Lacrosse League. Boarding schools where Native children were sent banned lacrosse and promoted baseball instead (more on boarding schools in chapter 22). World Wars took away the men who knew the game, and many never came home. Hockey, which was an evolution of lacrosse, became more popular in a state where there is more ice than grass much of the year.

To help set the stage on how close lacrosse was to becoming a major sport you need only look to the President of the United States at the time, Theodore Roosevelt. During the 1905 season, football had 18 deaths. States were calling for lacrosse to replace college football. This included the state of Minnesota.

DEAN LIGGETT HAS A REMEDY

Head of Agricultural School Favors the Strenuous Game of Lacrosse.

DEAN LIGGETT.

Minneapolis Journal March 20, 1906

    The President of the Minnesota Agricultural College, Dean Liggett, offered up one of the first solutions to the disaster that was the sport of football: play lacrosse. He predicted that football would not be a sport in the future because of player deaths, and that the public would demand a new sport to replace it. He offered that lacrosse was the natural replacement sport. Other states, mainly in the west, agreed with him. Colleges began to talk about ending their football programs.

Chapter Twenty - 1906, The End of Midwest Lacrosse

President Roosevelt saw that football was in trouble, and he was a big fan. Although he never actually played the game, he acted as only a President can: he called eastern colleges to the White House to discuss the future of football. College administrators from Harvard, Yale, and Princeton.

The President asked them to come up with an alternative to the rules to stop the rugby-like scrums, and create a safe zone or neutral zone where play could safely start for each down. The leaders, including Walter Camp from Yale, (creator of American Football), took the President's advice to heart.

Walter Camp and others sat down and developed rule modifications to resist the challenge from lacrosse to replace football. They accomplished this with just three rule changes. The first rule change was that a first down had been moved from 5 yards to 10 yards. This stopped plays from always running up the middle and creating mass brawls on the field.

The next rule change was that the President got his neutral zone, where players could not enter before the ball was snapped. And the last and probably most significant rule change was stolen from lacrosse: the forward pass. Up until 1906, a player could not pass the ball forward in football, rugby, hockey, and most other field team sports. Only lacrosse as a team sport allowed the ball to move in a forward motion by passing past the defense and creating a scoring chance. All offense in these other field sports were based on the ball being tossed backwards and allowing the defense to play very aggressively. This style of play put players in tough positions to block and move the ball without every play being a major collision.

Hockey started allowing limited forward passing in 1918, but only in the neutral zone. Then defensive zone forward passing was allowed in 1927, and finally a player could forward pass into the offensive zone in 1928, and in 1929 you could forward pass from zone to zone. That last rule change in hockey, in 1929, doubled the number of goals scored in a single NHL season.

When Dr. Beers wrote his rules of lacrosse, he did not base them on the typical European rules, but rather on how the Mohawk played the game. He wanted to stress the importance of a team game and allowed players to pass the ball forward in the first set of rules. By not basing lacrosse rules on European standards, he had created a more exciting game. Other sports, after watching lacrosse, eventually started to copy this forward pass concept and it is what saved the sport of American football.

Minnesota Lacrosse: A History

Strike one against lacrosse: in 1906, American football made the three major rule changes that defeated the challenge by college presidents in the west to end football and adopt lacrosse.

St. Paul Lacrosse Club Team 1900s
Minnesota Historical Society (GV3 14 p7)

Strike two: the game of lacrosse was taken from the Dakota and Ojibwe. In 1906 the St. Paul Lacrosse Club wanted to get the Ojibwe involved in lacrosse games and practices. They visited Mille Lacs in April but found no team willing to play them. By this time, the boarding schools were in full swing and teenage boys were gone from the area, and the kids were no longer allowed to play lacrosse at these schools. As part of "civilizing" or "assimilating" the First Nation children, they had to stop everything their cultural tradition taught them. This included language, how they dressed, skills they needed to survive a Minnesota winter, and their sports. (A future chapter will discuss more about the impact of boarding schools.)

Strike three: in 1906, the first formal efforts to start a collegiate lacrosse conference in Minnesota failed to regain interest. The schools back east, such as Harvard, Yale, Johns Hopkins, Cornell, Hobart, Swathmore, and Stevens Tech, all played in an Eastern College Conference.

Chapter Twenty – 1906, The End of Midwest Lacrosse

LA CROSSE NOT FOR CONFERENCE

Little Interest in the Game Displayed at Semi-Annual Meeting.

The semi-annual meeting of the Minnesota athletic conference was held Saturday at the Ryan hotel. The following faculty representatives were present: L. W. Chaney, Carleton; H. D. Funk, Macalester; Father Doyle, St. Thomas; P. M. Glasoe, St. Olaf; A. Z. Drew, Hamline.

The only matter of importance to come before the meeting concerned two protests filed by Hamline. The eligibility of two St. Thomas and three Macalester players was involved. The conference decided that Hamline's position was not well taken, and the protests were not allowed. The baseball pennant for the season of 1906 was formally awarded to St. Thomas.

Following is the order in which the conference teams finished the season:

	Won.	Lost.	Pct.
St. Thomas	10	0	1.000
Macalester	7	3	.700
St. Olaf	6	4	.600
Carleton	3	7	.300
Hamline	0	10	.000

The efforts of lacrosse enthusiasts to have the conference adopt this game on the basis of a conference sport received little encouragement. The recent talk that the local colleges were to adopt lacrosse is not taken seriously by any of the athletic authorities of these institutions. St. Thomas, Macalester and Hamline have no intention of even trying the experiment. Baseball and football have such a strong following at these institutions as to preclude the adoption of any new game for at least years to come. The next meeting of the conference will be held in September.

Minneapolis Journal – June 11, 1906

In the west, the colleges had not yet embraced lacrosse, having as the article says, "no intention of even trying the experiment (of lacrosse), baseball and football have such a strong following at these institutions as to preclude the adoption of any new game for years to come."

Local colleges have no interest in adding a conference schedule for lacrosse. St. Thomas, Hamline, and Macalester refused to try lacrosse as an experimental conference game.

> Carling club schedule follows:
> June 24, Calumets at St. Paul.
> July 15, St. Paul vs. Calumets at Chicago.
> Aug. 5, Chicago vs. St. Paul at Chicago.
> Aug. 19, Calumets vs. Chicago at Chicago.
> Sept. 16, Chicago vs. St. Paul at St. Paul.
> Sept. 23, Chicago vs. Calumets at Chicago.

Minneapolis Journal – June 13, 1906

Back to the Northwestern Lacrosse League in 1906, the season kicked off and published a formal schedule between the three remaining elite teams south of the Canadian border. Above is the schedule published for a series of lacrosse games played to decide the Carling Cup for the season. This series for the Carling Cup became the fourth strike against lacrosse. Violence.

At the June 24 game in St. Paul, Saints player Treherne hit a Calumet player over the head in an "honest attempt" for the ball (as defined by the local media). The official sent Treherne to the sideline with a penalty. Treherne was slow to get off the field, which gave Collins, the Calumet player who was struck, a chance to run over and hit Treherne over the head, sending him to the ground.

The fans who saw the hit were enraged and started to storm the field. The police who were present surrounded Collins to protect him from the crowd. After the situation calmed down, the game was finished and St. Paul won 5-3. But this was only a sign of things to come.

The next game was between a new Chicago team and the Calumets. The Chicago team had recruited three players from the Iroquois. Peter Hill, one of those Iroquois players, made a play and sat upon a Calumet player, Ollie Barret. Hill then made a scalping motion on the top of Barret's head, sending the crowd into a frenzy.

Chapter Twenty - 1906, The End of Midwest Lacrosse

The Calumet goalie then attacked the official, Danny White of the St. Paul Lacrosse Club, and chaos ensued. The green jerseys of Chicago and red jerseys of the Calumets starting fighting and a "battle royal" began. They did manage to control the situation and finish the game, but it was clear the gloves were off this year.

At the next Chicago and Calumet game, the league recruited St. Paul member Big Ed Murphy to officiate the game. At 235 pounds, he was called the *"Husky Minnesotan."* Before the game, he announced that it would be a clean game even if he had to whip every player himself to achieve it. The game was clean and the Calumets won.

The next game did not go so well. The season had ended in a tie with Chicago, the Calumets, and St. Paul having won two games each. Playoff games were scheduled. Since St. Paul was the previous champion, it was decided that Chicago and the Calumets would play first, and the winner then would play St. Paul for the Carling Cup and Northwestern Championship.

On September 24, 1906 Chicago and the Calumets squared off at the West Side Ball Park. This time the officials could not control the game. Several fights broke out, including near the grandstands. By the time the third quarter came around the players were less interested in the game and more interested in fighting. With ten minutes left, the police had to take over the game as players and fans collided on the field. The game was called and the league had to decide what to do.

LACROSSE GAME ENDS IN A ROW.

Calumets Have Ten Goals to Chicago's Four When Contest Is Stopped.

Chicago Tribune – September 24, 1906

On September 30, 1906 the Northwestern Lacrosse League suspended the playoffs and ended the season. Since St. Paul had won the Carling Cup the previous year, they were allowed to keep it and the championship. The Northwestern Lacrosse League never fully recovered from this event and the league was disbanded.

After this happened in Illinois, colleges like Northwestern—that had actually stopped playing football and were considering lacrosse—found a way to return football to the schools. Lacrosse's chance to take the place of football was finished on a major scale because lacrosse players could do no better than their comrades in football. The sport was not safe to continue.

1906 brought the official end of midwest lacrosse. After this year, many tried to revive the sport and there was some success, but no midwest league ever again formed that included the teams from the midwest United States.

Chapter Twenty - 1906, The End of Midwest Lacrosse

Minneapolis Journal, 1906 showing the waning interest in lacrosse

Minnesota Lacrosse: A History

Winnipeg Lacrosse Club in 1907
Archives of Manitoba, O'Dowda Collection #177

Although the Northwestern Lacrosse League ended in 1906, Duluth, St. Paul, and other cities continued to play the Canadians with informal games. No more games were played against Chicago or any other American teams outside the state.

Chapter Twenty - 1906, The End of Midwest Lacrosse

Souris Lacrosse Club of 1905
Archives of Manitoba, O'Dowda Collection #182

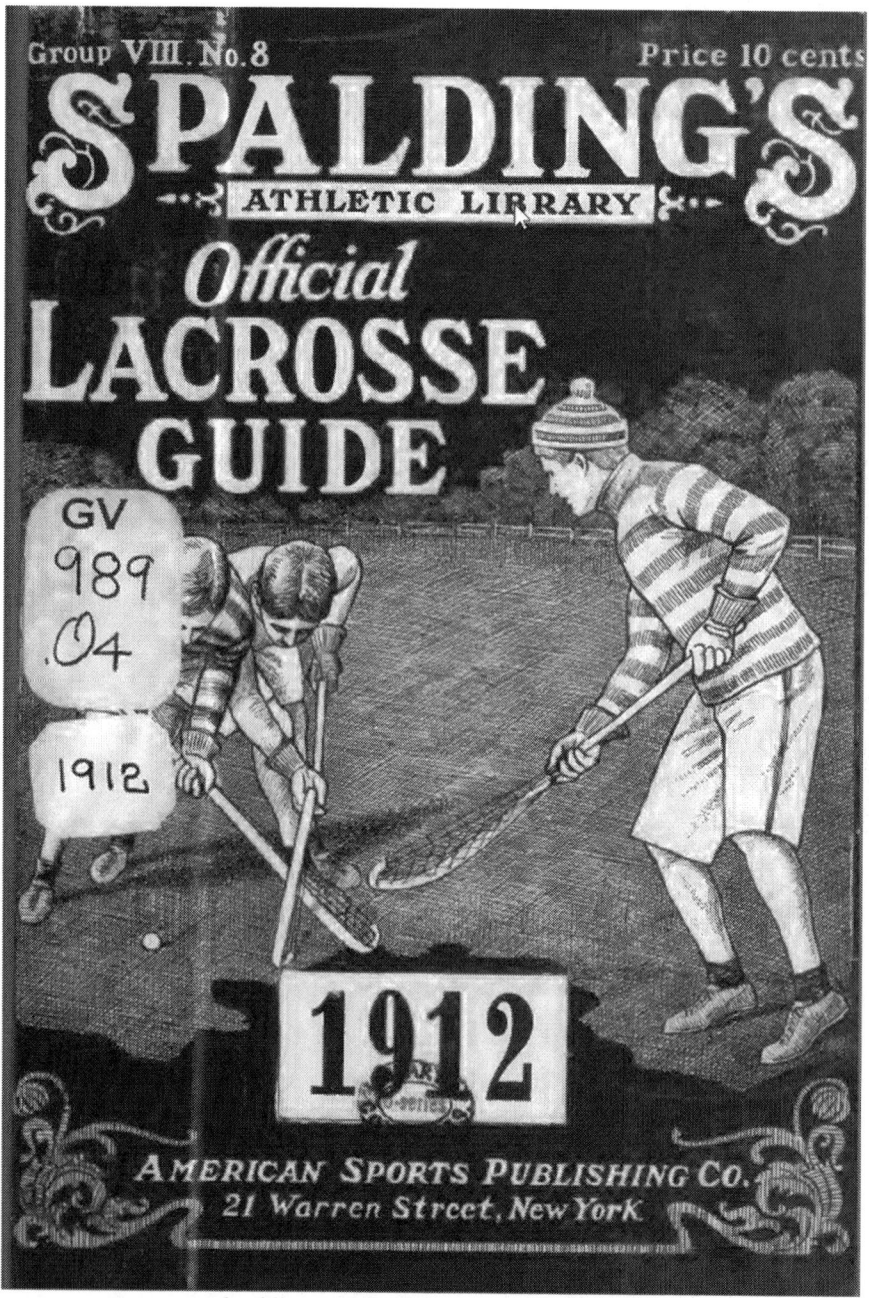

Spalding's Official Lacrosse Guide 1912

CHAPTER 21

GOPHER LACROSSE

As the efforts to grow lacrosse continued after 1906, the President of the St. Paul Lacrosse Club, W.D. Stewart, approached the University of Minnesota to start a lacrosse program. Since no college conference had been developed in the midwest, Stewart thought the best approach to grow lacrosse would be to create a team, and other colleges would join them. Stewart also reached out to local high schools to develop and start programs. Specifically he reached out to Minneapolis North and Minneapolis West high schools.

Stewart knew to attract interest he needed to find a coach that the players could relate to and understood college lacrosse. Early in 1911, Steward connected with Coach John Trott, who moved to the Twin Cities to become the first collegiate coach of lacrosse in Minnesota history.

At Columbia University from 1905 to 1909, John Trott was a highly regarded player and served as team captain during his senior year. He graduated from Columbia in 1909 and found an opportunity to teach and coach at the University Minnesota in 1910, becoming an instructor in the Architectural Department. (80)

When Coach Trott arrived, Mr. Stewart discussed how to go about recruiting players to join the Gopher lacrosse program. The program began in early 1911.

Coach John Trott

The first article describing the coach was found in the Minneapolis Tribune March 17, 1911.

Start Lacrosse Practice
University of Minnesota Athletics commence work at new game

The article discusses the start of the lacrosse program with Coach Trott and games to be scheduled with Northwestern University. Northwestern had replaced football with lacrosse in 1906, and they had already started a lacrosse team. Practices were announced as daily events or on every "fair-weather day," with inclement days being "chalk talk" with the coach. The assistant coach was listed as Malcolm Grant, a former player with the Toronto Lacrosse Team that had won the amateur lacrosse championship in Canada.

The first twelve players to commit to play collegiate lacrosse in the state of Minnesota were:

```
Ted Anderson
Harold Hull
John Lewis
C.W. Smith
P.W. Forsberg
Harold Swanson
Ivan O. Hanson
W.S. Schouler
T.H. Granfield
H.E. Karnofsky
Arthur Winter
S.P. Albee
```

Chapter Twenty One - Gopher Lacrosse

Stewart worked with Coach Trott, and practices were held with the Gopher lacrosse team and St. Paul Lacrosse Club. Little is mentioned about practices or development of the team, other than that Gopher players were taking to the game.

To this point, game schedules or scores from the Northwestern or other college games in 1911 cannot be found.

Sadly, after the season ended there is a tragic story. On June 12, 1911 Coach Trott was in a canoe on Lake Minnetonka with a coed named Miss Eva Kaye.

The story of lacrosse and the first coach for the Gophers ends quickly with this tragedy. The following story was reported by the Tribune:

University Instructor Drowns in Saving Girl

Minneapolis Tribune – June 13, 1911

"Mr. Trott, who was a graduate of Columbia University, New York, class of 1909, and who was an instructor in the architectural department of the university college of engineering, was also the coach of the university lacrosse team, having been captain of the Columbian team in 1909. Miss Kaye is a sophomore student in the academic course at the university and lives with her parents at 2413 Hennepin Avenue.

"Miss Kaye was attending a picnic of her sorority yesterday afternoon on Big Island. Mr. Trott, who was attending a house party at the lake offered to take the girls across the lake in his canoe, as she wished to telephone to some friends. The couple started, Miss Kaye seated in the bow of the canoe and Mr. Trott paddling at the stern.

Just as the canoe pushed out beyond the lee of Gale's Island and into the open lake it capsized in the waves. Both occupants in the boat caught the sides of the canoe when they came to the surface. They were clinging to the sides when Mr. Trott realizing that the girl's strength was fast giving out, started to swim for the shore at Tonka Bay. Striking out with strong strokes, the athlete swam away, telling the girl that he would be back soon with help.

"He had not gone far before he was overcome by the weight of his garments and sank beneath the water. A launch which passed soon afterward rescued Miss Kaye in a fainting condition, clinging to the overturned canoe."

Just like that, the Gopher Lacrosse program—less than one year old—ended in tragedy with the loss of its first coach. The newspapers noted that even though he had been in town less than one year, the funeral was well attended and that the loss hit home with a lot of students and faculty.

Coach Trott was not buried in Minnesota, but was returned to his parents in Brooklyn, New York.

Born John Clinton Trott in Brooklyn, New York – boyhood picture

As the 1911 fall semester started, Stewart and Murphy of the St. Paul Lacrosse Club were still not willing to let the sport die. They convinced the track coach, Dick Grant, to call a meeting and ask for support from the players. They responded and Dick Grant filed for the position as head lacrosse coach.

The newspapers discussed Coach Grant's experience in lacrosse, but no details were revealed. Mike Murphy of the South St. Paul Mohawk Junior Lacrosse Club stepped in to teach the game at daily practices. Murphy also recruited his junior lacrosse team to attend practices with him to train the players.

Chapter Twenty One – Gopher Lacrosse

Their biggest recruit was Jim Walker from the Gopher football team. He was an All-American football player who took to the game of lacrosse and loved it. They made Walker the captain and he recruited many football players to come out for the lacrosse team.

Death Certificate from Hennepin County – June 1911
Courtesy of the Minnesota Historical Society

The 1911-1912 Yearbook posted the following roster for the Gopher lacrosse squad:
```
Jim Walker - Captain
C.J. Smith
Bert Hull
Tom Crocker
J.E. Power
C.L. Richards
Ted Anderson
Sidney Stadsvold
John Shine
M.O. Nelson
R.A. Johnson
Clark Shaughnessy
```

237

Minnesota Lacrosse: A History

No more records appear for the Gopher lacrosse team after this report in the fall. Assuming the team was formed and the yearbook recorded the team in the spring yearbook, it can be assumed they were still playing in 1912. But no reports of games or scores were reported. However, after this season the yearbook and annual reports make no record of the Gophers having a lacrosse team.

So, the first experiment of lacrosse at the college level ended after only two seasons and the tragic loss of a coach from the east coast, Coach Trott.

1897 University of Minnesota Yearbook

Since the Gophers had the first collegiate lacrosse team in Minnesota, a simple explanation of how the Gopher name came to be is in order.

Gopher Timeline: [81]

1858 – Political Cartoon
In 1857 the legislature passed a railroad "loan bill" for five million dollars. Many of the legislators who backed the bill just happened to have interests in those same railroads benefiting from the loan bill. The loans were never paid back and the state of Minnesota was saddled with bad bonds for the next twenty years.

238

Chapter Twenty One - Gopher Lacrosse

In 1858, a satire cartoon was published by R.O. Sweeny (next page). The cartoon shows "gophers" pulling the gopher train. Although at the time many felt Minnesota should be called the "Beaver State," others felt the destructive nature of beavers should not be glorified. After this cartoon appeared, Minnesota began to be called the "Gopher State" both at home and nationally.

1888 – First UMN yearbook was published as "The Gopher"

At first many did not want to nickname the state after a cartoon depicting the politics of the railroads and the lost loan money. However, over time Minnesota came to accept its fate as the Gopher State. The naming of the First University of Minnesota Yearbook started this acceptance.

1897 – First image of the Gopher appears on the cover of the yearbook

The gopher drawing depicted on the previous page was the first image of the gopher published in connection with the University of Minnesota and it appeared on the cover the yearbook.

1926 – First time UMN football coach Clarence Spears refers to his team as the Gophers.

As other college sports teams had adopted mascots, the University of Minnesota started using the name Gophers for its sports teams, with football being the first.

Go Gophers!

Minnesota Lacrosse: A History

BROADSIDE RIDICULING THE FIVE MILLION LOAN OF 1857
This cartoon by R. O. Sweeny was widely circulated and gave Minnesota its nickname, the Gopher State

CHAPTER 22

THE BOARDING SCHOOL EXPERIMENT

This chapter could just as easily be called The Boarding School Tragedy. Boarding schools were developed as a "well-meaning" premise to avoid extermination of the First Nation people, and to instead "civilize" them.

So why did they start? The people of the United States had become weary of the military violently removing First Nation people from the land. In reaction to this sentiment, politicians started to propose a new approach to dealing with the original people, and that was assimilation.

The experiment started in 1879 with the founding, by Richard Pratt, of the Carlisle Indian Industrial School in Pennsylvania.

The goal was to, within a few generations, make the "American Indian" cease to exist. Taking the model made famous by the 19th century missionaries, the idea was to remove the children from their families, and to teach them to have a structured life—through restricted and labored activities—that reflected an agricultural society. These advocates saw themselves as "Friends of the Indian," saving them from certain destruction. The infamous tag line was *we can make the Indian "civilized."*

American society was so impressed with the *concept* of Carlisle that soon schools popped up around the country. States with the largest First Nation populations like Minnesota, Wisconsin, Oklahoma, and the Dakotas built many of these schools. By the late 1800s, Minnesota had over a dozen boarding schools. What did not come out from the Carlisle school reviews were the beatings, sexual abuse, and overall impact of trying to assimilate these Nations. (82)

First Nation children were now being asked to "forget" their past, reject their language, culture, and other items that made them non-American. The boarding schools began with a religious influence, using priests and nuns as teachers. Later on, as the system became "Federalized," the religious aspects were drowned out.

Giving up their culture included all First Nation games like double ball, snow snake, the moccasin game, and of course lacrosse. Instead, their cultural games were replaced with American football and especially American baseball.

Richard Pratt, founder of the Carlisle Indian Industrial School, made the following statement regarding sports at the boarding schools:

```
"If it was in my power to bring every Indian into the
game of football, ... I would do it, and feel that I was
doing them an act of the greatest Christian kindness,
and elevating them from the hell of their home life and
reservation degradation into paradise."
```
Letter to Bishop McCabe 1897

This statement clearly articulates the view of the boarding school founder, and shows how little he understood of the First Nation involvement in sports. When Dr. Beers wrote his book on lacrosse, he noted how much better the First Nation players were at sports, their superiority in conditioning, and their strength. He admired their training programs, their skill development, and their ability to play for hours without getting injured.

Admiration for native athletic ability had been replaced by the thought that First Nation sports like lacrosse could not be allowed to endure because it was "uncivilized."

Stories from interviewed families vary. There are stories of families being torn apart when authorities physically removed children from their homes. There was often violence, and parents were sent to prison for resisting the

Chapter Twenty Two - Boarding School Experiment

process. Students were beaten for speaking their native tongue, or for not being obedient to teachers. There were even sexual assaults by staff.

On the other hand, some families handed over their children in the hopes that they could escape the poor and desperate conditions on the reservation. These parents hoped that their children would have a better life off the reservation. Some parents felt they had no other option for the survival of their children. In addition, the children were often sent to schools far away from home to discourage runaways.

Even with the loss of lacrosse and other First Nation games, kids were kids and embraced competition in many American sports. Baseball proved to be successful in many boarding schools including Pipestone, Collegeville, and Morris in Minnesota. These schools encouraged assimilation through sport.

To encourage players to participate, some schools gave privileges to ball players. These privileges included the ability to leave school grounds to play games in other cities, or the ability to participate at "unsupervised" practices so they could speak their own language and name their own teams.

At the St. Johns Boarding School in Collegeville, the priests were the most generous in this area and allowed ball players to speak the Ojibwe language. This team was even allowed to name their baseball team, "NinSongideeminanig," or "Brave Men," often shortened to just Braves. [83]

These privileges led players to embrace baseball in order to escape boarding school life and compete against other schools—including whites. Headlines from the Pipestone County Star included the following:

```
Scalped the White Boys   (April 29, 1898)
Indians to Play Indians (April 21 1905)
Indians Great Record - Win 27 of 35 games (July 13, 1906)
Play "Heap Good" Ball (July 26, 1907)
```

These headlines were obviously written to sell newspapers, but they also talk to the popularity of baseball at the boarding schools. Even though they could not play their traditional sports, they were still great athletes.

Despite the great successes of the boarding school baseball programs, player rosters were very limited in area newspapers, and accounts of games very difficult to find. Pride in the boarding school players was not celebrated as it was in the white settler communities of Minnesota.

The achievements of these baseball players was not overlooked by the professional teams. Though much has been made of the color barrier being broken by Jackie Robinson in 1947, Ojibwe players had joined white professional teams over 30 years earlier.

The Baseball Hall of Fame inducted the Ojibwe star Charles Albert Bender or "Chief" Bender in 1953. Bender was born on the White Earth Reservation and attended Carlisle. Charles Bender has been credited as the inventor of the "slider" pitch, and was the First Minnesotan inducted into the Baseball Hall of Fame.

Back at Carlisle in Pennsylvania, Glenn "Pop" Warner, the father of junior football in the United States, decided to keep his football players in better shape by introducing the sport of lacrosse. Warner won his arguments and in 1910 the Carlisle school switched their spring sport to lacrosse and stopped playing baseball.

Just as each individual is different, so was the experience of the First Nation people at the boarding schools in Minnesota. Some students talked about leaving their parents for a chance at learning, while others spoke of being dragged out by police who hunted them down and forced them to leave their homes. Others talked about how sports gave them the freedom and the chance to survive, giving them hope and the opportunity to speak their language with teammates.

Many of the traditions, stories, and culture around the medicine game of lacrosse in Minnesota were set aside. Symbols remain around the area, such as "Ball Club Lake" near the Leech Lake Reservation.

Thomas Vennum and authors like George Catlin and Stephen Culin offer great insight into the traditions and culture of lacrosse as it was found at the time of their writings. Vennum noted that the historical game of lacrosse "almost disappeared," being replaced by baseball as the summer game of choice.

Boarding schools impacted the Ojibwe and Dakota communities very hard by forcing the loss of language, tradition, culture, and sport. The culture and sport of lacrosse and its traditions are being reintroduced to native youth.

SUGGESTED FURTHER READING

- *American Indian Sports Heritage*, Joseph B Oxendine
- *Thesis: Indian Summers: Baseball at Native American Boarding Schools in Minnesota*, David J. Laliberte
- *To Show What an Indian Can Do – Sports at Native American Boarding Schools*, John Bloom
- *The Native American Identity in Sports*, Frank A. Salamone

CHAPTER 23

OLYMPIC LACROSSE MEMORIES

Lacrosse was featured as an "official sport" in only the 1904 and 1908 Olympic games. Since very few countries had formal teams, and only Canada, Great Britain, and the United States had participated in lacrosse at the Olympics, the International Olympic Committee (IOC) removed lacrosse from the official games after 1908.

1908 Olympics

The 1908 games returned to Europe, and were played in London. Since the midwest lacrosse league had failed, St. Paul and other midwest teams had no interest in trying to attend the Olympic games in London. In fact, no eastern teams seemed to have an appetite to play lacrosse at the Olympics either. Thus, the United States was not represented in lacrosse during the 1908 games.

Only two teams competed in the 1908 games: the host country, Great Britain, and Canada. A team from South Africa was scheduled to attend the games but withdrew shortly before the event.

One lone game of lacrosse was played, on October 24, 1908 at White City Stadium in London. Here is the newspaper summary:

```
"At the end of the first quarter Canada led 5-1
and then 6-2 at half-time after which some
```

brilliant play by England tied the game at 9-9, before Canada rallied to win an excellent game, 14-10.

Excellent sportsmanship was demonstrated during the match. When Canada's Angus Dillon broke his stick and was having difficulty finding a replacement, England's R. G. Martin agreed to stay out until Dillon returned. At the end of the game, the players exchanged sticks, shook hands and congratulated each other on a well-played match."

Team Canada 1908

1908 Olympic Lacrosse Rosters

Team Canada (Gold Medal)	Team Great Britain (Silver Medal)
Paddy Brennan	Gustav Alexander
Jack Broderick	George Buckland
George Campbell	Eric Dutton
Gus Dillon	S. N. Hayes
Frank Dixon	Wilfrid Johnson
Richard Duckett	Edward Jones
Tom Gorman	Reginald Martin
Ernie Hamilton	Gerald Mason
Henny Hoobin	Johnson Parker-Smith
Clary McKerrow	Hubert Ramsey
George Rennie	Charles Scott
Sandy Turnbull	Norman Whitley

Chapter Twenty Three - Olympic Lacrosse Memories

Great Britain goalie makes a save on a Canadian Shot 1908 Olympics

Lacrosse had struggled with statistics even in the Olympics. Below is a compilation from various sources on the scoring of this game. In the stats there is a "?" for goals that were not awarded to a player, but just the team. At one point the game was tied 9-9 in the fourth quarter before Canada went on a 5-1 run to finish the game 14-10.

1908 Lacrosse Game Scoring:
FIRST QUARTER (4-1):
Canada: Gorman, Broderick, Turnbull (2);
England: Buckland
SECOND QUARTER: (6-2)
Canada: Brennan, ?;
England: Buckland
THIRD QUARTER (9-7):
Canada: Turnbull (2), Brennan;
England: Jones (2), Buckland (3)
FOURTH QUARTER (14-10):
Canada: Brennan (3), Gorman (2);
England: Jones, ?, ?

This weak appearance is probably what led to lacrosse not being represented in the Olympics.

Minnesota Lacrosse: A History

1928 Olympics

Lacrosse returned to the Olympic games—held in Amsterdam—as a demonstration sport in 1928. This time there were three countries representing the sport: Canada, Great Britain, and the United States.

Hosting countries of the Olympics are given permission to select the demonstration sports, in order to promote local activities at the world level. Since Holland had few sports to promote, they allowed participating countries to suggest demonstration sports.

Here is the write up from the Olympic Committee Report in 1928:

"After much correspondence and consideration the choice fell on 'Lacrosse', proposed by the Canadian Olympic Committee on behalf of the Amateur Athletic Union of Canada, and unknown in Holland. The Union saw a possibility of interesting teams in other countries and correspondence was opened with the English Lacrosse Union and the American Olympic Association, with the result that demonstrations were given by teams from the three countries named, on August 5th, 6th and 7th."

Canada successfully lobbied to get lacrosse back into the Olympics, and convinced Great Britain and United States to participate.

Lacrosse in the 1928 Olympics
LOUIS S. NIXDORFF 1928 OLYMPIC GAMES COLLECTION
1926-1978 #443 – Smithsonian Institution

Chapter Twenty Three – Olympic Lacrosse Memories

Here is the Official Lacrosse Program. It was handed out at the games so that fans could understand the game of lacrosse:

DEMONSTRATION OF LACROSSE.
Is Lacrosse the national game of Canada? Strictly speaking it is an old Indian game; the Indians played it in their leisure hours and differences between tribes were often decided by the game of Lacrosse.

The game is played by two teams of twelve players styled as follows:
Goalkeeper, point, coverpoint 1st, 2nd and 3rd defence, centre, 1st, 2nd and 3rd outside and inside home.

The players from the goalkeeper to the 3rd defence inclusive, are to try to prevent the other side from scoring.

"Centre" is the hub and must not only assist the defence, but also feed the "Home".

There are further 4 reserves including a reserve goalkeeper. Three of the reserves may take the places of other players at any time provided the game is interrupted, but the goalkeeper may only be replaced when he is forced to leave the field owing to an accident.

The playing time is 80 minutes divided into 4 periods of 20 minutes, with 10 minutes' rest at halftime and 5 minutes' rest between periods 1–2 and 3–4. Ends are changed after each period.

The team scoring the highest number of goals, wins. In the event of a draw 10 minutes extra time will be played with a change of ends after 5 minutes. Should neither team win after playing half an hour extra, the match will be declared a draw.

The Lacrosse pitch measures 125 yards by 55 yards, with goals placed 110 yards apart; the space behind the goals is intended for fielding the ball in case of an attack on goal.

There are a couple of items to point out. The field is referred to as the "pitch," similar to cricket and soccer. The game time is made up of 20 minute quarters. Overtime is 10 minutes, switching ends after 5 minutes.

The games were played as scheduled with the following results:

```
August 5, 1928 United States 6 - Canada 3
August 6, 1928 Great Britain 7 - United States 6
August 7, 1928 Canada 9 - Great Britain 5
```

Each team had won one game and lost one game. Also, each team scored 12 goals—so even a tie breaker of goals could not decide a winner. This was the first time that the United States defeated Canada in lacrosse during the Olympics.

The United States wanted a winner, and offered the option of a 3-game playoff series to settle the order of medals. Canada agreed to a playoff series to decide a winner, but Great Britain refused to play on.

The Olympic Committee was forced to make a decision, and they declared the games a tie and awarded everyone gold medals.

1928 Olympic Rosters

Canada	United States	Great Britain
J. Stoddart	W. F. Logan	P. L. V. Astle
L. Gregory	T. N. Biddison	L. Clayton
C. Grauer	G. Helfrich	A. B. Craig
R. A. Mackie	J. K. Eagan	H. H. Crofts
A. Farrow	L. S. Nixdorff	S. M. Fleeson
W. Fraser	J. D. Lang	G. F. Higson
A. Brown	J. W. Boynton	F. E. Johnson
J. Vernon	R. H. Roy	H. G. Johnson
N. Atkinson	W. A. Kegan	O. J. Knudsen
J. Wood	C. G. Mallonee	E. Parsons
C. Doyle	C. Leibensperger	F. C. G. Perceval
A. W. Wilkie	R. M. Finn	A. J. Phillips

Chapter Twenty Three – Olympic Lacrosse Memories

1932 Olympics

The next games were back in Los Angeles. The lacrosse community, which was largely based on the east coast, was excited to bring the game to a wider audience and to hopefully grow the game. The Los Angeles Olympics, they thought, would be a great format for this exposure.

The lacrosse demonstration sport included only two teams: the host country and Canada. They agreed to a best-of-three-games match played over several days.

The United States, knowing the Canadian team was very talented, took a different approach this time and selected a college team to represent the USA. The thought was that a team that had been playing together all season would improve their chances to beat the more talented Canadian team. This model was copied in 1980 by coach Herb Brooks when the U.S. hockey team used college players to defeat the Soviet Union.

Johns Hopkins University was selected to represent the United States in lacrosse at the 1932 games. Both the US and Canadian lacrosse teams were allowed to stay in the Olympic village, even though they represented a demonstration sport.

United States vs Canada in the Los Angeles Memorial Coliseum, 1932

The first game on August 7, 1932 was made famous by the picture above, showing the United States playing Canada in the Los Angeles Memorial Coliseum in front of 75,000 fans.

Of course the caveat of this photo is that the audience was really there to watch the end of the marathon race that was going on outside the Coliseum.

Even as of the printing of this book in 2015, this event is recorded as the largest audience to ever watch a lacrosse game in person.

The Coliseum audience was treated to a great game of lacrosse that showed the teamwork of the United States outmaneuver the individual talent of the Canadians. The United States won a close contest with a score of 5-3.

On August 9, 1932 the Canadian team rebounded, playing a very aggressive style. With seconds remaining in the game, the score was 4-4. Canada managed to score a last-second goal, giving them the win in the second game. The series was now tied 1-1, and the winner of the last game would be the champion.

On August 12, 1932 the two teams met for the final game. Again the United States went back to their teamwork model, earning a 7-4 victory, and the series win over Canada.

1932 Complete Rosters

United States	Canada
Francis Henry Beeler	Henry Baker
Walter Francis Kneip, Jr.	J. Stuart Gifford
Douglas Hoffman Stone	Anthony Pelletier
Joseph Cavendish Darrell	Joseph W. Bergin
Millard Tuttle Lang	William Harrison
Fritz Rudolph Stude	Matthew F. Rohmer
Lorne Randolph Guild	Richard Buckingham
Marshall Duer McDorman	F. A. Hawkins
William Harrison Triplett	A. Norman Russell
James Wilcox Ives	Kenneth E. Calbeck
James Merriken	Rowland W. Mercer
John Iglehart Turnbull	Bryce Spring
Caleb Redgrave Kelly	W. Fraser
George Frederick Packard	Bernard McEvoy
Church Yearley	H. D. Wallace
Donaldson Naylor Kelly	J. Frasir
Peter William Reynolds	John G. McQuarrie
William Frederick Weitzel	J. A. Worthy
	Norman A. Gair
	Yvan Paquin

Chapter Twenty Three – Olympic Lacrosse Memories

1948 Olympics

Because of World War II, the Olympics were on hold for twelve years. They resumed in 1948, and were held in London, England. This was the first Olympics held since the famed 1936 games hosted in Berlin by Hitler.

It was only three years after the end of the war, and England was still rationing food and rebuilding. Germany and Japan were not allowed to send athletes, and the Soviet Union was invited but declined to send any participants.

England was hosting the Olympics and again selected lacrosse as their demonstration event. The British still considered the game of lacrosse a beloved sport to be shared with the world.

This time, only the United States and Great Britain played in the games. Again the United States went with a college team to represent the USA. Rensselaer Polytechnic Institute (RPI) from Troy, New York was selected. RPI was coached by the legendary Ned Harkness, who coached RPI to National Championships in both lacrosse and hockey.

In the 1948 lacrosse season, RPI had gone 13-0 and was the obvious choice to represent the United States.

A series of games were set up to promote lacrosse around Great Britain. A final game, with an All-England team, played the USA at Wembley Stadium. The tour included games at Oxford and Cambridge. The United States team went 8-0 during the exhibition games and entered Wembley Stadium to face the all-England all-star lacrosse team.

LACROSSE
PROGRAMME

THE
ENGLISH UNIVERSITIES
v.
THE AMERICANS
(R.P.I.)

THURSDAY, 29th JULY, 1948 at 6.30 P.M.
on the
UNIVERSITY RUGBY GROUND, CAMBRIDGE

Price 3d.

From the Official Record of 1948:

```
LACROSSE
The organisation of the Lacrosse Demonstration
was carried out by the English Lacrosse Union and
this body invited a team from the United States
of America to play a match at the Empire Stadium
against an All-England Lacrosse side. The
visiting team was the Rensselaer Polytechnic of
Troy, New York State. The U.S.A. team had carried
out a tour in Great Britain, and concluded this
with the fitting finale of the match at Wembley.

The modern game of lacrosse is believed to have
originated from a tribal game known as "ball
game" of the North American Indians and was
brought to England by the settlers in Canada in
the 18th or 19th Century. It is played not only
```

Chapter Twenty Three - Olympic Lacrosse Memories

in Great Britain, but also in Australia and Canada and, most prominently of all, in the United States of America. The teams at Wembley proved to be excellently matched, and the resulting game was both close and exciting, in addition to being one of the best exhibitions of lacrosse ever seen in England.

During the first quarter (the game consists of four 20-minute periods), Whittaker opened the scoring for the English side, but the Americans soon asserted themselves and went away to a 4-1 lead with goals by Coleman, Myers (2) and Wood. Before the end of the period, however, Little had reduced the margin.

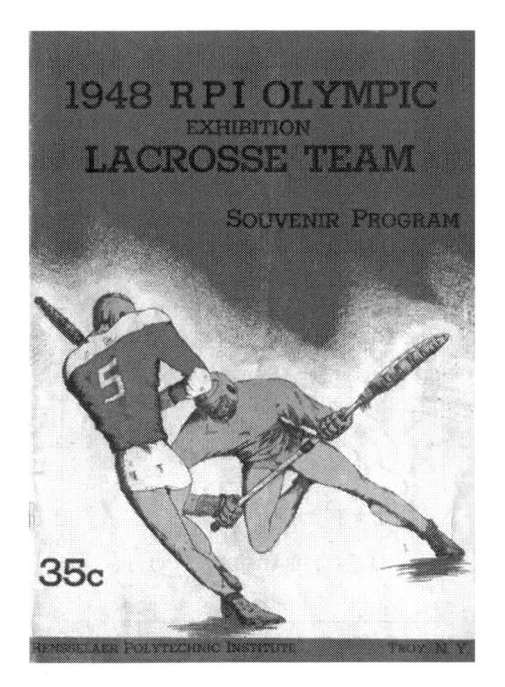

An Exciting Finish

There was no such goal-scoring rush in the second and third periods, a single goal by Wilson, which reduced the margin to one goal, in the second period, being the only score. The English team, however, turned on full pressure at the start of the final twenty minutes and first Whittaker equalised with a brilliant goal, and then Dennis put them ahead. It seemed likely that they would hold their lead, for the defence was now closely knit, but, in a most exciting finish, Myers put the Americans on level terms with only three minutes left for play.

Even though lacrosse was a demonstration sport, the players for the United States were all awarded gold medals for their amazing record of 8-0-1 in the Olympics.

1948 Lacrosse Olympic Rosters

United States	Position	All-England
R. Cambell	Goal	H. Wyatt
S.W. Spaulding	Point	J.P. Foy
R.E. Koch	Cover Point	J. Fletcher
R.M. Wood	3rd Defence	J.I. Whitehead
A.D. Beard	Left Defence	B.C. Makin
C.J. McCann	Right Defence	A.L. Dennis
M.T. Davies	Centre	H. Prime
R. Coons	Left Attack	R.N. Whittaker
J.A. Meyers	Right Attack	J. Buckland
W.L. Coleman	3rd Home	R.T. Renshaw
R.E. Powell	2nd Home	J.H. Little
D.E. Jordan	1st Home	R.V. Wilson
D.R Sutton	Substitute	J. Swindells
R.J. Sneedon	Substitute	N.R. Coe
R.F. Ball	Substitute	H.J. Ginn
R. Frick	Substitute	J. Griffiths
R. Hutcheon	Substitute	R.F. Zimmern
O. Cook	Substitute	

Goal Umpires
D. Pollack, A.J. Beinschroth, F.D. Ewen

Referee - A. Howarth

Lacrosse has not been featured in the Olympic games since 1948. There have been many reasons for this loss—waning interest, small number of countries playing the sport, and other new sports coming into the Olympics.

As of the printing of this book, there are many efforts to grow the game in countries around the world and develop an international body that can bring the event back to the Olympic games.

Because of the origins of the game of lacrosse, the Iroquois, Ojibwe, Dakota, and other nations should be represented as their own nations when it does return.

Imagine—the original medicine game could be on the world stage to help "heal" the world.

How exciting would an Iroquois versus Ojibwe or Dakota gold medal game be in the Olympics? Here's to daring to dream for that game.

CHAPTER 24

WOMEN'S LACROSSE

One of the questions most frequently asked is, "why is girls' lacrosse so different from boys' lacrosse?" Anyone who has watched both versions of the game can come away with the feeling that "these are two totally different sports. Why are they both called lacrosse?"

In the 1990s, Minnesota girls' lacrosse was quite different from other sports. The girls' lacrosse game had a *no boundary rule* and high school teams often played at local parks to allow more field on which to play.

It was not uncommon for a ball to roll down a hill, and instead of a whistle to stop play the girls charged down the hill and kept playing. Sometimes they weren't even visible for several minutes while they and the officials were out of sight. There were only two equipment rules for players: a mouth guard and a stick.

At this same time, boys' lacrosse was played with very different rules. Required equipment included a helmet, shoulder pads, gloves, stick, arm pads, and mouth guard. And while the Minnesota boys also tended to play at parks (football coaches were reluctant to hand over their fields to a game that tended to create "crop circles" on their grass), the boys' lacrosse game had painted lines on the field to show the fixed size that kept the players in a confined space.

Back in the 1990s, Minnesota boys mainly played with their hockey equipment. US Lacrosse was formed in 1998, and equipment rules requiring different helmets or other specifications had not yet reached the hockey-based culture.

One wonders how both games could be called lacrosse. The girls had minimal equipment, no lines and no boundaries. The boys played on a fixed-size field with full equipment and body contact similar to hockey. Which is closer to the original game as developed by the First Nations? That would be girls' lacrosse, with little equipment and no field restrictions.

How did this happen? How did girls' lacrosse not evolve by adding more and more rules, equipment, and contact similar to the boys' game? To answer these questions, we need to review the origins of the girls' game, and how it evolved on another continent and not Turtle Island (North America).

After George Beers wrote his book on the sport of lacrosse in 1869, he became a great promoter of the game. He took teams all over the world where the British Empire had been established. England, Australia, Scotland, Ireland, and others were visited, and he helped form local lacrosse programs. Beers' passion for lacrosse seemed endless as he spent his life sharing the game around the world teaching others to fall in love with his version of the Mohawk game.

As discussed in the First Rules Chapter, Dr. Beers toured England in 1876 where his teams played before Queen Victoria. The Queen was taken with the game and wrote about it in her journal. She detailed much about the visiting First Nation team Dr. Beers had brought with him, and their unique dress. She wrote in her diary that the game was "pretty to watch" and that there was "much running" involved in the game. Her approving words about lacrosse helped develop interest in girls' lacrosse in Europe.

These promotional games helped spread the word about lacrosse and also helped grow the sport. In 1883, a Canadian team, along with several Iroquois, played games of lacrosse in Scotland. This lacrosse tour included the cities of Dundee, Edinburgh, and Glasgow. The Edinburgh lacrosse game was set on the Queen's birthday celebration, which drew over three thousand spectators.

In the next year, 1884, Miss Lumsden and Miss Frances Dove of St. Leonards School for Girls traveled to Canada to attend the British Association Conference for the Advancement of Science. [84] The conference was held in Montreal, Canada. While in Montreal the ladies went to see a game of lacrosse between a local Montreal lacrosse club and the Canghuwaya national team.

Miss Lumsden, who was the first headmistress of St. Leonards School for Girls, wrote in a letter home that it was a "wonderful game, beautiful, and graceful."

Chapter Twenty Four - Women's Lacrosse

St. Leonards School for Girls is located in St. Andrews, Scotland and was one of the first schools to introduce lacrosse as a girls' sport. It's "one of the first schools" because St. Leonards was lucky enough to have their school records and archives remain intact through the two World Wars in Europe. It seems reasonable to assume that other girls' schools in Great Britain, where Dr. Beers held lacrosse games, would have developed lacrosse programs. Sadly many of those schools were lost during the European wars and few school records survived.

Regardless, St. Leonards played a key role in developing girls' lacrosse, and their graduating players were instrumental in spreading the game regionally and internationally. It is those players, like Rosabelle Sinclair, who introduced the sport back to North America and developed girls' lacrosse programs.

In 1890, St. Leonards formally introduced lacrosse as a new spring sport to be played by the girls' houses. The previous spring sport was called "goals," a precursor to girls' field hockey. Field hockey became very popular with prep schools as a spring sport. As lacrosse was introduced many people felt the posture of girls playing a sport upright versus bent over—as in field hockey—would be more lady-like.

At the St. Leonards School, dorms or "houses" were named after the house mistresses (the women who lived and supervised the girls at the school). On March 17, 1890 the first girls' lacrosse game was played between the houses of Sandy and Tulloch.

The game was played with 8 girls on each team and lasted one hour with a 10 minute break for halftime. Since lacrosse was new, there were no teachers or coaches for the lacrosse teams. The Sandy house is credited with winning the oldest recorded game of European girls' lacrosse, 3-1 over Tulloch. [85]

Since no one made lacrosse sticks in Europe yet, the St. Leonards' lacrosse sticks are assumed to have been imported from Canada. This could be the reason that while Miss Lumsden saw lacrosse played on her trip to Canada in 1884, she had to wait to introduce the sport until 1890; perhaps she had to import lacrosse sticks to play the game.

Miss Dove (who accompanied Miss Lumsden on the trip to Canada) left St. Leonards to found another school, Wycombe Abbey, and brought lacrosse with her. Miss Dove had become very excited about lacrosse as a sport for girls. Miss Dove published a book in 1898 where she discussed the reasons she felt lacrosse was a great game for girls to play.

> Lacrosse, a game which requires the same qualities of combination, obedience, courage, individual unselfishness for the sake of a side – a player who attempts to keep the ball instead of passing it being absolutely useless – and is full of interest on account of the various kinds of skills required, fleetness of foot, quickness of eye, strength of wrist, and a great deal of judgement and knack. The game of lacrosse well played is a beautiful sight, the actions of the players being so full of grace and agility. (86)

At St. Leonards, like other communities in the 1890s, sports were isolated and infrequent events. It was difficult to keep up to date with all the rules and vocabulary for a sport. Dr. Beers frequently traveled to help form lacrosse programs and returned at times with revised rules and techniques. In his writings, Dr. Beers never mentions the girls' programs that had started in Europe. Because of this isolation from outside programs, St. Leonards stayed with the original versions of the game as seen in Canada and Scotland.

Sport vocabulary evolves, and this helps to make each sport unique. Like most new sports, girls' lacrosse borrowed terms from other sports. Over time, players and coaches came up with terms to create distinction for items such as the "draw."

The term "love" was used in girls' lacrosse, as in tennis, to represent a score of zero. Several game records include scores of 3 goals to love. Field hockey and other sports at English and Scottish girls' schools also used the word love for no score by a team.

At the beginning of a lacrosse game a "draw" or "face-off" began on the ground as it was done by Dr. Beers' traveling teams. The girls' lacrosse games started this same way, with the face-off or draw on the ground. The draw was originally called a "face" or "face-off." Like the men's game, however, by 1902 most game articles called the face-off a "draw."

The term "draw" was used because the girls' rules at the time only allowed the ball to be drawn backwards on the face-off. Thus, the ball was "drawn" backwards. This name of a "draw" was only used by the girls' lacrosse programs in Europe.

As of the early 20th century, no girls' lacrosse program had been started in North America.

Chapter Twenty Four - Women's Lacrosse

In 1927, girls' lacrosse made a rule change that the draw would take place with the players standing. The reason presented was, "why should a sport that is played in the air start on the ground?" As discussed earlier in the book, the original lacrosse games of the Iroquois, Dakota, and Ojibwe Nations all tossed the ball into the air. Only when Dr. Beers wrote his book on lacrosse did the game start from the ground.

In 1901, the concept of two 25-minute halves was formally introduced. This is the time format used today in many levels of girls' lacrosse.

At St. Leonards, the number of players on a team started at 8. As the school grew in size, the number of players on a team grew to match the number of players originally played by the men's teams—twelve. (87)

1890 – 8 players
1895 – 10 players
1913 – 12 players

In 1912, the first formal lacrosse association for women was formed. The name they chose was "Ladies Lacrosse Association" or LLA. The word chosen was not girls or women, but ladies. This choice was intentional. Using the word ladies was meant to remind everyone that they were not trying to create women's lacrosse to compete with men, but a completely separate sport and reason for playing.

Lacrosse was to be played by ladies for recreation, not for sporting or competitive purposes. The men's game of lacrosse had developed a reputation of being a violent sporting event, which was yet another reason to create a different set of standards and rules. The Ladies Lacrosse Association did not adopt any equipment requirements (such as helmets or gloves) and created rules to keep the game safe and lady-like by not being too aggressive.

If history considers John Flannery the father of modern day American lacrosse, than its mother must be Rosabelle Sinclair. Rosabelle attended St. Leonards and graduated from Dartford College. While attending St. Leonards, Rosabelle Sinclair had been captain of her house lacrosse team. She was a very aggressive player who led by example, and by all accounts got the most out of her teammates on the field. At her graduation, she received First Class Honors in teaching, along with field hockey, lacrosse, and cricket.

Sinclair, who had lived in the United States before attending St. Leonards, moved back to the United States in 1925 to take the job as Athletic Director at Baltimore's Bryn Mawr School. In the spring of 1926 she introduced lacrosse. Their first game was held against the Friends School in Baltimore, and Roland Park School was mentioned as another team in the league later that season. Sinclair was credited with being willing to teach and coach girls' lacrosse teams from Virginia to Boston. Rosabelle Sinclair's most famous quote to her players was, "Pass the ball! Any fool can run with it!"

The game that Sinclair brought back with her was the same version she learned at St. Leonards, not the men's game now being played in the United States. The men's lacrosse game by the 1920s had morphed into using equipment for protection, had only 10 players on a team, and emphasized violence over skill. She had no desire to change the version of lacrosse she had grown up with to compete with the men's game, and stuck to her view that the game was a ladies game and should be played without protective equipment.

While Sinclair was successful at getting lacrosse going for girls, others had gone before her to start the process, and later worked with her to promote women's lacrosse in the United States.

In 1924, Helen Thompson introduced the sport of lacrosse to Wellesley College. She did not stay long and was soon replaced by Joyce Cran, who continued the sport. In fact, Cran was getting ready to board a ship to return to England when Wellesley College reached out and asked her to take over for Thompson. Joyce Cran had been in town coaching field hockey clinics and had brought lacrosse sticks with her to introduce the sport to her field hockey campers.

In 1929 Joyce Cran married a man named Tom Barry. Cran was key in developing the United States Women's Lacrosse Association, becoming its first President from 1931 to 1935.

Seeing the need for "good" field hockey sticks in America, Joyce Cran and her husband Tom Barry formed a company called "CranBarry." Later on, when promoting girls' lacrosse, she needed a "balanced" lacrosse stick. She designed a girls' stick and CranBarry began to manufacture them. CranBarry became the first lacrosse equipment company to specialize in making girls' lacrosse sticks. She often gave away her equipment or sold it for no profit to help grow the game. She was truly a pioneer in lacrosse. Her students fondly remember her and her legendary motorcycle, ridden to games and practices.

Chapter Twenty Four – Women's Lacrosse

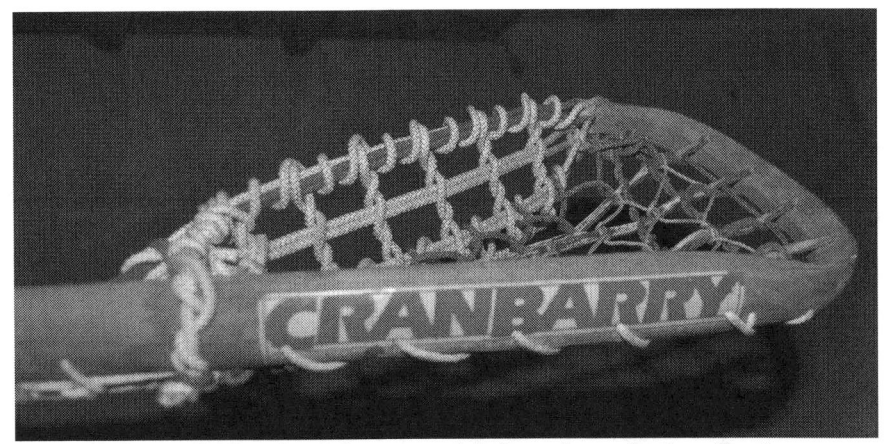

Photo of a Cranbarry lacrosse stick from the author's collection

At the American Physical Education Association Convention in 1929, it was Joyce Cran who officially promoted that "Lacrosse was the ideal game for girls" as compared to the awkward crouching positions in field hockey. In lacrosse, girls played upright and achieved proper posture. (88)

Thompson, Cran, and Sinclair all promoted the girls' lacrosse game through lectures and sports camps. (89) Rosabelle Sinclair stayed at Bryn Mawr for twenty-five years promoting lacrosse throughout the Baltimore area. Her efforts, along with the success of men's programs at Navy and Johns Hopkins, are the primary reason the Hall of Fame and US Lacrosse headquarters are in Maryland.

After World War II and following the first wave of girls' lacrosse, England's Margaret Boyd continued the movement in the United States. She taught the game of lacrosse up and down the east coast. Boyd published the book, *"Lacrosse Playing and Coaching"* in 1959, documenting her thoughts and ideas on how the game should be played.

Margaret Boyd established the International Federation of Women's Lacrosse Associations (IFWLA) in 1972. This organization helped start international lacrosse competitions in women's lacrosse.

As of the printing of this book, the ladies lacrosse game has added some equipment rule changes, such as requiring a mouth guard and goggles. It now has a defined field length of 120 yards by 70 yards, and more rules to protect players from dangerous play. But they have not adopted helmets, shoulder pads, gloves, or other protective equipment as "required" for play, except for the goalie position. With the increased emphasis on head injuries and concussions, this may change in the future. The game that would have been seen in 1890 at St. Leonards would look very similar to a high school game being played today. The same cannot be said if you watched a men's game in 1890 Minnesota and a high school boys' lacrosse game today.

To recap, girls' lacrosse was started around 1890 in an isolated environment at an all-girls prep school. The game remained this way, with very few rule changes or advancements in the sport, while the boys' game in North America continued to develop and change rules to make the game faster and more physical.

This version of girls' lacrosse was then reintroduced back to North America in the 1920s. The ladies choose not to adopt the changes made in the men's game and to keep the lady-like sport simple, fun, non-competitive, and recreational.

> **SIDE WALL:**
> *Women's role in First Nation Lacrosse.*
> *There was a large difference between east and midwest First Nations approaches to women in the game of lacrosse.*
>
> *The east coast First Nations created the game and stayed with a hard line that women could not play lacrosse or even touch a lacrosse stick. This had continued until very recently, with girls now being allowed to form their own teams.*
>
> *The midwest First Nations, such as the Dakota and Ojibwe, had a different view, and allowed women to play their own lacrosse games and even held mixed games where women and men played together on the same team.*

SUGGESTED FURTHER READING

- *St. Leonards Cradle of Lacrosse,* Jane Clayton
- *Lacrosse Playing and Coaching,* Margaret Boyd

CHAPTER 25

LACROSSE RESTORED TO MINNESOTA

Even though the lacrosse leagues had ended by 1906 and most white settlers had stopped playing lacrosse by 1914, the Ojibwe continued to play lacrosse in the northern part of Minnesota. The Bemidji Pioneer Newspaper recorded lacrosse events, fairs, and gatherings occurring in the area near Red Lake, Leech Lake, and White Earth in the early 20th century.

SECOND ANNUAL
RED LAKE INDIAN FAIR

WILL BE HELD AT

RED LAKE INDIAN FAIR ASSOCIATION FAIR GROUNDS

September 3, 4 and 5, 1914

Many improvements are being added to the fair grounds to make them more attractive and convenient to the fair visitors. The exhibits, agricultural and domestic, school booth, Indian bead work, etc., will excell former displays.

The Live Stock Exhibit will not be surpassed in Beltrami county or any adjoining county, this fall

There will be something to amuse you all the time

BEMIDJI DAY Friday, Sept. 4, will be the **BIG DAY**

The object of our association is the promulgation of industrial activities among our people; the education of our neighbors as well as ourselves. Better farming and more farming. Plenty of cattle and more cattle, etc.

Indians Only Can Compete for Prizes or Premiums
to be given for the best exhibits. However, persons on or near the reservation are cordially invited to display their agricultural products, as well as live stock

Good Program Every Afternoon and Evening
of our fair. Indians only participating. There will be an Indian Lacrosse game each day of the fair, tug of war, foot races, etc.

Bemidji Pioneer, 1914

Minnesota Lacrosse: A History

> **FIELD SPORTS AND CALEDONIAN GAMES FOR RED LAKE FAIR.**
>
> Red Lake Falls, Minn., Sept. 8.—A schedule of field sports and Caledonian games will be featured at the ninth annual Red Lake county fair and homecoming celebration September 29, 30 and October 1, according to directors of the association.
>
> Some of the events to be held are a 1-mile run, ½-mile run, ¼-mile run, ½-mile relay race, 100-yard dash, pole vault, standing high jump, broad jump, running broad jump, hurdle race, tug of war, hammer throwing and tossing the caber.
>
> A game of lacrosse between the Red Lake Indians and the Ponomah Indians also has been scheduled.

Bemidji Pioneer, 1919

Lacrosse games continued at local and county fairs and at the State Fair for years after the St. Paul and Minneapolis lacrosse clubs lost interest in the game. The First Nations held on to the game of lacrosse, especially in the northern part of the state, but assimilation, boarding schools, poverty, and other cultural losses eventually took its toll on the game.

Bemidji Pioneer, 1912

Chapter Twenty Five - Lacrosse Restored to Minnesota

Minnesota State Fair Ad

Minnesota Lacrosse: A History

Jerry Morgan's Play LaCrosse book cover

272

Chapter Twenty Five - Lacrosse Restored to Minnesota

Jerry Morgan of the Leech Lake Band wrote a book in 2004 documenting the history of lacrosse in the Leech Lake and Red Lake areas. Morgan describes the history of games being played at Oak Point on Leech Lake up until the late 1930s.

Spiritual leader Mr. Rueben Goggleye told him of families who played lacrosse at the end of that era. The Dunn, Cloud, Fairbank, and Raisch families were the last to play the game of lacrosse as it fell out of favor.

Red Lake Nation Lacrosse Photo

Mr. Goggleye discussed the town of Ball Club with Morgan, and how the lacrosse games were played on both sides of the lake and along the Mississippi River. People traveled by canoe and later on horseback to come together to play and watch games.

The games were used to settle differences between families or bands, and teams had as many as 40 people per side. The games included a time of feasting and prayers, and offered a true healing among the people.

By the end of World War II, as men who fought did not return home to the reservation, the game of lacrosse was no longer alive in Minnesota.

Minnesota Lacrosse: A History

> **SIDE WALL:**
> *One of the consequences of the GI Bill was that Ojibwe or Dakota men who fought in the war could now get a free college education, allowing them to pursue a life off the reservation.*
>
> *Many young men did this, and another generation of young people left the reservation, leaving behind their culture and traditions.*

By the 1940s, it had been less than 100 years since the treaties were signed, and reservations began in Minnesota. The cultural loss was nearly complete.

The impact of poverty, language, cultural loss at boarding schools, and young men leaving for college or jobs had taken a severe toll. Like any person or people who lose hope, a dark time began for the First Nations.

During the 1940s, 1950s, and 1960s, there was no lacrosse in Minnesota.

The 1970s arrived and so did a man from Pennsylvania, Dave White. He attended and played lacrosse at Dickinson College in Carlisle, Pennsylvania. He worked for Dayton's, and was transferred to the Twin Cities in 1976. During a trip to California for business, Dave saw an announcement for a game being played at UC-Davis, between the San Francisco Lacrosse Club and UC-Davis Lacrosse Club. This game, played outside of the east coast hot beds for lacrosse, prompted him to think maybe lacrosse could work in Minnesota.

When White returned home from this trip, he took out an ad in the Star Tribune's Sunday Sports Section asking people to join him in playing lacrosse. He got a few answers—about 9 to 10 people—but not enough to field a team. One of the contacts was Tom Oaster, who put White in touch with Julius Sante, who was attending the University of Minnesota. Sante was a native of Jamaica, had learned the game of lacrosse there, and had classmates interested in the game.

With one phone call to Sante, White had a team. The first official lacrosse club in decades was formed in 1976. Together, they were able to secure a practice field on the University of Minnesota grounds near the baseball fields. The official club name was the Twin Cities Lacrosse Club.

Part of White's campaign to recruit players was a bumper sticker, meant to get the attention of people who might have moved to the Twin Cities from other parts of the country. The bumper sticker worked and people approached him, saying they knew what it meant and that they had played the game when they were young.

Chapter Twenty Five – Lacrosse Restored to Minnesota

LACROSSE,
IS NOT JUST A CITY IN WISCONSIN !

Dave White's famous bumper sticker in 1976

The first event in the spring of 1977 was an away game. The Twin Cities team traveled to play their first game against Iowa State.

Since the team did not have any money, Steve Hill, a doctor on the team, "borrowed" medical gowns for uniforms. It is hard to tell, but the photo of the first home game shows the medical gowns being worn (see below).

Just before the first home game, the Star Tribune ran an article on the "new" sport for Minnesota. The article included pictures of the ragtag team.

There were many challenges for starting the lacrosse renaissance in Minnesota. The first was that none of the local sports shops carried lacrosse equipment. White said there was not a single stick, helmet, or even lacrosse ball to be had in the Twin Cities. All equipment had to be ordered by mail from Brine and Bacharach Rasin. Another challenge was distance the nearest competitor was over 200 miles away and officials.

First home game of the Twin Cities Lacrosse Club, May 1, 1977 Southwest corner of Lake of the Isles - Courtesy of Dave White

Minnesota Lacrosse: A History

Minneapolis Star Tribune 1976 Photo by Mike Zerby

Chapter Twenty Five – Lacrosse Restored to Minnesota

Minneapolis Star Tribune 1976 Photo by Mike Zerby

Minnesota Lacrosse: A History

Although Dave White wanted to play, the reality was there were no officials in the midwest to run the lacrosse games. Therefore, White decided he would officiate the lacrosse club games, and later college and high school games. For years White was the ONLY official in Minnesota.

Dave White, 1977   *Dave White, 2014*   *Dave's equipment*

Dave White's legendary Steel Shaft Long Pole

During the 1970s and 1980s, games were far away with limited competition. Early programs included Iowa State, Ripon College in Wisconsin, Madison Lacrosse Club, and the University of Iowa. Teams from further away met at neutral locations like Iowa State. These included Knox College, Kansas City Lacrosse Club, University of Missouri, and Western Illinois.

Chapter Twenty Five - Lacrosse Restored to Minnesota

Dave White's handwritten jersey list for the Twin City Lacrosse Club

In 1977, the Twin Cities Lacrosse Club traveled to La Crosse, Wisconsin to play a game at the Oktoberfest celebration. At that event White met Mick Walker. White and Walker partnered to create the Great Plains Lacrosse League in 1978.

In 1978, White organized a trip to the Aspen Lacrosse Shootout in Colorado. The team included 28 players from all over the midwest. There were only 8 teams that attended the tournament. This tournament then moved to Vail and has become a mainstay for Minnesota Travel Lacrosse teams to visit each summer. The beautiful mountains make it a great place to hang out and enjoy lacrosse games.

Twin Cities Lacrosse Club, Photo provided by Dave White

White stayed active in the lacrosse community for decades, serving many roles. As lacrosse grew in the midwest, he became "that guy from Minnesota" who helped get officials trained and organized in a new area. White then started the e-mail newsletter for Lacrosse Officials from 1995–2003. This email list of over 700 officials became the way colleges and tournaments arranged officials. Newsletters were random but constant, sometimes going out three to four times a week.

Fun trivia: during the last home game of the 1992 Minnesota Vikings football season, against the Green Bay Packers, a halftime lacrosse game was played with teams from the Twin Cities Lacrosse Club. It was officiated by Dave White and Terry Brennan.

Chapter Twenty Five - Lacrosse Restored to Minnesota

Twin Cities Lacrosse Club, Photo provided by Dave White

1980s

As club teams grew in the midwest, so did interest in colleges joining the scene. The first was Carleton College in 1981, started by Bruce Wall. In 1985 programs were started at St. Johns University by Karl Koller, and St. Thomas University, by Chris Larson.

St. Johns

As the following photos show, this was a ragtag group of players with non-matching equipment and random uniforms. But they were also a community of players having fun.

Minnesota Lacrosse: A History

St. Thomas sidelines 1980s

St. Johns 1985 team

St. Johns vs St. Thomas 1980s

Chapter Twenty Five – Lacrosse Restored to Minnesota

St. Thomas 1980s

1990

Dan Ninham began getting involved in a very different way for lacrosse in Minnesota. Ninham is Oneida and originally from Wisconsin. He was recruited to Bemidji State University on a basketball scholarship in 1981, and after college he returned home to the Oneida reservation to teach. Ninham started a lacrosse program there, which he ran from 1983 to 1990.

Dan Ninham coaching, 1995

Ninham's wife Susan was from the Red Lake Reservation in northern Minnesota, and in 1990 they moved to Bemidji. It was here that he started building a lacrosse program called Northern Minnesota Lacrosse.

He brought his passion for education and lacrosse to northern Minnesota and began teaching and traveling around the state to coach lacrosse on and off the reservations. Many in the Native lacrosse community are disciples of Ninham. Max Kelsey makes wooden lacrosse sticks, Jerry Morgan writes books, John Hunter started the Twin Cities Native Lacrosse program, Franky Jackson coaches at Lower Sioux, Lukas Fineday coaches at Pine Point Lacrosse on the White Earth Reservation, and Pete Neadeau at Red Lake makes traditional wooden sticks. Ninham touched many lives because of his leadership and passion for restoring the game of lacrosse.

1991

As colleges joined the ranks, they needed to develop a league in which to play. In 1991 the Upper Midwest Lacrosse League (UMLL) was started. UMLL was founded by Stan Shei, Rob Graff and Chris Larson. Gustavus Adolphus College won the first championship in 1993.

Men's collegiate teams prior to 2000
1981 – Carleton College
1985 – St. John's University, St. Thomas University
1991 – UMN-Twin Cities, MSU-Mankato, Gustavus Adolphus
1993 – UMN-Duluth, St. Cloud State, St. Mary's
1996 – Bethel, St. Olaf, MSU-Moorhead

1992

In 1992 a job transfer brought another person to Minnesota. This time it was Mark Hellenack, from New Jersey. Hellenack had run the New Jersey Chapter of The Lacrosse Foundation. He brought with him a wealth of knowledge about organizing lacrosse clubs. Back in New Jersey, his lacrosse club was called the "Hammerheads."

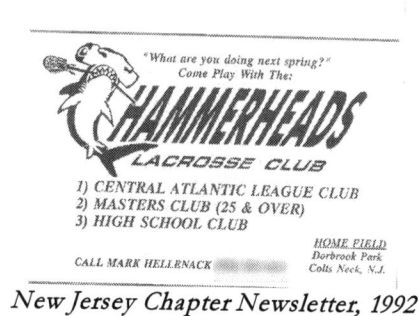

"What are you doing next spring?"
Come Play With The:

HAMMERHEADS LACROSSE CLUB

1) CENTRAL ATLANTIC LEAGUE CLUB
2) MASTERS CLUB (25 & OVER)
3) HIGH SCHOOL CLUB

CALL MARK HELLENACK

HOME FIELD
Dorbrook Park
Colts Neck, N.J.

New Jersey Chapter Newsletter, 1992

Chapter Twenty Five - Lacrosse Restored to Minnesota

1993

As Hellenack settled into Minnesota, he wasted no time and started sharing his passion for lacrosse. 1993 brought the first clinics to the city of Hopkins. Hellenack looked at the culture of Minnesota and figured that the best way to fit in was to do indoor lacrosse. It was more like hockey, and he found indoor time at the Hopkins arena. That became home base for indoor lacrosse clinics and leagues.

Hellenack also went out into the community to teach at schools anywhere he could get time to share his passion and vision of the game.

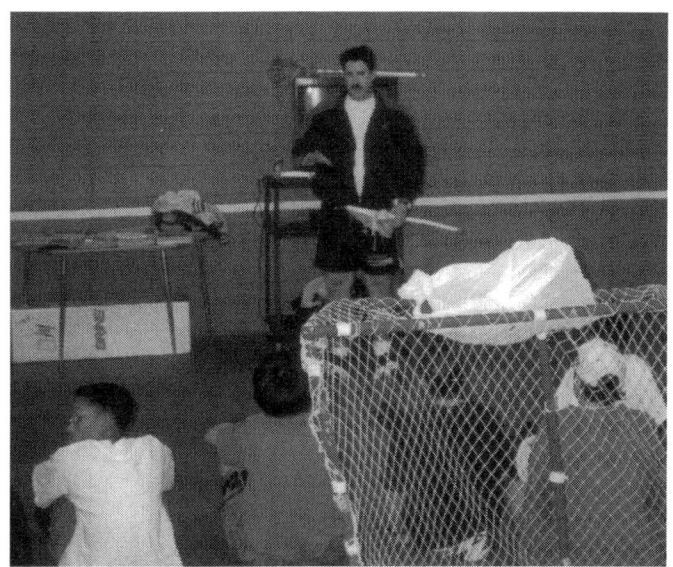

Mark Hellenack at North Hopkins School

Hellenack also started getting busy making Minnesota a Chapter in The Lacrosse Foundation (US Lacrosse was formally organized in 1998).

1994

In 1994, Dan Ninham reached out to the Twin Cities area after he heard about Mark Hellenack. Hellenack was not familiar with the full heritage and history of lacrosse in Minnesota. He learned from Dan Ninham, the Minnesota Historical Society, and others about the history of the game in the state. This union of Hellenack and Ninham spurred the first lacrosse tournament at Treaty of Traverse de Sioux site in 1994.

Ninham brought his lacrosse players from the north and met Hellenack, who hosted the event under the new Minnesota Chapter. Ninham hosted a

Minnesota Lacrosse: A History

traditional game with traditional sticks, while Hellenack ran a modern lacrosse tournament. They used the tag line *"Where old meets new."* They were joined by the Minneapolis Lacrosse Club, MN College All-Stars, and the Ojibway Nationals from Winnipeg.

Minnesota Lacrosse NEWSLETTER

Minnesota Lacrosse — Volume: 1 — Issue: 1 — Date: 3/25/95

Inside this Newsletter

2 What's Up
A listing of the lacrosse events going on this spring and summer.

3 Team Contacts & Schedules
Club and College contacts, game dates, and locations.

1 "Old Meets New"
A look at the upcoming River Rendezvous Tournament in Bloomington this Sept. 21-24.

3 Join Us!
A word about the benefits of joining the Lacrosse Foundation.

Old Meets New...

When I started the Chapter, I was not aware of the history of lacrosse in Minnesota. Even though it's actually our oldest sport and has been played by the local college clubs for 15 years, it is still a new sport for many Minnesotans. The "ball game" as it was called by the local Dakota, Ojibway, and other Great Lakes tribes was played over 150 years ago. The game's rich history was recorded by fur traders, missionaries, and famous painters like Eastman and Catlin. I credit Tom Vennum's book, "Native American Lacrosse", with my enlightenment and the idea to hold a traditional ball game at the Chapter's Fall-Ball tournament.

With history in mind, in Sept. of 1994, the Traverse Des Sioux Encampment was the venue for our traditional ball game and modern tournament. Frank Meyer's painting depicts the Dakota playing the game during the treaty signing of 1852 at the site in St. Peter, MN. Meyer's works are in the Goucher College Gallery in Baltimore. With traditional Dakota style sticks, players from the Minneapolis LC, MN College All-Stars and the Ojibway Nationals from Winnipeg, delighted the crowds as they did their best to demonstrate how the game was played 100 plus years ago. (see below photo)

Traditional ball game reenactments, a clinic and club tournament will be part of the 1995 River Rendezvous in Bloomington, MN. This Sept. 23-24 food, music, Native American dancers, fur traders, and crafts demonstrators will transport you back to frontier life in the 1800's. Over 15,000 people are expected to attend the event. On hand, once again, will be Bud Davids, storyteller and last of the Dakota style stick carvers. Dan Ninham, an Onieda and founder of the Northern MN LC, will run the youth clinic and provide sticks for the reenactments. Players from the tournament will have the opportunity to help reenact a ball game between Cloudman's and Shakopee's villages that took place at the Pond-Dakota Mission property 140 years ago.

Photo: Ball Play at Traverse Des Sioux
Dan Ninham (Bemidji) and college players play ball at the Encampment.

IT'S FUN & FOR A GOOD CAUSE:
Minutes from the airport, Mall of America and Minneapolis, the River Rendezvous is a great weekend of lacrosse & history. Men's & women's college and post-college teams from the US and Canada are invited to compete in the tournament which is also a fund raiser for the Minneapolis Native American Inner City Youth League. *Sponsors and teams are needed. For more details call Mark Hellenack at the Minnesota Chapter (612) 938-5241.*

The Lacrosse Foundation
Minnesota Chapter

First Minnesota Chapter Newsletter March, 1995
Provided by Mark Hellenack

Chapter Twenty Five - Lacrosse Restored to Minnesota

In March of 1995 the first newsletter of the Minnesota Chapter recounted the September 1994 event. This ignited a passion in many people who learned about the history of the game and how it was being played again.

Hellenack expanded the indoor lacrosse league with new levels including to an arena in Apple Valley. The games were rough at first, because the hockey-players-turned-lacrosse-players brought physical play. Hellenack observed that as lacrosse skills improved, the players learned to move the ball and not just hit, reducing the rough play.

Meanwhile, the girls started lacrosse with early participation at The Blake School. Sarah Hemmingway, a student who had moved from Connecticut, and Debra Wood, a teacher who had relocated from Pittsburgh, started throwing the ball around at school and shooting at a net made of PVC piping.

First Minnesota Chapter Tournament held at Traverse des Sioux
Provided by Mark Hellenack

1995

1995 brought some of biggest game changes in Minnesota. High school leagues started, travel teams started, field games started, and new tournaments were held.

Hellenack added to his knowledge about the history of lacrosse, and learned about the great 1852 game at Oak Grove, now Bloomington, Minnesota. Bloomington holds an annual River Rendezvous event at the Gideon Pond house site. Hellenack moved the tournament to this location in 1995 and again Dan Ninham brought his players down to support the event.

1995 CDH Lacrosse Team

Player
Steve Gaida
Marty Haugh
John Hunter
Jim Jordan
Joe Jordan
Chris Knapp
Mark Krenz
Brendan McInerney
Josh Meyer
Zack Roberts
Tom Sampair
David Tierney
Brennan Townley
Tully Velte
Jim Wilson

Cretin-Derham Hall 1995 Indoor Lacrosse Roster
Provided by John Hunter

1995 also brought a unique event to the National Sports Center in Blaine. They hosted the North American Indigenous Games, which included games of lacrosse. The new local fans got to watch lacrosse games and were even treated to the Iroquois teams who attended and won at the Bantam Boys level. Dan Ninham also placed Northern Lacrosse teams in this special tournament.

Chapter Twenty Five – Lacrosse Restored to Minnesota

1995 North American Indigenous Games Lacrosse

August 3-5, National Sports Center, Blaine...Many of you may not have realized it but lacrosse history was made in Minnesota this summer. This marks the first time the Indigenous Games 17 Olympic style sports and Native cultural events were held in the US. And for the first time in over 90 years the Games brought back lacrosse, a once proud tradition for the Ojibway and Dakota people of Minnesota. All native teams from Alberta, Winnipeg, Saskatchewan, Ontario, North Dakota and New York competed in field lacrosse for gold, silver and bronze medals in four age groups. Ontario dominated the competition with a strong well coached group of players from the six nation reserve, easily taking the Gold in the boy's Bantam and Midget competitions. On the Juvenile level (ages 17-18), the New York Girl's beat Ontario 15-9 and NY's Boy's beat Saskatchewan 20-0 for the Gold. Winnipeg handled Alberta 22-19 in the Men's Senior Game, while their Bantam boy's came away with a Bronze defeating North Dakota. I think the coaches, officials and event organizers all agree that every players left a winner, especially the North Dakota boys who only started playing 3 months prior to the Games. The goal of the Games is to promote participation in sports and as the Games grow so shall the sport of lacrosse in the indigenous communities of North America.

(Ontario "Six Nations" Boy's Bantam Team)

Minnesota Chapter Newsletter Volume 2, 1995

In 1995, the Minnesota Chapter, also called the Minnesota Lacrosse Association (MLA), ran all the events under one organization. There were few officials (such as Dave White, Paul Smith, Dave Rundquist, and the Yates brothers) who could officiate games.

River Rendezvous Flyer
Provided by Mark Hellenack

The boys' high school league in 1995 consisted of three teams: Breck, Tonka (western suburbs), and Valley (southern suburbs). This was the first outdoor lacrosse league; others continued to play indoors.

289

Minnesota Lacrosse: A History

So you want to play LACROSSE

1996 TWIN CITIES INDOOR LACROSSE LEAGUE

"All it takes is a lacrosse stick and we will teach you the rest."
Call today for more details !

LEAGUE DIRECTORS: Matt Pietrafitta Mark Hellenack

AGE LEVELS: Pee Wee (12 & under) Bantam (13-14), Midget (15-16), Junior (17-18), **Men** (19 & over)

PLAYERS PER TEAM: Minimum of 12, maximum of 15 players per team. Teams can have players from the other schools. Younger players can also play up an age group.

GAME SITES & DATES: West Metro Games will start March 10 - May 19 on Sun mornings and Thurs. evenings at the Hopkins Pavilion, Excelsior Blvd. in Hopkins. South Metro games start in Feburary on Mon. and Wed. eves. at the new Apple Valley Arena.

LEAGUE FEE: The League Fee is $85 per player and includes a jersey, free clinic and player recruitment night at your school. The League also provides training for the coaches and players, discount coupons for equipment, indoor playing fields and locker rooms. Exact clinic and game dates/times will be finalized in Dec..

EQUIPMENT: Players are required to provide their own lacrosse stick, hockey or lacrosse: helmet, gloves, elbow and shoulder pads, mouth guard, sneakers and shorts. Some loaner equipment is available. Teams are responsilbe for finding an adult coach, transportation and equipment. For a list of local new and used lacrosse equipment dealers call the League Directors.

LEAGUE HISTORY:
Invented by the North American Indians, lacrosse is America's oldest know team sport and it is just starting to grow on the Youth and H.S. levels here in Twin Cities, Mankato and Bemidji. The Twin Cities Indoor (6 on 6) Lacrosse League was first formed in 1994 with four teams, in '95 league participation jumped to 10 teams including, Apple Valley, Champlin Park, Cretin Durham Hall, Eagan, Eden Prairie, Edina, Hopkins, Minnetonka, Orono, and Rosemount. The Indoor League offers newcomers to the sport the opportunity to learn and develop their lacrosse skills without the body contact. As many players are finding out lacrosse is fun and a great cross-over sport for football, soccer. and hockey players. Indoor lacrosse is also the *national summer sport of Canada* and a new professional sport as seen on ESPN. Many of the NHL's top scorers, Wayne Gretsky, Joe Nieuendyke, Brenden Shanahan, and Brian Oates attribute box lacrosse with sharpening their on ice skills. Players will also have the opportunity to participate in field (10 on 10) lacrosse leagues and traveling teams this summer. Traditionally a spring sport here in US over 300 universities and 1,500 high schools from Maine to California have varsity field lacrosse programs. In Minnesota there are eleven men's and two women's field lacrosse clubs at local colleges. Ohio St., Penn St., Notre Dame and Michigan St. offer both men's and women's lacrosse scholarships.

Coaches and Officials are needed ....
With the combind rules of basketball and hockey lacrosse is a highly skilled, fast moving, high scoring and exciting game to to watch and play. Lacrosse has caught on in Minnesota and it's growing so fast we need more coaches and officials. Interested parent's and former players are encouraged to call the League directors for more details about upcoming coaching and officials clinics and for rule books. Officials from other sports especially basketball and hockey make great lacrosse refs.

The Lacrosse Foundation — Minnesota Chapter
Lacrosse is experiencing such tremendous growth in Minnesota. Anyone interested in playing or learning more about the sport is encouraged to call the Lacrosse Foundation (612) 938-2723. Ask about the free in-school clinics, and leagues that are geared to teach the basic skills, rules, strategy and build player confidence.
Mark Hellenack, Chapter President

Twin Cities Indoor Lacrosse League Application Request

NAME:_____ AGE:___ GRADE:___ SCH:_____

ADDRESS:_____ CITY:_____ ZIP:_____

HM. PHONE:(___)____-_____ POSITION:_____ TEAM:_____ Yrs. of Experience_____

PARENTS' NAMES_____ OTHER SPORTS COMPETED IN:_____

Send no money. Mail your application request to the Twin Cities Indoor Lacrosse League, 138 14th Ave. North, Hopkins, MN 55343 or call the League directors with your questions. (612) 938-2723 or (612) 935-2583

1996 Indoor Lacrosse Signups – Provided by John Hunter

Minnesota Chill started in 1995 – Provided by Mark Hellenack

290

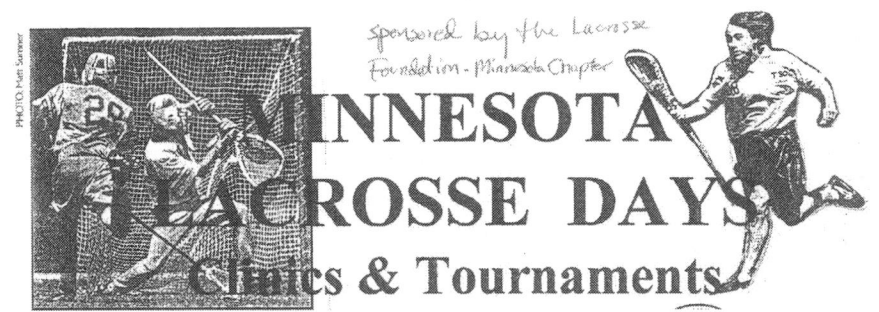

Chapter Twenty Five - Lacrosse Restored to Minnesota

1995 Minnesota Lacrosse Chapter Flyer

Travel teams began again and continued the tradition that Dave White started by going to Colorado. Art Ayers took a team called the Minnesota Chill to Vail. The Coach of the Year was often named coach of the Chill, then the team traveled to Vail to represent Minnesota.

River Rendezvous Tournament Program, 1995
Provided by Mark Hellenack

Minnesota Lacrosse: A History

CONGRATULATIONS TO:

1995 Twin Cities Indoor Lacrosse League Champions
ST. PAUL (Youth) and CRETIN DERHAM HALL (H.S.)
Hopkins Pavilion...Sunday, May 20th, (Youth Division) The St. Paul team of 7th and 8th grader players from Nativity and Holy Spirit went undefeated this season and easily handled Minnetonka 7-3 in the League Championships. League MVP's included forwards Josh Cohen, Jon Hedberg, Andy Stringer, Drew Payne, Nick Krunkkala, Dan Spooner, Ryan Sauter and goalie Kyle MaGaa. (High School Division) Cretin Derham was by far the most physically talented team in the League, defeated Rosemount 11-7 in the finals. Even Rosemount's high scoring young offense lead by juniors, Brad Gobar, Jason Endely and soph., Josh Kuhn, was no match for the size and speed of Cretin's senior dominated team lead by high scorers Brendan Townley and Marty Haugh. Other outstanding players from the League include Anderw Gorton (AV), Mark Kielucki and Scott Holm (Cham Pk.) and Matt Witham (Hop).

The 1996 Twin Cities Indoor League starts in March at the Hopkins Pavilion. Tentitive plans include Bantam, Midget and Junior age divisions and a south metro League site in Apple Valley. In July, League champs will get to play in Winnipeg, Canada.

(St Paul Youth Team, 1995 Indoor League Champions)

Minnesota Chapter Newsletter, 1995
Provided by Mark Hellenack

The girls' lacrosse team at The Blake School now had real nets to shoot at and played the Twin Cities post-collegiate team called the Hoydens. The Hoydens were founded by Mary Scott Hunter, Holly Souza, and Chris Duca. The Blake School also played a group of young women at Carleton College that year.

1996 - 1999

The 1990s saw fast growth in lacrosse in the Twin Cities area. Dan Ninham was also very successful up north. By 1998 Ninham had 64 middle school age players and a traveling program that went to Winnipeg, Milwaukee, and other destinations.

In the Twin Cities, the boys' high school league grew from 3 to 13 teams. Minnesota led the nation in growth with an amazing 70%+ growth rate by 1998.

The girls' game was growing as well. In 1996, a Hopkins, Eden Prairie, and St. Louis Park single team split into multiple teams. Janet Holdsworth coached Hopkins, Judy Baxter and Holly Souza coached Eden Prairie, and student/coach Arianna Gavzy took St. Louis Park.

By 1998 the girls had formed a league with Janet Holdsworth and Debra Woods, creating the Northcentral Schoolgirls Lacrosse Association.

The River Rendezvous tournament continued to grow and Dan Ninham kept the First Nation teams coming. The photo here shows an Oneida youth team at the tournament.

Chapter Twenty Five – Lacrosse Restored to Minnesota

Oneida Youth team at the River Rendezvous Tournament

With lacrosse growing for players and communities, there was a need to get officials in order to make these game happen. The next step was to create a formal officials organization and build a team to train and develop rules for the evolving game. Matt Dempsey and Harold Buck stepped forward as officials, and together they formed The Upper Midwest Lacrosse Officials Association (UMLOA). This organization has grown to serve Minnesota's youngest levels through the collegiate level in the upper midwest.

1998 River Rendezvous Flyer

Minnesota Chill in 1997 at Baltimore, National Junior Lacrosse Festival
Photo provided by Howard Rogers

High School Team Timeline from 1995 - 1999

This detailed history concludes at 1999 because it is a good transition point in the evolution of lacrosse. Around that time, the popularity of lacrosse quickly grew. The teams below are the early participants.

Boys' Lacrosse High School Teams
1995   Breck, Tonka (western suburbs), Valley (southern suburbs)
1996   Robbinsdale Cooper, Hopkins
1997   Mankato, Minnetonka, Orono, Roseville
1998   Bloomington Jefferson, Eden Prairie
1999   Academy of Holy Angels, Edina

Girls' Lacrosse High School Teams
1994   The Blake School
1995   Eden Prairie, Hopkins
1996   n/a
1997   Academy of Holy Angels, Robbinsdale Cooper
1998   Bloomington Jefferson
1999   Bloomington Kennedy, Mahtomedi, Mankato, St. Louis Park

One of many snow lacrosse games in Minnesota, UMN vs UMD, 1999

Select Events from the 2000s

During the 90s the majority (if not all) of the lacrosse events—leagues, clinics, tournaments and more—were run by the Minnesota Lacrosse Association (MLA). The River Rendezvous no longer allowed lacrosse games after 1999. Determined to go on, Mark Hellenack moved the event to Brooklyn Park. It was renamed the Hot Dish tournament. Participants brought a hotdish to share at the tournament. Prizes were awarded for the best hotdish, and a silent auction at the tournament was started to support the American Cancer Society.

Dan Ninham's work in northern Minnesota did not fall under MLA, and he kept the game growing while he remained in the state. In 2000, he and his wife Susan were awarded a grant from the Bush Foundation to pursue doctoral studies. (They were the first husband and wife to be honored with grants at the same time from the Bush Foundation, founded by Archibald and Edyth Bush of Granite Falls, Minnesota.)

The Ninham's moved to Colorado in 2000 to pursue their studies. By the time they returned in 2002, Northern Lacrosse had folded. Ninham stayed involved by mentoring coaches like Jerry Morgan, who had started other lacrosse programs. Morgan brought a team from Red Lake and Leech Lake to play in the Hot Dish tournament in 2002.

In 2001, Janet Holdsworth led the charge to get girls' lacrosse approved as a sanctioned high school sport. It passed and girls began a new era of high school lacrosse.

In 2004, Minnesota purchased a franchise in the National Lacrosse League and named it the Swarm. The first professional lacrosse game took place on December 10, 2004 in a pre-season game against the Colorado Mammoth. The first regular season game took place on January 1, 2005 against the Rochester Knighthawks; the Swarm won 12-11.

In 2006, Howard Rogers led the charge for boys' lacrosse to become a sanctioned high school sport like the girls. Rogers had campaigned unsuccessfully since 2004. In 2006 he got the approval of the Minnesota State High School League (MSHSL). The first state lacrosse tournament, hosted by the MSHSL, began in 2007.

In 2008 the first Men's NCAA Division 1 (D1) game was played in Blaine, Minnesota. With the help of the Minnesota Swarm, Notre Dame and Army came to Blaine to play a D1 Men's game of lacrosse.

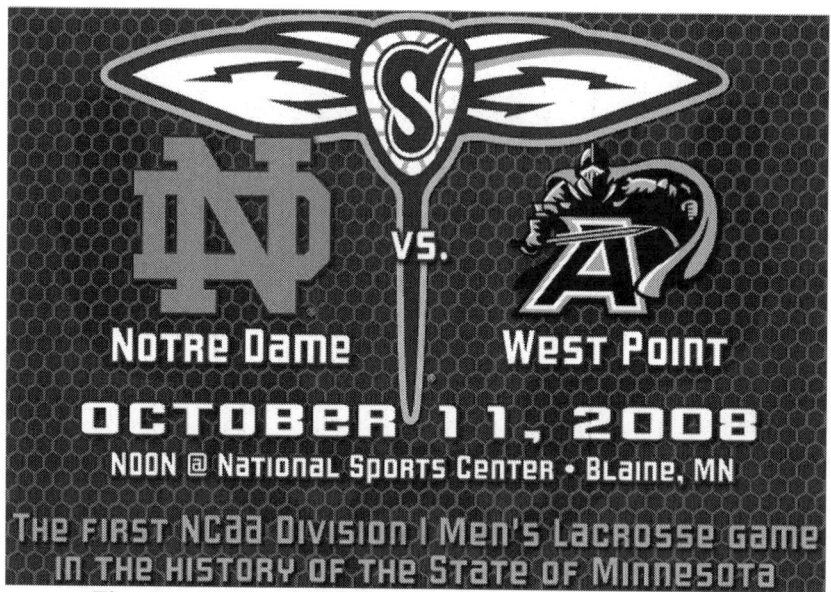

First Men's Division I Lacrosse game held in Minnesota

In 2014 women's lacrosse led the way again by offering the first Minnesota collegiate NCAA lacrosse team. Augsburg College began NCAA lacrosse on February 22, 2014 against Midland University. Augsburg won the game 12-10.

As of the printing of this book no Minnesota men's lacrosse team has gone to the NCAA level.

Chapter Twenty Five – Lacrosse Restored to Minnesota

Dan Ninham continues to teach kids to embrace the wooden stick game

Minnesota Lacrosse: A History

Mark Hellenack doing what he loves to do, share the game
Photo taken by author at Bloomington River Rendezvous in 2014

EPILOGUE

There are many reasons for my passion and love of lacrosse. It starts with my kids and their desire to bring our family into the game. Until they started playing I had never seen the sport. From those beginnings, I learned about the special history Minnesota had with the Ojibwe and Dakota Nations, and the early settlers who formed the St. Paul and Minneapolis Lacrosse Clubs.

I had three goals in mind while writing this lacrosse history book. First, that those who are the descendants of these great lacrosse players from the Ojibwe, Dakota, and early settler lacrosse clubs look in their basements and storage areas to see if any lacrosse sticks, balls, photos or more have survived. These are priceless to our heritage of the game. Please take pictures and share them with the community—a Minnesota Lacrosse Hall of Fame will be coming.

During one of my many visits to the Minnesota Historical Society Archives, Adam Scher opened a cabinet to show me lacrosse sticks that had been cataloged in their collection. When he opened the drawer I saw something that was not cataloged and it amazed me. It was John Stark's lacrosse stick. Stark was a member of the 1884/1885 National Champion St. Paul Lacrosse Club, and he later served as President of the St. Paul Lacrosse Club in 1901. This discovery was awesome—we had a lacrosse stick that has survived from that unique championship era. So maybe there is more out there—go look, ask, and discover.

Second, that we all find a way to return the game to the descendants of the creators of the sport, the Minnesota Ojibwe and Dakota Nations. Many challenges stand in the way of making this happen. I am convinced, however, that as projects such as Dr. Treuer's passion to restore the Ojibwe language (see Appendix E), or the efforts of leaders like Dan Ninham, John Hunter, and many more, this will take hold. Their versions of the game may be different from what we play today, but that version has a truth, a spirit, and a role to play in the community.

I can tell you from personal experience that playing the wooden stick game with no equipment, body on body collisions, and trying to hit a post with a ball creates a special bond among players, and brings an honor that exists in no other sport I have ever experienced. There is a special respect among these players, and a special medicine I cannot even say I truly understand—but I feel it.

How fun would it be to hold an annual lacrosse tournament in Minnesota with tribes, bands, and Nations from all over Canada and the United States coming together to celebrate the origins of the game. Remember that the game is not just about competition, but a celebration of life, community, and healing of our lives.

Finally, my third goal is to get you involved. Join your local lacrosse club and help improve, develop, and grow the game. If this book has inspired you at all, let that be the message: get involved, stay involved.

Long Live Lacrosse

George Kervin's "Duke's Special" Lacrosse Stick
Minnesota Historical Society (9079.2)

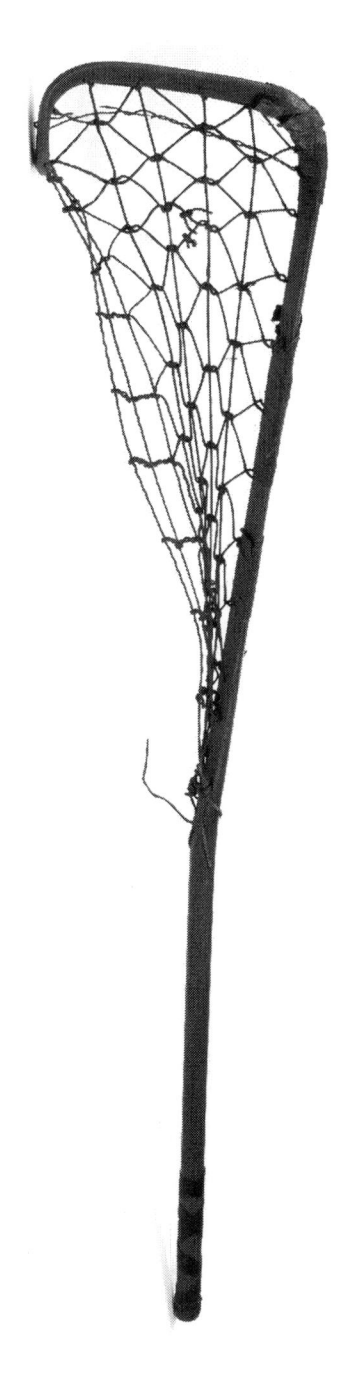

John Stark's "Lally Special" Lacrosse Stick
Minnesota Historical Society (9079.1)

REFERENCES

(1) – Peacock, Thomas D., page 16, *Ojibwe Waasa Inaabidaa*

(2) – Peacock, Thomas D., page 22, *Ojibwe Waasa Inaabidaa*

(3) – In 1994 the Walam Olum was declared a hoax. I present the concept of the Walam Olum because some parts of the Ojibwe Nation believe it to be a reasonable account of their creation story. Oestreicher took stories he heard from the Nations and the concepts from Joseph Smith who had recently published the Book of Mormon to create Walam Olum in 1836. David M. Oestreicher, Unmasking the Walam Olum: A 19th Century Hoax, Archaeological Society of New Jersey, 1994

(4) – Peacock, Thomas D., page 24, *Ojibwe Waasa Inaabidaa*

(5) – Warren, William W. page 78-79, *History of the Ojibway People*

(6) – Kammerer, J. C. Largest Rivers in the United States

(7) – Benton-Banai, Edward. page 89-95, *The Mishomis Book – The Voice of the Ojibway*

(8) – Benton-Banai, Edward. page 102, *The Mishomis Book – The Voice of the Ojibway*

(9) – Miceli, Augusto, Page 96, *The Man With the Red Umbrella*

(10) – Warren, William W. page 146-154, *History of the Ojibway People*

(11) – Warren, William W. page 123, *History of the Ojibway People*

(12) – Warren, William W. page 264, *History of the Ojibway People*

(13) – Warren, William W. page 265, *History of the Ojibway People*

(14) – Warren, William W. page 82, *History of the Ojibway People*

(15) – Bruchac, Joseph. *The Great Ball Game*

(16) – Johnston, Basil. *Tales the Elders Told*

(17) – Vennum, Thomas, page 46, *American Indian Lacrosse – Little brother of war*

(18) – Greer, Allan. page 1, *The Jesuit Relations*

(19) – Brown, Craig. page 106, *The Illustrated History of Canada*

(20) – Donnelly, Joseph. page x, Preface, *Jean de Brébeuf 1593-1649*

(21) – Donnelly, Joseph. page xi Preface, *Jean de Brébeuf 1593-1649*

(22) – Greer, Allan. Page 72, *The Jesuit Relations*

(23) – Vennum, Thomas, page 28, *American Indian Lacrosse – Little brother of war*

(24) – Vennum, Thomas, page 18, *American Indian Lacrosse – Little brother of war*

(25) – Scott, Bob. page 7, *Lacrosse technique and tradition*

(26) – Brown, Craig. page 58, *The Illustrated History of Canada*

(27) – Brown, Craig. page 110, *The Illustrated History of Canada*

(28) – Donnelly, Joseph. pages 271-279, *Jean de Brébeuf 1593-1649*

(29) – Parkman, Francis. page 179, *Conspiracy of Pontiac Vol 1*

(30) – Parkman, Francis. page 203-205, Conspiracy of Pontiac Vol 1

(31) – Parkman, Francis. page 218-219, Conspiracy of Pontiac Vol 1

(32) – Parkman, Francis. page 230, Conspiracy of Pontiac Vol 1

(33) – Parkman, Francis. page 271, Conspiracy of Pontiac Vol 1

(34) – Parkman, Francis. page 275-276, Conspiracy of Pontiac Vol 1

(35) – Warren, William W. page 203, History of the Ojibway People

(36) – Warren, William W. page 205, History of the Ojibway People

(37) – Warren, William W. page 211, History of the Ojibway People

(38) – Hall, Steve. page 2, Fort Snelling – Colossus of the Wilderness

(39) – Don Dorman. Writ in Remembrance: 100 Years of LaCrosse Area History

(40) – McCracken, Harold. page 13, George Catlin and the Old Frontier

(41) – McCracken, Harold. page 138, George Catlin and the Old Frontier

(42) – McCracken, Harold. page 142, George Catlin and the Old Frontier

(43) – McCracken, Harold. page 147, George Catlin and the Old Frontier

(44) – Warren, William W. page 359, History of the Ojibway People

(45) – McCracken, Harold. page 174, George Catlin and the Old Frontier

(46) – McCracken, Harold. page 175, George Catlin and the Old Frontier

(47) – National Park Service, Pipestone: The Rock pamphlet

(48) – Eastman, Mary H. page 53, The American Aboriginal Portfolio

(49) – Vennum, Thomas, preface xii, American Indian Lacrosse – Little brother of war

(50) – Vennum, Thomas, page 221, American Indian Lacrosse – Little brother of war

(51) – Vennum, Thomas, page 47, American Indian Lacrosse – Little brother of war

(52) – Vennum, Thomas, page 85, Lacrosse Legends of the First Americans

(53) – Vennum, Thomas, page 226, American Indian Lacrosse – Little brother of war

(54) – Vennum, Thomas, page 45, American Indian Lacrosse – Little brother of war

(55) – Vennum, Thomas, page 46, American Indian Lacrosse – Little brother of war

(56) – Vennum, Thomas, page 248, American Indian Lacrosse – Little brother of war

(57) – Vennum, Thomas, page 127, American Indian Lacrosse – Little brother of war

(58) – Vennum, Thomas, page 248, American Indian Lacrosse – Little brother of war

(59) – Vennum, Thomas, page 219, American Indian Lacrosse – Little brother of war

(60) – Vennum, Thomas, page 185, American Indian Lacrosse – Little brother of war

(61) – Clapesattle, Helen, The Doctors Mayo

(62) – Weyand. Alexander M. page 14, The Lacrosse Story

(63) – Fisher, Donald, page 24, Lacrosse: A history of the game

(64) - Vennum, Thomas, page 284, American Indian Lacrosse – Little brother of war

(65) – Fisher, Donald, page 52, Lacrosse: A history of the game

(66) – Fisher, Donald, page 53, Lacrosse: A history of the game

(67) – Fisher, Donald, page 55, Lacrosse: A history of the game

(68) – Fisher, Donald, page 97, Lacrosse: A history of the game

(69) – Weyand. Alexander M. page 36, The Lacrosse Story

(70) – Lacrosse Tribune, April 28, 2011

(71) – Rippel, Joel A.. page 65, Minnesota Sports Almanac

(72) – Shakespeare, William Act III, Scene 1, Romeo and Juliet

(73) – Rippel, Joel A.. page 312, Minnesota Sports Almanac

(74) – O'Coughlin, Seamus. page 34, Squaw Valley Gold: American Hockey's Olympic Odyssey

(75) – History of Stevens Institute of Technology, page 67

(76) – Weyand. Alexander M. page 73, The Lacrosse Story

(77) – Weyand. Alexander M. page 71, The Lacrosse Story

(78) – Godin, Roger A. page 6, Before the Stars, Early Major League Hockey and the St. Paul Athletic Club

(79) – St. Paul Globe, page 14, November 29, 1903

(80) – Minnesota Engineer, page 39, November 1911

(81) – Savage Pacer, B3, June 29, 2013

(82) – Blom, John page 14, To Show What An Indian Can Do

(83) – Atkins, Annette, page 235, THE STATE WE'RE IN

(84) – Clayton, Jane, page 16, St. Leonards Cradle of Lacrosse

(85) – Clayton, Jane, page 20, St. Leonards Cradle of Lacrosse

(86) – Clayton, Jane, page 34, St. Leonards Cradle of Lacrosse

(87) – Clayton, Jane, page 67, St. Leonards Cradle of Lacrosse

(88) – Clayton, Jane, page 86, St. Leonards Cradle of Lacrosse

(89) – Clayton, Jane, page 80, St. Leonards Cradle of Lacrosse

Bibliography

Alumni of Stevens Institute of Technology. *Stevens Institute of Technology Lacrosse: A Proud Tradition.* Web. 3 May 2011.

Arneach, Lloyd. *The Animal's Ballgame: A Cherokee Story from the Eastern Band of the Cherokee Nation (Adventures in Storytelling).* New York: Childrens Press, 1992. Print.

Atkins, Annette, and Miller, Deborah. *THE STATE WE'RE IN.* St. Paul: Minnesota Historical Society Press, 2010. Print.

Banai, Edward Benton. *The Mishomis Book – The Voice of the Ojibway.* Hayward: Indian Country Communications, Inc., 1988. Print.

Beers, George. *Laws of Lacrosse*, 1869. Print.

Beltrami, Giacomo Costantino. *Pilgrimage in America,* London, 1828. Print

Bernstein, Ross. *"Frozen Memories" Celebrating a Century of Minnesota Sports.* Minneapolis: Nordin Press, 1999. Print.

Bloom, John. *To Show What an Indian Can Do – Sports at Native American Boarding Schools.* Minneapolis: University of Minnesota Press, 2000. Print.

Bruchac, Joseph. *The Great Ball Game – A Muskogee Story.* New York: Scholastic, 1994. Print.

Catlin, George. *Letters and notes on the manners, customers, and conditions of North American Indians.* Mineola: Dover Publications, 1973. Print

Claydon, Jane. St. Leonards *Cradle of Lacrosse.* St. Andrews: Westport Print & Design, 2009. Print.

Culin, Stewart. *Games of the North American Indians.* New York: Dover Publications, Inc., 1975. Print.

David M. Oestreicher, *Unmasking the Walam Olum: A 19th Century Hoax.* Archaeological Society of New Jersey, 1994. Print.

Donnelly, Joseph Peter. *Jean de Brebeuf 1593-1649.* Chicago: Loyola University Press, 1975. Print.

Fisher, Donald M. *Lacrosse: A history of the game*, Baltimore: The Johns Hopkins Press, 2002. Print.

Fisher, Douglas. *"Our national game that never was"*, Canadian Geographic. 104 December-January 1984. Print.

Godin, Roger A. *Before the Stars – Early major league hockey and the St. Paul Athletic Club Team.* St. Paul: Minnesota Historical Society Press, 2005. Print.

Greer, Allan. *The Jesuit Relations.* New York: Bedford/St. Martins, 2000. Print.

Hall, Steve. *Fort Snelling – Colossus of the Wilderness.* St. Paul: Minnesota Historical Society Press, 1987. Print.

Hardy, Stephen. *"Polo at the Rinks": Shaping Markets for Ice Hockey in America 1880-1900.* University of New Hampshire, 2006. Print.

Heilbron, Bertha L. *With Pen and Pencil on the Frontier in 1851.* St. Paul: Minnesota Historical Press, 1986. Print.

Johnston, Basil. *Tales the Elders Told – Ojibway Legends.* Toronto: Royal Ontario Museum, 1981. Print.

Kammerer, J. C. *Largest Rivers in the United States.* USGS, 2011. Print.

Klein, Jeff Z. *The Hockey Compendium: NHL Facts, Stats, and Stories.* Toronto: McClelland & Stewart, 2001. Print.

Krout, John Allen. *Annals of American Sport.* New Haven: Yale University Press, 1929. Print.

Laliberte, David J. Thesis: *Indian Summers: Baseball at Native American Boarding Schools in Minnesota.* St. Cloud University, 2008. Print.

Manchester, Herbert. *Four Centuries of Sport in America (1490-1890).* New York: Derrydale Press, 1931. Print.

Mann, Charles C. *1491 – New revelations of the Americas before Columbus.* New York: Vintage Books, 2006. Print.

McCracken, Harold. *George Catlin and the Old Frontier.* New York: Dial Press, 1959. Print.

McDermott, John Francis. *Seth Eastman*. Norman: University of Oklahoma Press, 1961. Print.

Miceli, Augusto P. *The Man with the Red Umbrella*. Baton Rouge: Claitor's Publishing, 1974. Print.

Mitchell, Michael. *TEWAARATHON (LACROSSE) Akwesasne's Story Of Our Nation Game*. Cornwall Island: North American Indian Traveling College, 1978. Print.

Morgan, Jerry. *Baaga'adowe Play Lacrosse*. St. Paul: Minnesota Historical Society, 2004. Print.

O'Coughlin, Seamus. *Squaw Valley Gold: American Hockey's Olympic Odyssey*. iUniverse, 2001. Print.

Oneroad, Amos E., and Skinner, Alanson B. *Being Dakota*. St. Paul: Minnesota Historical Society Press, 2003. Print.

Oxendine, Joseph B. *American Indian Sports Heritage*. Lincoln: University of Nebraska Press, 1988. Print.

Parkman, Francis. *The Conspiracy of Pontiac Volume 1*. Lincoln: University of Nebraska Press, 1994. Print.

Parkman, Francis. *The Conspiracy of Pontiac Volume 2*. Lincoln: University of Nebraska Press, 1994. Print.

Peacock, Thomas. *Ojibwe Waasa Inaabidaa – We look in all directions*, Afton: Afton Historical Press, 2002. Print.

Pond, Gideon. *Dakota Friend*. August 1852. Print.

Porter III, Frank W. *The Ojibwa*. New York: Chelsea House Publishers, 1992. Print.

Rippel, Joel A. *75 Memorable Moments in Minnesota Sports*. St. Paul: Minnesota Historical Society, 2003. Print.

Salamone, Frank A. *The Native American Identity in Sports*. Lanhm: The Scarecrow Press, Inc., 2013. Print.

Scott, Bob. *Lacrosse: technique and tradition.* Baltimore: The Johns Hopkins University Press, 1976. Print.

Treuer, Anton. *Living Our Language: Ojibwe Tales and Oral Histories.* St. Paul: Minnesota Historical Society Press, 2001. Print.

Treuer, Anton. *Ojibwe in Minnesota.* St. Paul: Minnesota Historical Society Press, 2010. Print.

Vennum, Thomas. *American Indian Lacrosse Little Brother of War.* Baltimore: The Johns Hopkins Press. 2008. Print.

Vennum, Thomas. Lacrosse Legends of the First Americans. Baltimore: The Johns Hopkins Press. 2007. Print.

Warren, William W. *History of the Ojibway People.* St. Paul: Minnesota Historical Society Press, 1984. Print.

Weyand, Alexander & Roberts, Milton. *The Lacrosse Story.* Stamford: Garamond/Pridemark Press, 1965. Print.

Wissler, Clark. *Adventures in the wilderness.* New Haven: Yale University Press, 1925. Print.

Appendix A
Minnesota Lacrosse Hall of Fame
(one man's humble suggested starting point)

Originators of Minnesota Lacrosse
Ojibwe Nation
Dakota Nation

Minnesota Club Lacrosse Founders
St. Paul Lacrosse Club - 1883
President   Dr. Angus MacDonald
Vice President   Thomas McCann
Secretary   G.W. Purdy
Captain   A.A. Dennie

Minneapolis Lacrosse Club - 1883
President   J.T. Lee
Vice President   S. Freelander
Secretary   R.M. Jaffray
Captain   J. Gray

Minnesota Settler Players (1883 – 1912)
St. Paul Lacrosse Club Members

1884 St Paul Lacrosse Club Members		
Arthur Ault	George Lovell	John Stark
A. Dixon Warner	Geo Smith	Lewis Martin
Adrian Giberton	George Macauley	Robert Devine
E.F. Walsh	Henry Warwick	Sam W. Chivrell
Eugene Giberton	James Shea	William Fry
F.B. Peters	John Moir	

1885 St Paul Lacrosse Club Members		
A. Dixon Warner	George Lovell	J.B. Clark
Adrian Giberton	H. Beasley	John Moir
Chip Sherwood	H. Larkin	John Stark
D.J. Mahoney	Henry Warwick	Lewis Martin
Eugene Giberton	J. Burns	P. Costello
G. Warwick	J. Hughes	William Fry

1886 St Paul Lacrosse Club Members		
Adrian Giberton	G. Warwick	McGuire
Chip Sherwood	H. Quigley	R. Warner
D.J. Mahoney	Henry Warwick	Robert Devine
Eugene Giberton	James Shea	
G. Smith	Matthews	

1899 St Paul Lacrosse Club Members		
A.D. Strachan	Hamilton	R. Agnew
Bailey	Howard	Ralph Martin
Colvin	Jack Elliott	T. McMillan
Dan Whyte	John Stark	W.D. Stewart
Dr. Burdett	Jones	Webster
E.J. Murphy	Moore	William Fry
Fink	Newson	

1900 St Paul Lacrosse Club Members		
Bailey	Fink	Strachan
Brown	Hamilton	W.D. Stewart
Dan Whyte	Hartney	Webster
E.J. Murphy	John Stark	William Fry
Jack Elliott	Oehme	

1901 St Paul Lacrosse Club Members		
Armstrong	Jack Elliott	Oehme
Bailey	Frank Thompson	Sheppard
Dan Whyte	Hartney	W.D. Stewart
Dr. Burdett	John Stark	
E.J. Murphy	Jones	

1902 St Paul Lacrosse Club Members		
Allen	Dr. Burdett	Newson
Armstrong	E.J. Murphy	O'Brien
Bailey	Flett	Oehme
Best	Gaiseford	Raymond
Brown	Jack Elliott	Sheppard
Clarke	Jones	Slattery
Cowie	Macauley	W.D. Stewart
Dan Whyte	Mossop	Wadsworth

1903 St Paul Lacrosse Club Members		
Allen	E.J. Murphy	Mossop
Armstrong	Gaiseford	Oehme
Bailey	Jack Elliott	Raymond
Barclay	Kervin	W.D. Stewart
Brown	McAuley	Wadsworth
Cowie	McCarthy	Wood
Dan Whyte	Monkman	

1904 St Paul Lacrosse Club Members		
Allen	Haines	Oehme
Armstrong	Jack Elliott	Raymond
Brown	Kerwin	Sellers
Dan Whyte	MacDonald	W.D. Stewart
E.J. Murphy	Monkman	
Gaiseford	Mossop	

1905 St Paul Lacrosse Club Members		
Allen	Gaiseford	Mossop
Armstrong	Haines	Raymond
Brown	Jack Elliott	Sellers
Dan Whyte	Kervin	W.D. Stewart
E.J. Murphy	MacDonald	

Minneapolis Lacrosse Club Members

1883 Minneapolis Lacrosse Club Members

Bicer	Hollowell	O'Connor
C. Esplin	J.I. Brown	R.M. Jaffray
C.A. Harrington	J.J. Gethin	W. Thompson
Dafoe	J.S. Gilkinson	W.H. Patton
Donahue	J.S. Thompson	Whiting
George Wilson	McWalters	Wood
Gray	Moore	

1884 Minneapolis Lacrosse Club Members

A.W. Stone	F.E. Whiting	J.S. Thompson
Andy Grant	G.E. Wilson	R.M. Jaffray
C. Esplin	J.J. Gethin	W. Thompson
C.A. Harrington	J.S. Gilkinson	W.H. Patton

1885 Minneapolis Lacrosse Club Members

Andy Grant	J.S. Gilkinson	Stewart
B. Dickinson	J.S. Thompson	W. Thompson
C. Esplin	Lawrence	W.H. Patton
Carroll	Orr	
George Wilson	R.M. Jaffray	

1889 Minneapolis Lacrosse Club Members

A. Raymond	Lalonde	Taylor
Baird	Lawrence	Vance
Best	Miller	Wall
Currie	Raines	Webber
Danz	S. Raymond	Wilson
Deslauries	Seller	
Hall	Tate	

1900 Minneapolis Lacrosse Club Members		
A. Raymond	McBride	Sullivan
Baird	McLeod	Walls
Best	Raine	Webber
Currie	S. Raymond	
F.E. Taylor	Seller	

Stillwater Lacrosse Club Members

1885 Stillwater Lacrosse Club Members		
Charles Merry	George Cushing	Nat Roney
Cowan	Grosvenor	Norris
Dr. Watier	Joe Bellisle	Robert Welsh
Ed Butts	Kennedy	W. Newberry
Ed Osborne	McRobie	William Birge

Winona Lacrosse Club Members

1885 Winona Lacrosse Club Members		
C. Forbush	George Booth	O.H. Webber
E.C. Smith	George Gartside	T.E. Higgins
E.D. DeGroff	J.D. Miller	William Wells
Ed Porter	J.R. Marfield	
F. Fenell	John Hollowell	

Owatonna Lacrosse Club Members

1885 Owatonna Lacrosse Club Members		
Austin	Leick	Racy
Chesley	McClintock	Schunaann
Foster	Misgen	Scott
Gramps	Potter	
Hoffman	R White	

Duluth Lacrosse Club Members

1902 Duluth Lacrosse Club Members		
Cargill	Grimes	Towers
Fauble	McDonald	Trask
Foreman	McMullen	Wink
Gillson	Prouix	
Grant	Saunders	

1904 Duluth Lacrosse Club Members		
Blaize	Grimes	Malcolm
Cargill	Hogarth	McKay
Ellert	Hunter	Mcmullen
Forman	Jefferson	Proulx
Grant	Jimmy Murphy	

University of Minnesota Gophers 1910 – 1912

1910-1911 Minnesota Gophers Lacrosse Players		
Arthur Winter	Harold Swanson	S.P. Albee
C.W. Smith	Ivan O. Hanson	T.H. Granfield
H.E. Karnofsky	John Lewis	Ted Anderson
Harold Hull	P.W. Forsberg	W.S. Schouler

Head Coach   *John Trott*
Assistant Coach   *Malcolm Grant*

1911-1912 Minnesota Gophers Lacrosse Players		
Bert Hull	J.E. Power	R.A. Johnson
C.J. Smith	Jim Walker – Captain	Sidney Stadsvold
C.L. Richards	John Shine	Ted Anderson
Clark Shaughnessy	M.O. Nelson	Tom Crocker

Head Coach   *Dick Grant*
Assistant Coach   *Mike Murphy*

Restorers of the game in Minnesota
Dan Ninham
Dave White
Mark Hellenack

Appendix B
Minnesota and Lacrosse Timelines

This appendix has been included to show the timeline of events associated with lacrosse and Minnesota history. By showing these timelines, it helps to visualize what was going on in both the sport and culture, and their impact on one another.

Year	Event
900-1100	Ojibwe begin migration from the east coast
1604	Samuel de Champlain arrives in Nova Scotia
1609	Jesuit missionaries arrive in New France
1620	Mayflower arrives at Plymouth Rock
1636	Jean de Brébeuf writes about a First Nation game he calls lacrosse
1650	Dakota meet Europeans
1662	French trader Nicolas Perrot records that the game of lacrosse played by First Nations had rules and that the game was played to three goals
1670s	Ojibwe begin to migrate from Madeline Island to the area that becomes northern Wisconsin and eastern Minnesota
1679	Dakota/Ojibwe Treaty allowed Dakota to trade with the French trader Daniel du Luth via Lake Superior, and in return the Ojibwe could hunt in the area
1680	Father Hennepin reaches a large waterfall near what is now Minneapolis. He names the falls after his favorite saint, St. Anthony
1740	Horses arrive in the area that is now Minnesota
1750	Mohawks teach the game of lacrosse to French Canadians in Montreal
1756 - 1763	French and Indian War; French lose and British take over forts and trade
1763	Fort Michilimackinac attacked by Ojibwe and Sauk Nations using a lacrosse game as a ruse
1776	Americans declare independence from British rule
1782	Smallpox epidemic reaches the area that is now Minnesota
1790	After Revolutionary War, Canadian First Nations served as stewards over the land in Canada. Local Nations changed lacrosse rules to 60 players and field-length of about 500 yards. This started to move the game towards being a sport and less warrior training and healing games

1803	Louisiana Purchase
1805	Pike's Treaty signed to acquire land for a fort, to be built near the confluence of the Minnesota and Mississippi Rivers
1807	First sporting club in North America founded: Montreal Curling Club
1820	Fort St. Anthony construction begins
1823	First steamboat arrives at Fort St. Anthony
1825	Fort St. Anthony finished and renamed to Fort Snelling
1825	First Nation players near Montreal change lacrosse to a 7 v 7 game and a 50 yard field
1830	Seth Eastman arrives at Fort Snelling
1834	Pond brothers Gideon and Samuel arrive in Minnesota. The brothers start to document the Dakota language
1834	Exhibition lacrosse game by Caughnawaga Nation players in Montreal made the newspapers and began to generate interest in the game by white settlers in the area
1835	George Catlin visits Fort Snelling in order to watch and paint images of lacrosse
1838	Nicollet and Fremont engrave initials in the sacred red clay at Pipestone
1839	Paul Bunyan first appears and timber industry begins in the area that is now Minnesota; trees over 200ft tall and 5ft in diameter begin to fall
1844	Stillwater becomes the hub of the lumber industry in the area that is now Minnesota
1844	White settlers in Montreal (7 players) begin to play lacrosse against the Iroquois Nation (5 players). Easy win for the Iroquois who begin a 17-year winning streak against the settlers
1847	Harriet Bishop starts First Public School in St. Paul
1849	Minnesota Territory established; Alexander Ramsey appointed Governor
1849	Minnesota Pioneer newspaper starts
1851	Treaty of Traverse de Sioux; Treaty of Mendota
1851	University of Minnesota founded
1851 - 1860	Settlers begin moving in great numbers after treaties, growing from a population of 3,814 to 172,072 in ten years' time
1856	First white settler lacrosse club formed in Montreal: The Montreal Lacrosse Club
1858	Minnesota becomes 32nd state in the union; Henry Sibley First Governor of Minnesota

1862	Abraham Lincoln passed Homestead Act, giving settlers 160 acres if they stay for 5 years
1862	Railroad opens in Minnesota - St. Paul to St. Anthony
1862	US/Dakota War – 38 Dakota hung in Mankato in largest public mass execution in United States history
1864	Sakpe (Shakopee) and Medicine Bottle kidnapped in Canada, then executed at Fort Snelling
1865	Civil War ends
1867	Canada Confederacy formed; George Beers declares lacrosse the national sport of Canada. Parliament was not in session and this was never formally approved
1867	First college lacrosse team formed at Upper Canada College of Toronto
1867	Other lacrosse clubs form this year, going from 3 to 80 clubs in the Montreal area
1867	In Troy, New York a lacrosse demonstration game held in the United States
1868	First United States lacrosse club formed in Troy, New York and go 0-4 in first year against Canadian teams
1868	"Fireball" lacrosse experiment was held at night in Ottawa. Ball was soaked in kerosene and lit on fire. Game was played with the fireball. The ball caught sticks and nets on fire. The game was not repeated
1871	Prince Rupert Lacrosse Club established in Winnipeg
1872	Epizootic Fever strikes horses; horse power reduced for three months plunging Minnesota into its first energy crisis
1873-1878	Grasshopper plague in Minnesota lasts five years
1874	Laura Ingalls first settles in Minnesota
1874	First lacrosse club in Australia is started by L.L. Mount of the Montreal Lacrosse Club after a visit by George Beers
1875	A lacrosse ball, with the top and bottom cut off, is the first recorded use of the modern form of the puck in a hockey game. Until then, rubber balls, wooden balls or pucks had been used. (Montreal on March 3, 1875 @ the Victoria Rink)
1876	Queen Victoria watches and "endorses" a lacrosse game in Windsor, England and is quoted as noting "The game is very pretty to watch"
1877	First United States lacrosse game played in Central Park, New York between Manhattan College and NYU. NYU was winning 2-0 when game was called for darkness

1878	Washburn Flour Mill explodes in Minneapolis, killing 18 and destroying five mills. Shockwave felt in Stillwater
1879	First public art gallery in the Northwest founded by lumber baron Thomas Walker in his house. He deeded it to the city, which later became the Walker Art Center
1879	John Flannery forms the United States Amateur Lacrosse Association
1879	First annual contest for the lacrosse championship of the US held at Newport, Rhode Island. Referee was James Gordon Bennett, president of Westchester Polo Club, and editor of the New York Herald. Union (Boston) won over Ravenwood (New York) 3-0
1880	Maria Sanford hired as first female professor at the University of Minnesota
1880	Canadian National Lacrosse Association votes to no longer allow "professional" lacrosse teams to compete for championships. Essentially geared at First Nation teams to keep them from competing against white teams
1880	One of the first night games under the new "electric light" was played in August of 1880 at the Shamrock Lacrosse Field in Montreal. In order to help the fans follow what was occurring on the field at night, in a second game the promoters decided to coat the ball with phosphorous (note that the more famous first game under lights in baseball was 50 years later in 1930!)
1880	Union (Boston) defeats the Independent Club of Montreal 3-1, marking the first time a US team had ever defeated a Canadian Club team
1881	Minnesota State Capitol building burns down
1881	Lacrosse match held between Montreal Shamrocks and the New York Lacrosse Team for the "Championship of America"
1882	Philips Exeter Academy (New Hampshire) and the Lawrenceville School (New Jersey) were the first high school teams in the United States
1882	On a trip to visit the Garry Lacrosse Club of Winnipeg, the Montreal Lacrosse Club visits Chicago and St. Paul
1882	Badger Lacrosse Club founded in La Crosse, Wisconsin
1883	Mayo Clinic Founded
1883	St. Paul Lacrosse Club formed; Minneapolis Lacrosse Club formed
1884	Merritt discovers Mesabi Iron Ore Range

1884	First All-American team for any sport is selected for lacrosse – No Minnesota players named
1884	St. Paul Lacrosse Club wins National Lacrosse Championship over Calumets of Chicago 3-0
1885	School now required 12 weeks a year for all kids
1885	St. Paul Lacrosse Club travels back east to play top teams in the country, defeating all United States teams including New York, Detroit, and even John Flannery's team. Loses to Toronto in International Championship. Back to back National Champions of Lacrosse
1886	First Winter Carnival - Montreal cancelled theirs, and St. Paul copied the idea, wanting to show St. Paul was fun in January
1886	St. Paul Lacrosse Club loses to New York 1-3 in White Bear Lake in a controversial game
1888	National Lacrosse Association is disbanded and two associations take their place: Eastern and Western - Pittsburgh is considered the dividing line
1890	First girls' lacrosse game recorded at St. Leonards School in Scotland
1892	Owens College was the first team in the world to use a goal net. It was introduced by Norman Melland
1893	Lord Stanley of Preston awards first Stanley Cup to Montreal HC (Hockey Club)
1895	St. Paul Hockey Club formed; teams placed in Winter Carnival but winter was too warm and no games played until the next year
1897	First image of a gopher for University of Minnesota (UMN) appeared on the yearbook
1900	St. Paul and Minneapolis Lacrosse Clubs join the Western Canada Lacrosse Association
1900	St. Paul reaches the finals for the Drewry Cup against Winnipeg and loses 3-9. Ed Murphy is the Captain
1902	Chipman Cup is set up for the winner of the Western Canada and Western United States playoff game
1902	Shamrocks of Winnipeg won the first Chipman Cup at Lexington Park in St. Paul, winning two games in late September. St. Paul Saints Captained by Burnett
1904	Lacrosse in Olympics in St. Louis
1910	In 1910, Glenn "Pop" Warner, Athletic Director at the Carlisle Indian School, (and now famous for "Pop Warner Youth Football program) replaced baseball with lacrosse as the school's spring sport because of the "evils of professional

	baseball" and the fact that many Carlisle Indian School students had been lured away from school into "temptations and bad company by professional baseball offers." He is also quoted as saying "Lacrosse is a developer of health and strength. It is a game that spectators rave over once they understand it." The famed US Olympic hero Jim Thorpe played lacrosse at the School
1911	The Crescents Lacrosse Club have the distinction of being the first American lacrosse team to play for a US President. William Howard Taft watched the Crescents defeat the Montreal AAA at Bay Ridge on June 8, 1911
1914	Girls' lacrosse introduced in US by Miss Caroline Gascoigne from St. Leonards School at Sweetbriar College in Virginia
1921	W. Wilson Wingate, Baltimore sports writer, coins the famous lacrosse phrase "fastest game on two feet"
1923	After having two teeth knocked out, Vic Ross, the leading college scorer in 1923, introduced a face mask for the lacrosse helmet
1926	Another St. Leonards graduate, Miss Rosabelle Sinclair, brought girls' lacrosse to the US at Bryn Mawr School in Baltimore
1928	Lacrosse was a demonstration sport at the Amsterdam Olympics. The New Westminster Salmonbellies field lacrosse club represented Canada with the result being a three-way, one win-one loss-one tie with each of the three competing teams having scored 12 goals. The U.S. suggested a three-way playoff to decide a single victor; Canada agreed but England refused. The Olympic committee then declared all three teams gold medal winners
1931	Box Lacrosse starts with 7 v 7; "...[Jim McConaghy] apparently read a newspaper account of lacrosse being played in Australia with just seven men a side instead of the twelve men used in Canada, and that the Australians were playing the game in an enclosed indoor box (arena) instead of outdoors. Strangely enough, the story turned out to have no shred of truth in it whatsoever, but some old-timers insisted that it gave McConaghy the idea to go to the Canadian Amateur Lacrosse Association in 1931 with the idea for box lacrosse
1931	The first box lacrosse games in British Columbia were played at Queens Park Arena in Vancouver
1931	Women's lacrosse forms United States Women's Lacrosse Association

1932	Los Angeles Summer Olympics; Lacrosse was a demonstration sport. Teams from Canada and the United States played three games, with the team from the United States winning the series 2-1. Games were played in the Los Angeles Memorial Coliseum in front of large crowds of about 75,000 people
1937	Robert Pool introduced the first double-walled wooden stick, an early prototype for today's plastic sticks
1947	The men's field game positions change from goalkeeper, point, cover point, first defense, second defense, center, second attack, first attack and in home to goalkeeper, attack, midfield and defense.
1948	Lacrosse was a demonstration sport at the London Olympics. Teams from Great Britain and the United States played a single match, which ended in a 5-5 draw. The match was played in Wembley Stadium
1952	Box Lacrosse removes the "rover" position and settles on 6 v 6 game
1976	Dave White establishes the Twin Cities Lacrosse Club
1978	The first issue of Lacrosse Magazine is published by The Lacrosse Foundation.
1998	US Lacrosse is formed

Appendix C
Evolution of Men's Lacrosse Rules

Year	Rule Modification
1867	W. George Beers publishes the "Laws of Lacrosse" which includes the first rules of lacrosse:

1867 (continued)
12 players to a team
Crosse can be of any length but not more than 1 foot wide
Ball must be India Sponge rubber
Goals can be any length apart as agreed upon before the game and goal posts must be 6 feet high and have flags
Captains may or may not be a player in the game
When a foul is called players must stop at their positions and stay until play is resumed
Winner is best three of five games; each goal represents a game
No change of players is allowed after the game begins
Cannot touch the ball with your hand, except goalie who can use his hand to make a save
Balls out of bounds will be faced off to restart play
A player may be removed for foul play and if so his team will finish the game shorthanded

1876 Reduction of field size from 200 yards to 125 yards
Casper Whitney, the foremost American sports writer at the time, called it the most important rule change that crystalized the game taking hold in America

1879 Could not hit, punch, or threaten an opponent
No cross checking with two hands on the stick

1888 Game changed to have time limits, no longer the first team to score three goals
Games no longer be called because of darkness
Game time is in halves but not set formally; later on it was referred to as 30 minutes

1889 Could no longer stand in the goaltender's crease
Cannot hit an opponent from behind or push him into a fence
Cannot hit the goaltender
Cannot kneel down in front of an opponent attempting to scoop the ball

1892 College rule changes
Time of a half increased from 30 minutes to 45 minutes
Goal crease changed from 12 x 12 yards square to 18 x 12 rectangle
Face-off technique was clarified: ball must be placed on the ground, sticks are back to back and overlapping by two thirds of the netting
The ball had to be drawn backwards only
A field captain now had to be a player in the game
A player could only play for his college for a maximum of five years

1899 New rule book is published
Cannot intentionally delay the game by throwing the ball out of bounds
Cannot knock the stick out of an opponent's hand
Cannot threaten an on-field official
Cannot use foul language

1902 Collegiate goal crease returned to 12 x 12 yards
Overtime was reduced from 30 minutes to 15 minutes
Field length required to be between 110 and 125 yards
Top bar across the goal posts is now required

1906 Collegiate goal crease fixed at 18 x 12 yards
Players may substitute at any time but once they leave the game they cannot return

1914 With more football players joining the lacrosse for defense, rules were modified to take out the football blocks
Body checking below the knee illegal

1921 A center line is added to the field and "offside" era begins
The player who was offside is removed for 3 - 7 minute penalty
Required to have 3 players back at all times, not including the goalie

1930 Colleges require numbers on their jerseys for the first time

1932 Changed time from 45 minute running halves (no timeouts) to 15 minute quarters with timeouts
Tentative change: Player count reduced from 12 to 10 to help with travel costs
Clubs claimed having fewer players would also increase passing in the game

Players may have been lowered due to the success and interest in box lacrosse which started in 1931

1933 Rule formally changed to reduce players from 12 to 10 per team
Length between the goals reduced from 110 yards to 80 yards
Space behind the nets reduced from 35 yards to 20 yards
Teams must change field ends after each quarter

1935 Out of bounds rules changed
Previously if a ball went out of bounds, it required a face-off. Since in box lacrosse a ball did not go out of bounds, this made the game more exciting
If a ball went out of bounds on the side line, the opponent of the last player to touch the ball was allowed to throw the ball into play
If a ball went out of bounds on the end lines, the player who crossed the end line was awarded the ball - in the case of a tie a face-off would occur
The new rules worked and the game sped up and was more exciting

1937 Rule change made to address the clutter of players on a face-off
Wing lines added to isolate only the two players taking the face-off

1940 Field size changed to its final size of 80 yards between goals and 15 yards behind the goals
Field width set to 60 yards minimum and 70 yard maximum

1942 In case of a tie, play two five minute periods
Removed rule that a player could only be substituted once; could be substituted an unlimited number of times
This changed sped the game up again

1946 Rule change - if a defensemen knocked the ball out of the crosse of an attacking player, and the ball goes out of bounds, it is awarded to the defensemen
If an attacking team intentionally throws the ball out of play over an end line, it is awarded to the defensive team and not the player who crosses the end line first

1947 The men's field game positions change from goalkeeper, point, cover point, first defense, second defense, center, second attack, first attack and in home to goalkeeper, attack, midfield and defense

1948 It has always been a rule that a player who losses his crosse could not continue to play until he retrieved his crosse. A tradition developed after the center line was introduced: instead of reducing speed, a player would toss his stick on the ground marking the spot where he stopped playing. During an Army-Navy game a Navy player tossed his stick near the center line but a close-following official, Gard Mallonee, was hit, knocking out one tooth and chipping three others. After this event the rule was changed so that a player could not throw his stick under any circumstances

Players required to wear numbers on both the front and back of the jersey

First rule requiring face masks implemented

Goal crease changed from the rectangle of 12 x 18 to a circle with a 9 foot radius

Officials implement the first use of hand signals for penalties

1951 Rules were changed to remove the circle in the middle of the field

Body checking considered legal within 15 feet of a loose ball

The Shot Rule implemented with a shot going out of any line or deflected shot would be award to the player nearest the ball at the time it went out of bounds

All passes that went out of bounds continued to be awarded to the opponent

1953 The rule of a player having to freeze after play stopped was removed. Since 1867, if play was stopped with a whistle, all players had to freeze where they were on the field

A player could move freely after a whistle stopped play

1969 NCAA Rules Committee set up a formal "Sudden Death" rule to eliminate ties. After two overtime periods of four minutes each, and switching ends between periods, if the score remained tied there would be as many four minute "sudden death" periods as needed until a goal is scored. Overtime until this point was not well defined

1971 The double wall, molded plastic lacrosse head declared legal by the rules committee

1972 Nylon strings approved for use in the new molded lacrosse heads

To understand the impact of these two prior rules changes, one only has to look at the NCAA Championship game in 1971 and 1972. In 1971 all goals, assists, and saves were made with all-wooden sticks. In 1972 all goals, assists, and saves were made with the new modified head sticks. That is how quickly the new heads were adopted.

1973 A mesh-strung stick approved for play

1974 An aluminum handle approved for play

Rule changes obviously have continued after this date. The goal was to show the major rule changes and how the game evolved from standing still after a whistle, to goal creases, jersey numbers, offsides, face-offs, and new sticks making it into the game played today.

Sources of the rules changes come from the book "The Lacrosse Story", and rule books from Spalding, NCAA, and US Lacrosse.

APPENDIX D
Official National Collegiate Athletic Association (NCAA) Lacrosse Guide - 1914

Lacrosse vs. Base Ball
ONE SOLUTION OF THE SUMMER BALL PROBLEM.
By Glenn S. Warner,
Athletic Director, United States Indian School, Carlisle, Pa.

[Standing in the position of Athletic Director of the United States Indian School at Carlisle, Pennsylvania, it is particularly appropriate for Mr. Warner to express his views on Lacrosse, the Indian sport. The following solution to the summer base ball question offered by him must command the highest attention everywhere, coming as it does from an authority who has had an opportunity to work out both sides of the problem.]

I believe lacrosse to be an ideal spring sport for our schools, colleges and universities, and I am of the firm opinion that those who have the interest of school and college athletics and amateur sport at heart, should consider well the advisability of substituting this game for base ball as a college sport. Such a step would seem to be about the only feasible way to settle the ever present and much discussed evil of the so-called '"summer base ball problem."

As long as base ball continues to be a major college sport, no rules nor any amount of discussion can ever prevent college boys from playing it professionally in their summer vacation if they are developed at college to such a degree of skill that their services upon professional and semi-professional teams are in demand. The temptation of publicity and enormous salaries for doing something which is all play and no work is too alluring for college boys to resist.

Unlike base ball, lacrosse is not highly professionalized, as there are practically no professional lacrosse teams in the United States. Although I am a great lover of base ball and believe it the greatest game ever invented for the general public and the masses, yet I am convinced that lacrosse is better adapted for a college sport than is our great national game. One of the advantages of lacrosse as a school and college sport, in addition to the fact that it is a strictly amateur sport in this country, is that it can be learned and played skillfully by a boy who has never played the game, in one season, while rarely indeed is it that a college student wins a place upon the 'varsity base ball team unless he has played the game from his childhood days.

All other college sports, such as track athletics, rowing and foot ball, can be taken up successfully and skill acquired during a student's college days with no experience whatever before entering college, so that all these sports are open to the inexperienced student who wishes to engage in athletics when he enters college. In these sports students can be encouraged by the fact that it is possible for them to acquire skill enough during their college careers to win the coveted college or university letter. This is not so with base ball.

For many years the athletic and other authorities of the Carlisle Indian School were perplexed by the fact that the Indian boys who played upon the school's base ball teams could not be restrained from engaging in professional base ball during the summer. The students here, unlike at colleges, did not go home for their summer vacations, but were placed out in the country upon a farm or at some trade under the school's outing system, and it was impossible to convince the base ball boys that it would be better for them to spend their summers in this way for a small monthly wage when they could earn many times more by playing base ball.

The result was that many of them played professional base ball in the summer and while a few, like Bender of the Athletics, LeRoy of St. Paul and Johnson of Cincinnati, made a success of the profession, many others were unable to withstand the numerous temptations with which they were surrounded upon semi-professional and minor league teams and acquired bad habits. For this reason it was decided several years ago to discontinue base ball as a school sport and substitute lacrosse. The school authorities have never regretted this change and the summer base ball problem has been settled in a perfectly satisfactory manner at the Carlisle School ever since lacrosse was so substituted.

Base ball is still played and encouraged at the school, but the point is, that the players are not coached and developed to a point where they are in demand during the summer, and they play the game only for sport and recreation and not with the idea of making base ball their business or profession.

While lacrosse originated with the Indians, the game has not been played very much by them for many years except in Canada and New York State. Most of the students at Carlisle come from the West and Southwest and only a very few boys here had ever played the game when the sport was introduced at the school.

Nevertheless they took to it so readily and acquired skill so quickly that Carlisle's first season at the sport was a successful one and compared favorably with the teams of recent years after the sport was firmly established, thus proving that proficiency in the game can be quickly acquired.

Lacrosse is a highly interesting game which requires speed, courage, skill, and team work of a high degree. Besides this, the expense of outfitting teams and players is small. In my opinion lacrosse is especially adapted as a spring sport for schools and colleges, and would provide an excellent substitute for base ball if it should be eventually decided that the evils of college ball can only be corrected by eliminating it as a representative college sport.

Carlisle Lacrosse Team, 1910 - Courtesy of the Antique Sports Shop

Appendix E
Language of Lacrosse

Language is culture. And the language of lacrosse has been lost over the years. The Ojibwe and Dakota here in Minnesota are trying to keep the language of the First Nations from disappearing.

In his book *Ojibwe in Minnesota*, Dr. Anton Treuer estimated that there are fewer than 1,000 Ojibwe speakers left in America. Most of them reside in Minnesota, with the main area being around Red Lake.

Thanks to many people like Dr. Treuer, the Ojibwe language is making a comeback. Seeing success in other cultures like the Native Hawaiians, which went from 500 speakers to over 15,000, the Ojibwe language proponents are trying to replicate this same opportunity to restore their culture.

Their first efforts have been in the city of Bemidji, which is near the reservations of White Earth, Red Lake, and Leech Lake. The city started with simple bilingual restroom signs. Stores followed suit with new signs saying "boozhoo," which means "welcome." The University of Bemidji has gone further, with outreach programs and signs throughout their campus.

In the Twin Cities the Dakota have had similar efforts to document their language and signs have begun to appear around town. Lake Calhoun recently updated a sign to add the Dakota name "Bde Maka Ska."

Recently Dawí Huhá Máza completed a Go Fund Me campaign to record and document the Dakota language by visiting elders and collecting stories and lessons.

Our job as advocates of lacrosse should be to support the language of lacrosse. To help do this, some of the lacrosse words in the two main First Nation languages in Minnesota are included below.

Use this list to share with your coaches, players, parents, and fans of the game of lacrosse.

The University of Minnesota and the Minnesota Historical Society have many resources to help you learn to speak the language. In these languages, a single word can be an entire sentence.

English	Ojibwe	Dakota
Lacrosse	baaga'adowe	Tabkapsicapi
Lacrosse Ball	bikwaakwad	Tabkapsicapi tapa
Pass - Throw	gabikan	Tapa kah'od iyeya
Run	bimibatoo	Iayaaka
Crosse - Stick	baaga'adowaan	Canyankapi
Lacrosse Player	baaga'adowewinini	Takapsicapi ska'ta
Shoot	baashkiz	Kute
Score	gabenaage	Yawapi
Greetings	boozhoo	Hoyekiyapi
Thanks	miigwechiwi	Wopida

Thanks to those who contributed: Jerry Morgan, Sasha Brown, Lonna Hunter, Ryan Dixon, Jeremy Red Eagle, and the University of Minnesota Dakota-to-English online dictionary.

ABOUT THE AUTHOR

Childs' family photo
Taken at Cory Childs' wedding in St. Paul, Minnesota, April 2015
Brody, Courtney, Charlee (first granddaughter), Alan, Cory, Jace, Bailey, and Candy

Alan's family moved to Minnesota in 1992 from Los Angeles, California. Alan never played lacrosse while growing up in California, so it was his five children that started the family in the sport. His daughters Courtney and Bailey both played goalie in hockey, and midfield/attack in lacrosse. Cory, Jace, and Brody all played hockey and lacrosse.

The Childs' kids all wore the jersey #7, when available, because there are 7 in the family. Alan served on the YLM (Youth Lacrosse of Minnesota) board, started the Burnsville Lacrosse Club for boys and girls, and has coached his kids in various sports.

Today the family still plays, coaches, and mentors in the community of lacrosse. Alan's first book, *Flamethrowers,* was a young adult novel that he will return to, and finish the series, now that this book has been published.